KEY TEXTS

THOEMMES

Printed and bound by
Antony Rowe Ltd., Chippenham, Wiltshire

KEY TEXTS
Classic Studies in the History of Ideas

PHILOSOPHICAL STUDIES

J. McT. Ellis McTaggart

Edited with an introduction by
S. V. Keeling

With a new introduction by
Gerald Rochelle

THOEMMES
PRESS

This edition published by Thoemmes Press, 1996

Thoemmes Press
11 Great George Street
Bristol BS1 5RR
England

ISBN 1 85506 479 0

This is a reprint of the 1934 edition

© *Introduction* Gerald Rochelle, 1996

Publisher's Note

FOREWORD

In 1889, at the age of twenty-two McTaggart wrote to his lifelong friend, Roger Eliot Fry, 'I have got some ideas on the elimination of time – also, alas, some new books and clothes'.[1]

The seminal and notorious denial of the reality of time published in 1908 concludes that the relations past, present and future, though essential for time to be real, are self-contradictory. This paradoxical claim has stimulated a constant flow of philosophical discussion for most of the twentieth century. Indeed, any discussion on tense, even if not explicitly, draws upon McTaggart's thesis. His argument against time is well known: what he replaces time with, is not.

McTaggart was an exceptional philosopher, a visionary holding mystic beliefs about the nature of reality. His philosophy is an expression of his ontological quest; and understanding that intention reveals the denunciation of the reality of time as only part of a greater conception. A fuller appreciation of his metaphysical system leads us into a world that gives a coherent place to his unusual claim that we live in an atemporal world. That conception of reality is closely related to his views on our experience of life. Fully to understand his intention we need to appreciate something of his personality and how he lived.

---

[1] Letter, McTaggart to Roger Fry, 29 June 1889, King's College Library, Cambridge.

Life[2]

John McTaggart Ellis McTaggart was born in London
on 3 September 1866 to an upper class family with
antecedents in the law and academic life. His parents
were cousins, Francis and Caroline Ellis, who, to claim
an inheritance, adopted the name 'McTaggart'. He had
two surviving younger sisters, Margaret and Susan, and
a younger brother, Norman.

His earliest influences included anthropomorphic
images of romantic naturalism from his father (who
died when he was four) and stories of Maori canni-
balism and reincarnation from his mother. He was
something of a philosophical prodigy. By the age of
seven he was well read, studying Kant closely. He had
sufficient intellectual confidence to argue forcibly
against accepted dogma and many of his social classes
strongly held beliefs. Within weeks of entering his first
preparatory school in Weybridge whither the family
moved in 1872, he openly argued against the Apostles'
Creed and repudiated the existence of God. He was
removed from this school and, after a short period at
another, was educated privately. His head was
unusually large; he suffered from a spinal curvature
and walked crab-like, often with his back close against
walls. He was very sensitive and cried easily, usually
over poems or songs. He roamed the countryside,
swinging a stick and carrying on philosophical conver-
sations with himself. Because of his eccentricity
children called him a 'loonie'.

---

[2] For a detailed examination of McTaggart's life see Gerald Rochelle, *The
Life and Philosophy of J. McT. E. McTaggart, 1866–1925* (Lewiston,
New York, Edwin Mellen, 1991).

His childhood philosophizing was mainly concerned with death and God. He soon concluded that he was an atheist and immortal. He became convinced that the emotional state of love allowed him to transcend the apparent world and witness a reality beyond. Throughout his life he was to experience bouts of this overpowering emotion he came to call the 'Saul feeling' (after Browning's poem *Saul*). It revealed itself in ecstasies of love and mystic intuition. Sometimes, he was transported to a hallucinatory world where the only reality was a projection of his own mental state (for example, he would see blossom and leaves on bare trees in the winter). This belief in the transcendental power of love and the mental self ultimately came to underlie all his philosophy.

In January 1882, at the age of fifteen, he was sent to Clifton College in Bristol. His incompetence at games (he lay down on the games field refusing to take part), untidiness, absorption in philosophy and sensitivity, augured an unhappy life there. However, in his first year, he formed close loving relationships (including his lifelong friends Roger Eliot Fry and George Herbert Dolby) and won his victory over organized sport – he was allowed to walk on the Downs and philosophize instead. Also he developed a deep interest in the dogmas of religion. At the beginning of his second year, he became absorbed in debating and began to develop an extraordinary interest in the structure and management of organizations. His involvement in the Clifton Debating Society, ultimately as Secretary, convinced him that the use of intellectual powers would always take precedence over the physical aspects of worldly life. From his absorption in the conduct of affairs, administrative, ceremonial or legal, he derived a sense of well-being and in later life he became quite preoccupied with such matters.

In May 1885 he was admitted as Pensioner to Trinity College, Cambridge. He quickly developed a deep attachment to Trinity, always seeking out information on its tradition and workings. For the whole of his life, his love for Trinity, Clifton and Oxford never diminished. His circle of close friends at this time, apart from Fry and the brothers Ferdinand Nassau and Ferdinand Philip Maximillian (Max) Schiller (who went up with him from Clifton), included Nathaniel Wedd, Goldsworthy Lowes Dickinson, and Basil Williams. In May 1886 he was elected as a member of The Apostles (The Cambridge Conversazione Society) and remained an active and influential member until 1891. His commitment to the Society and its members was inviolable. His paper 'Violets or Orange Blossom?' (now lost), a defence of homosexuality, was treasured by the Society for many years. He was deeply loyal to his Apostolic 'brethren', always giving them the highest priority of devotion. During this period, he loved, in particular, Max Schiller, though his love was somewhat unrequited. However, this only caused McTaggart to believe more strongly the Platonic principle that the main course of love was to be found in the lover and not the beloved.

During his undergraduate years, McTaggart was particularly influenced by three of his moral science teachers. John Venn convinced him of the need for rigorous logic in argument, and James Ward inspired him with his distinction between the subject that has the experience and the experience in itself. Henry Sidgwick (who first made the distinction between 'psychological hedonism' and 'ethical hedonism' and was co-founder of the Society for Psychical Research), reinforced McTaggart's belief in the philosophical respectability of survival after death. He graduated in 1888, being placed in the first class of the Mental and Moral Sciences Tripos with Distinction in Metaphysics and awarded The Marshall Prize for Political Economy and The Members Prize. From 1888 to 1891 he worked on his Fellowship on Hegel; and this, with his studies of Plato, consolidated his idea that behind appearance lay a monistic world of loving harmony. Along with his philosophy, he became increasingly closely focused on his friends, joining summer house parties at the Schiller holiday home in Gersau, Switzerland, and revelling in their company.

In 1890 McTaggart's family emigrated to New Zealand for the sake of his brother Norman's health. McTaggart made two visits to New Zealand. He set off on his first trip at the end of 1891, stopping off in Calcutta to visit Ferdinand N. Schiller. Here he was introduced to horseback riding and his rides in the hills brought surges of the 'Saul feeling'. After visiting Australia, he arrived in New Zealand, staying first with his mother and then on the farm of some local landowners, the Halcombes. Here, he fell deeply in love with one of their sons, Norman (called 'N'). He also met Margaret 'Daisy' Bird who was later to become his wife. During his stay he rode, camped, helped herd sheep, gave lectures, made speeches, sang hymns and enjoyed country parties. Cut off from the life at Trinity he absorbed himself in philosophy and correspondence. He spent all his spare time studying Hegel and during this period became a confirmed idealist. Upon his return to Cambridge in February 1893, he submitted his dissertation on Hegel's Dialectic and was duly elected to a Prize Fellowship at Trinity.

He then settled into his life as a Fellow of Trinity, a vocation for which he believed he had been destined. He enjoyed drinking and smoking and dined every evening in College – a life wittily reflected in his collection of anecdotes and observations which he wrote from 1896 onward, *College Stories*. In 1897 he was appointed a lecturer. His teaching consisted of three courses for the Tripos (essentially metaphysics but mainly on Hegel), an advanced class in 'The Problems of Philosophy' and, from 1899 to 1924, his Friday evening lectures for non-philosophers 'Introduction to the Study of Philosophy'. When lecturing, he spoke rapidly, illustrating his arguments with images of dragons and griffins. He had little patience with ill-informed questioners and could be daunting as a supervisor. He became a formidable force in Cambridge, both as a philosopher and a personality, causing even Bertrand Russell to believe himself an Hegelian until 1898. McTaggart found it 'a very pleasant thing to be a Fellow'.[3]

In the summer of 1898 he set off again for New Zealand. He asked Bertrand Russell to stand in for his Lent term lectures on Leibniz. On his arrival he quickly reacquainted himself with 'N'. His love for 'N', their moonlit horseback rides and the wild country that surrounded them, took him to new levels of ecstasy. Again, he gave talks and speeches but for the most part he was absorbed with 'N'. He met Daisy Bird again and in January 1899 they became engaged (since 1892 a Cambridge Fellow could marry without resigning). Their relationship was to become a lifelong devotion of

---

[3] Letter, McTaggart to Rupert Brooke, 13 March 1913, King's College Library, Cambridge.

a very deep sort. Initially, the idea of loving a woman caused him confusion because hitherto his only 'love' (except for his mother) had been for male friends. However, he was convinced he could fit his love for her within the context of his existing love for his friends. She shared his feelings on schoolboys, 'women' questions and metaphysics. McTaggart judged her an acceptable lover as 'she wasn't in the least feminine'.[4] How his friends would take the news caused him some anxiety and for six months the 'Saul feeling' left him. On receiving their approval, it returned with greater strength than ever and he was overjoyed. In August 1899 he got married in New Plymouth and, with his new wife, left for England in September. In January 1900 they moved to 5 Benet Place, Lensfield Road, Cambridge, which remained their home for the rest of their married life. Eccentric as a child, now an adult he was a 'character'. Often in his red gown, he rode a tricycle along Trumpington Street to Trinity at precisely the same time each day. He saluted cats whenever he met them and observed (and in *College Stories* reported on) the conduct of College ceremonies in minute detail.

Until 1900, McTaggart expressed much of his own philosophy through exposition of Hegel, thereafter separating his own thoughts more distinctly with a range of works, all of which were ultimately to be distilled, after the war, into his *magnum opus*, *The Nature of Existence*. In 1907 he visited the University of California at Berkeley and delivered his paper 'The Relation of Time to Eternity'. Apart from Plato, philosophers of the nineteenth and the early part of the twentieth century were his main inspiration, Hegel

[4] Letter, McTaggart to Nathaniel Wedd, 24 January 1899, King's College Library, Cambridge.

being in his view an extension of Greek idealism. In addition, he admired Spinoza for his rigid and abstract method and the way he had allowed his philosophy to guide his life. Influenced by Leibniz's metaphysical method, he also echoes Leibniz's non-spatially extended monads in his notion of the atemporal self. In Schopenhauer, he found what had always been his own attitude to God reinforced. He was also interested not only in the contrast between Oxford and Cambridge but in work at St Andrews and Edinburgh. The critical reaction of Bertrand Russell and G. E. Moore helped him to refine his own arguments. Though McTaggart felt that neither the methods nor results of science could be usefully applied to philosophy, he kept himself in touch with contemporary thinking, being most interested in Albert Einstein's work and often visiting Arthur Stanley Eddington and Ernest Rutherford for their opinions on such matters. He was an avid reader of novels (good and bad) and poetry and is reputed to have read the whole of the Union Library collection by an early age. His favourite poet was Algernon Charles Swinburne who, he felt, expressed many of his own thoughts; and typically he was fond of Lewis Carroll's popular writing.

His philosophy matched his day-to-day life – his faithfulness and commitment to the truth, his deep-seated belief in immortality, and a mystic sensitivity to a world which he felt was only a second-rate impression of the true reality beyond, guided all his undertakings and in particular his friendships. For McTaggart these were evidence of his idealist belief. He believed all friends were friends from previous lives: if he recognized love, he recognized a previous love. Because he believed events accumulate in an atemporal series, faithfulness to love was inescapable. Based on this, he tried to ensure that his relationships persisted and continued to grow in content. Nearly all his relationships lasted for life. If they did founder then the reason could be found in political disagreement, misunderstanding over university policy or, what McTaggart considered, a lack of sincerity of the other. He did not generally go out of his way to befriend people outside his limited circle and indeed within the university he could be terse and very abrupt and was apt to ignore certain individuals.

His loving relationships fell into distinct categories. He was deeply attached to his mother. Believing as he did that children seek out the parents to whom they wish to be born his devotion to her was unassailable. Her death in 1909 caused him great sadness, a sadness compounded by the death of his sister, Margaret, in childbirth in 1910. The two deaths left him alone in a way for which he was not really prepared. Though he believed he would be with them again in the future, the mortal loss stirred in him a feeling of sadness he could never reconcile with his intuitive optimism. Then there were those he believed showed him that love was indeed the fundamental relation of all selves. This category included Fry, Wedd, Lowes Dickinson, the Schiller brothers, 'N', Dolby, and his wife. These, he believed, he experienced in an other-worldly sense and he bestowed on them a committed faithfulness. From these friends he often sought approval for his actions or thoughts and, in so doing, he integrated the will of others into his own actions. Sometimes, in his intimate correspondence, this appeal for approval seemed a weakness; but in truth it was a submission to love. Indeed, it was this surrender to mutual love that he most craved. This intensity, however, led him to bouts of jealousy, though this never led to separation. When he was the reason for another's jealousy he believed it only underpinned the strength of love the other had for him.

In a lower category, but still dear to him, were Basil Williams, Dalhousie Young, Donald McLachlan and Gerald and Arthur Balfour. Others in this category were those whom he hero-worshipped, most notably Henry Jackson, Maurice Marshall, James Ward, Ernest Rutherford and Henry Sidgwick. Yet often such friendships were based upon literary associations, either by McTaggart seeking out his inspirers, or he himself being sought out by those he inspired. George Fleming belonged to the former variety and Thomas Hardy and Sir Francis Younghusband to the latter. Some friendships occurred spontaneously and were outside his social class and away from his natural environs at Trinity and Cambridge. Seven years before his death, on one of his frequent train journeys to London, he befriended a boy of ten, who was returning home in disgrace from an open-air camp. Following this initial meeting, he often had the boy to stay in Cambridge and entertained him with dinners in town. This friendship continued until McTaggart's death.

His friendship with Russell and Moore, both of whom were his students, was of yet another sort. Although they were both Apostolic brothers, they were certainly not considered by McTaggart to be among his beloved. During the earlier years leading up to the war, Russell not only admired McTaggart but believed in the major points of his philosophy. Moore respected McTaggart as a senior Apostolic brother, an elder Don and the possessor of an exceptionally able and critical mind. Both Russell and Moore would submit their ideas to him for criticism and opinion. Though he hardly played a central role in their work his relationship with them was important and so too was his contribution to their development. His association with Moore continued throughout and after the war but his friendship with Russell was to come to an abrupt end.

From 1914 to 1918 McTaggart's life at Cambridge immunized him from many worst effects of the war. However, his feelings against Germany, born of a lifelong dogmatic adherence to a traditional English nationalism and an increasingly callous Toryism, were intense. This hatred was manifested in its full-blown form when the conflict came and he was seized with a determination that England should cause Germany's inglorious defeat. While he pressed on with his academic work in much the same way as before, he diverted any of his 'non-essential' energies into war work, working in a munitions factory and as a special constable. His enthusiastic support for the war effort (shared by his wife) caused an irreparable rift between himself and others who pleaded the case for peace. As opinions became polarized this led to his opposing the anti-war lobby in the university and, most notably, Bertrand Russell. Many of Trinity's younger Dons had joined the army. This meant that the College Council was controlled by the older, more conservative Fellows, of whom McTaggart was the epitome. Russell's lectureship term at Trinity was due to come to a close in October 1915. The Council was considering offering him a Fellowship. However, while it was deliberating, Russell applied for two terms leave of absence which influenced the Council simply to renew his lectureship. In Spring 1916 Russell published what became known as the 'Everett Leaflet', his defence of exclusion from military service on conscientious grounds. He was arrested, prosecuted and fined under the Defence of the Realm Act. In July 1916 Trinity Council unanimously dismissed Russell from his lectureship but then, under pressure from a powerful lobby within the College, offered it back to him again. McTaggart grudgingly acquiesced in the decision on the understanding that it did not involve a retraction. Russell, however, simply resigned the post. McTaggart had reasoned out his stand on the matter carefully – acting, as he saw it, correctly but with a heavy heart. The decisive point for him was that Russell had been convicted of a crime. Russell, for his part, held McTaggart to be the key figure in his dismissal, viewing McTaggart's Toryism and consolidated place on the College Council, together with his reputation and obvious diligence in his pro-war stance, as representing the older league of 'unenlightened' Dons, still holding tight to an outmoded and immoral imperialism. When, in February 1918, Russell was imprisoned for statements considered prejudicial to Britain's relations with America, McTaggart would not sign a petition to support improvement in the conditions of Russell's imprisonment.

When the war ended, McTaggart was overjoyed by Germany's capitulation and felt his single-minded nationalism vindicated. The affair over Russell, however, had created irreconcilable problems. In the years that followed, as Russell became a popular and distinguished philosopher, McTaggart became progressively viewed as an obscure Hegelian. The affair had a disproportionate effect on all the other work McTaggart did and on his view of life. It showed him that the idea that friendships once made were never broken, though in essence still true, was, in practice, far from true. This disturbed his previously confident stance on the nature of the loving self in its practical application. The result was that, after the war, though he continued to work out his philosophical claims with dedication, his enthusiasm for life and social contacts gradually and progressively became more desultory. He focused more closely on his love for his wife. The seemingly inappropriate love of his early years was now beginning to outlive the excitement he had derived from his male relationships. He wrote to her at the end of his first draft of volume two of *The Nature of Existence*, 'Heart of my heart have I done well?'.[5]

After the war, both the world and McTaggart had changed. He still believed, as he always had; but his enthusiasm had been diminished. His nationalism and belief in the dogma of the law had seemed to play a practical role in the war years, but now they seemed only the object of distaste for so many close to him. As he had gained by love in the early years, he now found that in losing friends, he had lost some of himself. He felt psychologically depleted and old. Nevertheless, the remaining friendships, the reading and the correspondence continued unfailingly, as did the belief in immortality as a necessary ingredient of the ultimate, all-consuming love. In 1919 he suffered another blow when 'N' died.

Throughout his last years he continued working strenuously on *The Nature of Existence*. His editorial practice was to complete five drafts before his work was ready for publication. The first volume was

---

[5] Note, 3 September 1917, MS. *The Nature of Existence*, vol. 2, draft A, Trinity College Library, Cambridge.

completed in July 1920 and published in 1921. He
planned to resume work on volume two straight away,
but felt depressed that the project had already taken
him eleven years. The second volume was bigger and
more complex and, although he was writing and
rewriting this throughout the war years, the final
version was still nowhere near completion. By 1921 he
had started experiencing periods of psychological
morbidity. Incidents, which had previously been only
part of his life's routine, became high points. He now
prepared weeks in advance for such things as visits from
the boy he met on the train or dinners with friends. As
his life seemed to contract, he even showed jealousy of
his wife's charity work and the involvement it
demanded. In 1922, after at least a four-year interval,
which had begun at the time of the dismissal of Russell,
he again saw Lowes Dickinson, when he sat opposite
him at dinner. He was pleased to find that he was quite
friendly again. Yet his pleasure was not the ecstatic
one that it would have been some years before. He
wrote to Wedd that after dinner, 'As usual, a large party
went round to Keynes' rooms but, as for me, I went to
bed'.[6]

A year later he retired from all his commitments
except the Friday evening lectures, 'The Problems of
Philosophy' class and his course on 'General History of
Modern Philosophy', so that he could devote himself to
finishing volume two of *The Nature of Existence*.
Typically, he laid definite plans for its progress. He
proposed that the second draft should be typewritten by
the end of 1923 and that the project should be ready for

[6] Letter, McTaggart to Nathaniel Webb, 22 June 1922, Cambridge
University Library.

publication in the summer of 1927. By now, he was even left out of the intellectual circles in which he had revelled for so much of his earlier life, though he was not so hurt by friendships that fell short of his model of perfect love, and continued to believe that his own ability to love never weakened. In 1923 he wrote to Walter John Herbert Sprott, 'My friendships no longer make me suffer, and yet I do not think I love less'.[7] He was fat, unfit and disinclined to put his energy into argument and verbal combat. He was happier at home, writing letters, or in his rooms, reworking his manuscript of *The Nature of Existence*.

He still took holidays with enthusiasm but, somehow, he now had to work harder to find pleasure in life. His own priorities became confused. He became upset by the selling of land and possessions at Trinity and with the same strength of feeling he mourned the death of a friend's cat. He was depressed by the closing of the old Combination Room, where he had spent so much of his life. Although the old friendships could occasionally kindle delight, the 'Saul feeling' seemed to have left him. He went on a final holiday to Italy during Easter 1924, preparing himself by studying an Italian translation of *Alice in Wonderland*, and, perhaps for the last time, felt the 'Saul feeling' again when he saw the Botticellis in Florence.

He became increasingly uninterested in Cambridge life. Towards the end of 1924, he attended a meeting of the Eranos (a philosophy discussion group originally formed by Whitehead, Russell, Lowes Dickinson and McTaggart in the early 1890s), keeping silent throughout and seeming detached. At the end of the

---

[7] Letter, McTaggart to Walter John Herbert Sprott, 30 January 1923, Cambridge University Library.

proceedings he went up to a friend and said, 'The longer I live, the more I am convinced of the reality of three things: truth, love and immortality'.[8] In December 1924 he was struck down with a painful thrombosis. He was told that he would die and told his wife, 'I am grieved that we must part, but you know I am not afraid of death'.[9] On 18 January 1925 he died at the age of fifty-eight. It was left to his executor and colleague, Charlie Dunbar Broad, to prepare the second volume of *The Nature of Existence* for print. After his death, Lowes Dickinson completed a memoir of McTaggart, Stanley Victor Keeling assembled McTaggart's philosophical essays and Broad published his own *Examination of McTaggart's Philosophy*.[10] In 1935 Broad, considering all his literary obligations fulfilled, consigned all the royalty rights of McTaggart's estate to Clifton College.[11]

Work

McTaggart's full metaphysical exposition is contained in *The Nature of Existence* and a popular version of the main course of his thinking can be found in *Some Dogmas of Religion*; but his important essays are collected in *Philosophical Studies*. *Philosophical Studies* contains the essence of his idealistic philosophy. All the fundamental aspects of metaphysical enquiry

---

[8] Basil Williams, 'McTaggart's Friendships', in Goldsworthy Lowes Dickinson, *J. McT. E. McTaggart* (Cambridge University Press, 1931), p. 77.

[9] Lowes Dickinson, *McTaggart*, p. 122.

[10] Charlie Dunbar Broad, *Examination of McTaggart's Philosophy* (Cambridge University Press, vol. 1, pts 1 and 2, 1938).

[11] Letter, Charlie Dunbar Broad to Cambridge University Press, 4 April 1935.

are tackled: the existence of God, belief and the nature of mysticism, time, eternity, causality and the nature of self. In addition, the central, and connected issues of immortality, the nature of good, individual purpose and value are scrutinized. There is also a brief clarification on the question of propositions applicable to themselves, his reasons for considering philosophy of prime importance, and an outline of how he thought metaphysics best defined. An overview of McTaggart's intention is best had from his essay 'An Ontological Idealism' published in 1924. Comparing this with one of his earliest works, 'The Further Determination of the Absolute' (written in 1893), we can see the remarkable consistency of his conclusions. It also shows the change from the earlier, Hegelian style of dialectical argument obviously influenced by Bradley, to the later style, influenced positively by the work of Russell and Moore.

Some Dogmas of Religion, though not a definitive exposition of his philosophy, does reveal the intention of his belief and the form in which he believed it could be accepted on the grounds of common sense. The first chapter, 'The Importance of Dogma', is based on the article 'The Necessity of Dogma', published in January 1895. The third chapter, 'Human Immortality' first appeared in 1903 and the fourth chapter, 'Human Pre-existence' in 1904. Both were published together in 1915 as *Human Immortality and Pre-Existence*. In addition there are chapters on 'Free Will', 'God as Omnipotent' and 'Non-omnipotent God'.

Whereas *Some Dogmas of Religion* tells us that there is nothing in common sense to make us disbelieve the existence of a mental self, *The Nature of Existence* tells us what self is and fits it into a universal scheme of selves. It is an essentially deductive argument based upon the most meagre self-evident truths: that something exists, that we know that something exists and that what exists is differentiated. By adopting these as a priori necessities, McTaggart completely sidesteps epistemology and aims straight for an absolutist metaphysical truth. The process leads to the conclusion that the self is real and will continue *sub specie temporis* ('under the appearance of time') until it reaches the final stage of endless eternality.

Much of McTaggart's early work is concerned with Hegel. His first book, *Studies in Hegelian Dialectic*, is an interpretation and defence of the general principles of the dialectical method. *Studies in Hegelian Cosmology* deals with special applications of the method. *Commentary on Hegel's Logic* is a rigorous exposition of the Hegelian process from the category of Pure Being to the Absolute Idea.

Philosophy
Rightly or wrongly, McTaggart sees in Plato, like Plotinus and Hegel, an other-worldly mysticism to which he can relate his own mystic intuition. Like Plotinus, McTaggart's mystic vision of idealistic reality reaches beyond the sensations of the world of appearance. As Plotinus seeks the fuller truth of Platonism, so McTaggart tries to reach the heart of Hegel's Absolute. Certainly we misread McTaggart if we accept the general view of his philosophical contribution as confined to the erection of a paradoxical argument about the unreality of time.

McTaggart imagines an idealistic self passing through a sort of spiritual metempsychosis. It progresses from fragmentary, misperceived experiences in the apparently material world of temporality, in stages of increased perception, towards the timeless, final stage of all-perceiving reality. It is a system of recurring 'self-rebirth' as new perceptions add to the total content of the perceiving self. The final stage is a state of everlasting, timeless and all-knowing lovingness. Like Plotinian souls in the world of intellect, McTaggart's selves in the atemporal world know 'nothing dark or out of rule'.[12]

Though McTaggart attempts to fit the self into a completely idealistic world, he is constantly concerned with our human condition and how this can be reconciled with an idealistic existence. This leads him to consider all elements of our experience that influence our view of self. Consequently, he re-defines many things that appear to us in the world of experience. He re-describes substance, what we are, the nature of time, change and the progress of the individual in the timeless world. He questions the nature of love and value and tries to answer why the world of appearance is riddled with error.

Though he believes that something exists, he thinks that most of what we commonly accept as existing is misperceived. What is correctly perceived, though substantial, is not materially real. This way of thinking leads him to propose a universe of spiritual selves, existing eternally in a timeless, non-material world. To develop his idea, he supposes that there must be something true about what exists, besides its existence. Such 'truth' exists in its qualities, which, though generally indefinable, are inescapable. Further, all qualities themselves will also have qualities to infinity,

---

[12] Plotinus, *The Enneads*, trans. Stephen MacKenna, Introduction and Notes by John Dillon (Harmondsworth, Penguin, 1991), vol. 3, chap. 8, p. 247.

so whatever qualities are, they at least have the potential to act as complete descriptors of substance. Because substance is related to its qualities, its qualities must be related to it. The consequent complexity of such qualitative description means that no two substances can be identical. Because the qualities of a substance have a relation to a perceiver, each substance must be different from another by at least one attribute (the individual's perception) and must therefore be capable of an exclusive and sufficient description. As far as McTaggart is concerned, if something is capable of complete description then it is entitled to be called real. So what exists, though non-material, because of its qualities and the way they are perceived, is substantial, describable and real. The content of any substance is therefore known when it is perceived by a non-material self.

Because perception is non-material, McTaggart considers it spiritual. Because spiritual selves perceive the content of substance, all selves have the content of perception and so are spiritual ('spirituality' simply means 'non-material', with no theological connotation). Neither matter nor sensa being required for this process, they are superfluous and, as neither can be shown to have content, they cannot be spiritual and so do not exist anyway. McTaggart splits the world of selves into four serial relations. He calls the relation 'past, present and future' the A series and the relation 'earlier and later' the B series. The real series that we misperceive as the B series he calls the C series. The increments of our misperception of the C series he calls the D series. The C series is the series of perceptions that are in the perceiver. Perception is the only quality of selfhood. It is known to us by introspection and not by our perception of the external world (that is 'external' to perception itself).

In McTaggart's system we are, therefore, spiritual entities, the primary quality of which is defined by our content and the secondary quality by our own perception. In this way selves are clearly defined as both the total content of the universe and the only medium by which their own spirituality can be known. Our situation is that all we think of as real, outside our own perception, is not real. The only reality is the 'direct perception' we have of ourselves or of other selves, everything else invoking unreal matter or sensa. Our misperception of the apparently real leads us to be continually mistaken about the nature of our own selfhood. As the whole content of McTaggartian selves is formed from mental states with no material charac-teristics, they are the only thing immune from error and, therefore, the only thing that can be depended upon to perceive clearly and distinctly.

We might think, therefore, that the self should be readily known. However, this seems far from the case and the self may be impossible to prove. Self-perception only proves that something is being perceived as a self and it is still possible that such perception is illusory, particularly given the high degree of error that McTaggart's theory proposes. However, the notion of the perceiving self is arrived at after removing the far more potentially error-ridden sensa and matter. In McTaggart's system, our individuality is guaranteed by our experience of self-perception. Whatever perceptions we have of ourselves we can be sure are to do with us alone. Even in the fuller system, the self retains individuality. No self forms part of another self, so we do not get lost in an amorphous world of confused spirituality. Even God could be a self if he were the content of one mind. All selves are part of the whole but the whole cannot be a self. It is only selves that can know the content of substantial existence and the whole is formed only of selves. As spirit is the quality of all content, then selves together form the total of all existence. In this system, we are only spirit in a totality of spirit, but our individuality is guaranteed by the very definition of self.

However, even if sensa and matter are thrown out, the self still seems to exist in time. Everything we experience seems to happen in time. Even direct perception seems to take time. The paradox of McTaggart's claim that time is unreal is heightened because, while he insists that its components are self-contradictory, he accepts that our experience of it is unavoidable. Yet the real world cannot, he thinks, be represented in time as we experience it, so his denial of its reality is an unavoidable component in his metaphysical scheme. He believes that it is possible to prove that nothing existent can possess the characteristics of being in time and that all statements involving time are erroneous. He acknowledges that this is more paradoxical than the idea of the unreality of space or matter, for, whereas our own introspective states are not material or spatial, they are unavoidably temporal. Still, no matter how much temporal misperception pervades our experience, it has no place in the serial existence of the self.

McTaggart's argument against time has two parts. Part one involves three steps: time involves change; change can only occur if there is a series of relations past, present and future (the *A* series); the *A* series involves a contradiction that leads to a vicious infinite regress: therefore there can be no time. Part two argues that the relation earlier and later (the *B* series) must be temporal, but that there can be no *B* series without an *A* series. As the *A* series is self-contradictory there can be no *B* series. We are then faced with two problems – our view of things changing in the *A* series is wrong and our experience of time in the *B* series is also wrong.

If time is unreal, then change, which is undeniably happening (even to selves), must be different from how we usually think of it. In McTaggartian change, real change occurs only if events change. It is not facts that change, because 'facts' are only facts about events, so if events do not change then facts do not change. Neither is it things nor facts about things, that change, because, as there is no materially objective status in the universe, all apparent changes to things must be changes in perceptions. In the atemporal world of selves, what changes is that new perceptions are added to their total content of perceptions. Nothing can be taken away; for, just as the universe cannot lose any of its contents, neither can selves. Selves are on a one-directional course in the *C* series. However, because of the inter-connectedness of the quality of selves, the substantial universe will be extrinsically altered by any additional perception of change in any self. Any such change, in any part of any characteristic in the universe, means that none of the substance that existed before the change, will exist in the same way after the change.

It is the perception of the substantial but non-material selves, of themselves and other selves, to a greater or lesser degree, that form the real atemporal *C* series. Though all empirical knowledge is either perception or knowledge based on perception, it is superficial because it only gives us knowledge about the characteristics of existent substance. It is knowledge by acquaintance with the substance and cannot give us knowledge of any real characteristics of the substance. When we perceive characteristics of a substance, we only perceive the particular substance's perception of the characteristics of other particular substances and so on. In this way a self's perception includes the perception of another self that it perceives. On the one hand, some apparent experiences may appear to us to be experiences and may be experiences of the real. On the other hand, some experiences may appear to us to be experiences and are only experiences of the apparent. Our experience of time, like our empirical experience, falls into the latter category.

Even though the ultimate nature of substance is simple, its appearance to us is that of unyielding complexity. To demonstrate its reality by complete description, and at the same time avoid a vicious regress, McTaggart introduces a system of perpetual determinacy he calls 'determining correspondence'. This is a one-to-one relation between members of the sets of parts such that a self A has a set of parts B and C (which could be a set of parts to infinity) and B and C has a set of parts corresponding to each set of parts of A. A sufficient description of C includes the fact of its relation to part of B and therefore determines a sufficient description of that part of B. So when one part is determined by another part that determining part includes, as part of itself, the determination of the other parts. In other words, anything that is itself perceived, has perceptions that have perceptions and so on and, although they are not directly perceived, any perception has, as part of it, all these other perceptions. Each perception in the universe increases the number of determining correspondence relations and ultimately all selves will stand in determining correspondence relations to all other selves.

Based upon his personal experience of love, McTaggart concludes that love between selves is the fundamental relation. He believes that the experience of love is the most direct experience any individual can have. He finds it difficult to define love other than in the way we experience it, but thinks it is never 'in respect of', but 'because of', qualities of the beloved. Although we may be caused to love by a person's qualities any resulting love we have is for the person and not for those qualities. Any love that is 'in respect of' qualities is only justified as long as those qualities hold, whereas love which is 'because of' those qualities, although it may be originally in respect of them, does not persist because of that original relation. For McTaggart, the essence of love 'springs from a sense of union with another self'.[13] In ultimate reality, when we can directly perceive another self, our experience of love, as an outcome of this 'sense of union', will therefore transcend all other relations we may hold to another self.

Because of the serial nature of the C series, selves must be 'heading' somewhere. McTaggart believes that the universe contains both good and evil but favours the idea that the C series will ultimately include more good. The thought, that we may exist eternally in a timeless universe of evil, he finds intuitively unbearable. He thinks that the increase of perception in the series equates with an increase in value and consequently an increase in good. Evil cannot be removed from the

---

[13] McTaggart, *The Nature of Existence*, §464.

system, but in the final stage, it will be insignificant compared to the amount of good. Again, this ties in with his idea of a 'growing love' being the fundamental relation.

As love 'grows', so will value. Value will increase as the number of incidents of value increases. Because time is misperceived, the repetition of values, such as pleasure or pain, will not become wearisome (we need not worry about getting fed up with pleasure) but will only add to the total sum of the value of pleasure or pain. Value is represented by quality and not quantity or duration. Value is not the possession or maintenance of high levels of good, it is the increase in good and the consequent reduction in evil. In this respect, it is not the ultimate amount, but the degree of change, which dictates the value. The conclusion of the C series will bring the union of the total of all value in the series at that stage, and the total increase in value throughout the series. In the final stage, the values of love, knowledge and virtue, will be at their highest because the C series will be in a state of the greatest unmixed non-hedonic good.

Throughout his metaphysical task, McTaggart, like Descartes, finds himself concerned that, having uncovered a universe of error, it may be impossible to know what is true. He can only fall back on his intuitive belief that the experience of love is neither a misperception nor an error of judgement. He believes it is the one thing that, in our mortal existence, gives us a hint of what is our immortal reality. By doing this, what he draws from his own life ultimately provides him with his philosophical stability. His philosophical faith in the spiritual self is combined with his intuitive faith in the reality of love.

Conclusion

The twentieth century has not had much sympathy for idealism of McTaggart's sort but that hardly decides the question of his relevance. Mathematics and science have had a strong influence on contemporary thinking. In philosophy the mechanics of logical positivism have made it more difficult to pursue metaphysics. However, as the century ends and philosophy of mind takes the high ground, we see a resurgence of interest in pluralism and, together with a contemporary dominance of the metaphysics of the absolute, a renewed interest in idealism. Thus Gödel expresses the universe as a scientific model but also recognizes the debt such thinking has to idealists such as McTaggart.[14] Indeed, according to Yourgrau, McTaggart's system can play an important role in our understanding of the fuller consequences of space-time theory.[15] Few have looked closely at McTaggart's fuller philosophy. Yet in *The Nature of Existence* we find a masterpiece of logical insight and philosophical vision. Not only can it help us understand metaphysics, but its ontology reveals how philosophy is still the tool for enquiry into psychological and spiritual concerns. *Philosophical Studies* provides a perfect introduction to what McTaggart has

---

[14] Kurt Gödel, 'A Remark about the Relationship between Relativity Theory and Idealistic Philosophy', in Palle Yourgrau, *Demonstratives* (Oxford University Press, 1991), pp. 261–5.

[15] Palle Yourgrau, *The Disappearence of Time: Kurt Gödel and the Idealistic Tradition in Philosophy* (Cambridge University Press, 1991).
See also: Stanley Victor Keeling, 'McTaggarts Metaphysics', in Lowes Dickinson, *McTaggart*, pp. 125–60; Peter Thomas Geach, *Truth, Love and Immortality* (London, Hutchinson, 1979); John Wisdom, 'McTaggarts Determining Correspondence of Substance: A Refutation', *Mind*, vol. 37 (1928), no. 148, pp. 414–38; John King-Farlow, 'The Positive McTaggart on Time', *Philosophy*, vol. 49 (1974), no. 188, pp. 169–78; William R. Shea, 'McTaggart and the Neo-positivist Entropists', *Philosophy*, vol. 50 (1975), no. 193, pp. 346–51.

to offer, and an ideal way of breaking through the paradoxical barrier he created when he denied the reality of time.

Finally, all who read these essays are indebted to the work of Stanley Victor Keeling who edited them and provided the Introduction. Keeling had a deep understanding of McTaggart's work. His introduction is concerned, in part, with the relation of McTaggart's idealist view and the logical atomism of Bertrand Russell. This should not be seen as simply an interesting piece of history; for as well as illuminating the nature of philosophical argument it provides a very enlightening contemporary view of a philosophical controversy. The discussion still has relevance and remains an important contribution to the debate. Keeling himself had a more Bergsonian view of time than McTaggart and put forward a strong argument in defence of the nature of time lying in its duration.[16] This alternative view, however, did not diminish his respect for McTaggart's lifelong dedication to rigorous metaphysics and his contribution to the way we view the temporal world.[17]

Gerald Rochelle
Shropshire, 1996

---

[16] Stanley Victor Keeling, *Time and Duration*, edited by Gerald Rochelle, Introduction by Edward Senior (Lewiston, New York, Edwin Mellen, 1991).

[17] Permission to reproduce Keeling's work is granted by his literary estate.

BIBLIOGRAPHY

'Trade and the Flag'. Lecture delivered to the Cambridge Economic Club, Lent term 1887, *Economic Club Essays* (Cambridge University Library, 1887), 4 pp.

'The Changes of Method in Hegel's Dialectic, I', *Mind*, vol. 1 ns (1892), no. 1, pp. 56–71.

'The Changes of Method in Hegel's Dialectic, II', *Mind*, vol. 1 (1892), no. 2, pp. 188–205.

Review, 'T. Mackay, ed., *A Plea for Liberty*', *International Journal of Ethics*, vol. 2 (1892), no. 3, pp. 391–2.

'Du Vrai Sens de la Dialectique de Hégel', *Revue de Métaphysique et de Morale*, vol. 1 (1893), pp. 538–52.

'The Further Determination of the Absolute', privately published pamphlet (1893). Substantially chap. 9 of *Studies in Hegelian Cosmology*.

'Time and the Hegelian Dialectic, I', *Mind*, vol. 2 (1893), no. 8, pp. 490–504.

Critical Notice, 'E. Caird, *The Evolution of Religion*', *Mind*, vol. 2 (1893), no. 7, pp. 376–83.

'Time and the Hegelian Dialectic, II', *Mind*, vol. 3 (1894), no. 10, pp. 190–207.

Critical Notice, 'F. H. Bradley, *Appearance and Reality*', *Revue de Métaphysique et de Morale*, vol. 2 (1894), pp. 98–112.

'The Necessity of Dogma'. Lecture delivered to the London Ethical Society. *International Journal of Ethics*, vol. 5 (1895), no. 2, pp. 147–62.

Review, 'W. Wallace, *Hegel's Philosophy of Mind*', *International Journal of Ethics*, vol. 5 (1895), no. 3, pp. 393–5.

Critical Notice, 'A. J. Balfour, *The Foundations of Belief*', *Revue de Métaphysique et de Morale*, vol. 3 (1895), pp. 734–53.

Studies in the Hegelian Dialectic (Cambridge University Press, 1896), 2nd ed., 1922. 255 pp. Chaps. 2–4 are based on McTaggart's Fellowship dissertation submitted for examination at Trinity College, Cambridge, 1891.

'Hegel's Theory of Punishment', *International Journal of Ethics*, vol. 6 (1896), no. 4, pp. 479–502.

'Hegel's Treatment of the Categories of the Subjective Notion I', *Mind*, vol. 6 (1897), no. 22, pp. 164–81.

'Hegel's Treatment of the Categories of the Subjective Notion II', *Mind*, vol. 6 (1897), no. 23, pp. 342–58.

'The Conception of Society as an Organism', *International Journal of Ethics*, vol. 7 (1897), no. 4, pp. 414–34.

Review, 'J. Watson, *Christianity and Idealism*', *International Journal of Ethics*, vol. 8 (1897), no. 1, pp. 123–4.

'Introduction to the Study of Philosophy'. McTaggart's personal notes of the course of Friday evening lectures held at Trinity College, Cambridge from 1899 to 1924.

'Hegel's Treatment of the Categories of the Objective Notion', *Mind*, vol. 8 (1899), no. 29, pp. 35–62.

'Hegel's Treatment of the Categories of the Idea', *Mind*, vol. 9 (1900), no. 34, pp. 145–83.

Critical Notice, 'J. Royce, *The World of the Individual, First Series*', *Mind*, vol. 9 (1900), no. 34, pp. 258–66.

Review, 'W. R. Inge, *Christian Mysticism*', *International Journal of Ethics*, vol. 10 (1900), no. 4, pp. 535–6.

Studies in Hegelian Cosmology (Cambridge University Press, 1901), 2nd ed., 1918, 293 pp.

Review, 'H. H. Joachim, *A Study of the Ethics of Spinoza*', *International Journal of Ethics*, vol. 12 (1902), no. 4, pp. 517–20.

Critical Notice, 'G. H. Howison, *The Limits of Evolution and Other Essays Illustrating the Metaphysical Theory of Personal Idealism*', *Mind*, vol. 11 (1902), no. 43, pp. 383–9.

'Hegel's Treatment of the Categories of Quality', *Mind*, vol. 11 (1902), no. 44, pp. 503–26.

Critical Notice, 'J. Royce, *The World of the Individual, Second Series*', *Mind*, vol. 11 (1902), no. 44, pp. 557–63.

'Some Considerations Relating to Human Immortality', *International Journal of Ethics*, vol. 13 (1903), no. 2, pp. 152–71.

Review, 'F. R. Tenant, *The Origin and Propagation of Sin*', *International Journal of Ethics*, vol. 14 (1903), no. 1, pp. 128–31.

'Hegel's Treatment of the Categories of Quantity', *Mind*, vol. 13 (1904), no. 50, pp. 180–203.

Review, 'R. Adamson, *The Development of Modern Philosophy*', *International Journal of Ethics*, vol. 14 (1904), no. 3, pp. 394–5.

'Human Pre–existence', *International Journal of Ethics*, vol. 15 (1904), no. 1, pp. 83–95.

Review, 'P. S. Tattvabhushan et al., *Aspects of the Vedanta*', *International Journal of Ethics*, vol. 15 (1904), no. 1, pp. 124–5.

Some Dogmas of Religion (London, Edward Arnold, 1906), 2nd ed., (with an introduction by C. D. Broad and including McTaggart's emendations extracted by S. V. Keeling), 1930, 299 pp.

Critical Notice, 'A. T. Ormond, *Concepts of Philosophy*', *Mind*, vol. 16 (1907), no. 63, pp. 431–6.

Review, 'E. Westermarck, *The Origin and Development of Moral Ideas*, vol. 1', *International Journal of Ethics*, vol. 17 (1906), no. 1, pp. 125–8.

'The Relation of Time and Eternity'. Address delivered to the Philosophical Union of the University of California, 23 August 1907. *University of California Chronicle*, vol. 10 (1908), no. 2, pp. 127–52. Reprinted as a pamphlet (Berkeley University Press, 1908), 28 pp. Reprinted in *Mind*, vol. 18 (1909), no. 71, pp. 343–62.

'The Individualism of Value', *International Journal of Ethics*, vol. 18 (1908), no. 4, pp. 433–45.

'The Unreality of Time', *Mind*, vol. 17 (1908), no. 68, pp. 45–74. Forms the basis of chap. 33, *The Nature of Existence*, vol. 2.

Critical Notice, 'W. James, *Pragmatism, a New Name for some Old Ways of Thinking; Popular Lectures on Philosophy*', *Mind*, vol. 17 (1908), no. 65, pp. 104–109.

'Mysticism', *The New Quarterly*, vol. 2 (1909), no. 7, pp. 315–39.

Review, 'E. Westermarck, *The Origin and Development of Moral Ideas*, vol. 2', *International Journal of Ethics*, vol. 20 (1909), no. 1, pp. 94–9.

'Dare to be Wise'. Address delivered to the 'Heretics' Society in Cambridge, 8 December 1909 (London, Watts and Co. (for The Rationalist Press Association), 1910), 9 pp.

Commentary on Hegel's Logic (Cambridge University Press, 1910), 311 pp.

Review, 'Hegel, *Grundlinien der Philosophie des Rechts*, G. Lasson (ed.)', *International Journal of Ethics*, vol. 22 (1912), no. 4, p. 480.

Critical Notice, 'B. Bosanquet, *The Principle of Individuality and Value: the Gifford Lectures for 1911*', *Mind*, vol. 21 (1912), no. 83, pp. 416–27.

Human Immortality and Pre-Existence (London, Edward Arnold, 1915), 119 pp. Reprint of chaps. 3–4 of *Some Dogmas of Religion*.

'The Meaning of Causality'. The Henry Sidgwick Memorial Lecture, delivered at Newnham College, Cambridge, 1914. *Mind*, vol. 24 (1915), no. 95, pp. 326–44.

'Personality', *Encyclopaedia of Religion and Ethics*, ed. J. Hastings (Edinburgh, T. and T. Clark, 1917), vol. 9, pp. 773–81.

The Nature of Existence, vol. 1 (Cambridge University Press, 1921), 309 pp. Reprinted in 1968 and 1988, 330 pp.

'Immortality and Monadistic Idealism', *The Monist*, vol. 31 (1921), no. 2, pp. 316–17.

'Propositions Applicable to Themselves', *Mind*, vol. 32 (1923), no. 128, pp. 462–4.

Critical Notice, 'A. S. Pringle-Pattison, *The Idea of Immortality*', *Mind*, vol. 32 (1923), no. 126, pp. 220–24.

'An Ontological Idealism', *Contemporary British Philosophy*, 1st Series, ed. J. H. Muirhead (London, George Allen and Unwin, 1924), pp. 251–69.

The Nature of Existence, vol. 2, ed. C. D. Broad (Cambridge University Press, 1927), 479 pp. Reprinted in 1968 and 1988, 526 pp.

Philosophical Studies, edited and introduced by S. V. Keeling (London, Edward Arnold, 1934), 292 pp.

PHILOSOPHICAL STUDIES

by the late

J. McT. ELLIS McTAGGART

Litt.D., LL.D., F.B.A.

Edited, with an Introduction, by
S. V. KEELING, M.A., D.-ès-L.
Senior Lecturer of University College, University of London

LONDON
EDWARD ARNOLD & CO.
1934

Printed in Great Britain by
Butler & Tanner Ltd., Frome and London

CONTENTS

5

ACKNOWLEDGMENTS

I thank the persons and publishers mentioned below for their courteous permission, so readily granted, to reprint the essays collected in this volume. The provenance of those essays is fully indicated for the convenience of readers wishing to refer to any of them in the place of its original publication.

For essay I, The Rationalist Press Ltd. ; for II, Messrs. J. M. Dent & Sons Ltd., The New Quarterly, vol. II, no. 7, July 1909 (pp. 315–39) ; for III, the representatives of the late Dr. Hastings and Messrs. T. & T. Clark of Edinburgh, Hastings's Encyclopædia of Religion and Ethics, vol. IX (pp. 773–81) ; for IV, The University of Chicago Press, International Journal of Ethics, vol. XVIII, July 1908 (pp. 433–45) ; for V, VI, VII, VIII, Professor G. E. Moore of Trinity College, Cambridge ;—V, Mind, vol. XVII, no. 68, October 1908 (pp. 457–74) ; VI, Mind, vol. XVIII, no. 71, July 1909 (pp. 343–62) ; VII, Mind, vol. XXIV, no. 95, July 1915 (pp. 326–44) ; VIII, Mind, vol. XXXII, no. 128, October 1923 (pp. 462–4) ; for IX, Mrs. J. McT. E. McTaggart ; for X, the Cambridge University Press, a substantial part of the essay being ch. ix of Studies in Hegelian Cosmology ; for XI, Messrs. Allen & Unwin Ltd., publishers of Contemporary British Philosophy, I, edited by Professor J. H. Muirhead (pp. 251–69).

My own heaviest obligation is to Mrs. McTaggart, both for the encouragement of her interest and help, and for her efforts to recover the unpublished MS. entitled ' The Empirical Element in Metaphysics '—from which McTaggart gave his last address before the Moral Sciences Club at Cambridge. Its omission from this collection is a very serious one. I also thank most cordially my friend, Dr. R. Leet Patterson, for his many sound suggestions, and for the pleasure and benefit I have derived from discussing with him various points in McTaggart's philosophy, during the last eight years.

ACKNOWLEDGMENTS

I acknowledge with gratitude the help and efficiency of Miss Marjorie Giuseppi and of Miss F. Leontinoff, B.A., to whom the typographical accuracy of the text is so largely due ; the former prepared the typescript of the essays, and the latter undertook that most ungrateful of tasks, the reading of proofs.

S. V. K.

July 1934.

Note.

I have not conceived it my business to change the typography of the original impressions of these essays beyond correcting some quite certain misprints. The reader may sometimes be puzzled at McTaggart's seeming nonchalance in using now capitals, now small letters, for the initials of certain recurrent words, such as ' Time,' ' Causality,' ' Reality,' ' Spirit,' etc., and often, too, in using both within the same paragraph. I resist the temptation to change this seemingly inconsistent usage of small and capital letters, since it does not follow that because I cannot see McTaggart's reason for his practice, that he had none, and it is an editor's duty to respect his author's text where doubt is possible.—*Ed.*

8

INTRODUCTION

There are reasons more than enough to justify the publication of this book. A casual glance at the titles of the studies assembled in it might suggest that their subjects are so diverse, and the connections between them so remote, that they have little in common save in being subjects which philosophers are wont to discuss. In preparing the material for publication, however, I have found not merely more connectedness than I had anticipated, but also an unmistakable unity of theme. On this account, collectively they present the essence of McTaggart's philosophy in a clear and impressive way, whilst individually many of them are concerned with the very key-problems of metaphysics. The intrinsic excellence of McTaggart's treatment of those problems more than justifies me in collecting his essays from journals now out óf print and sources difficult of access, and publishing them in a single volume. And for the student of philosophy at the universities these papers will have a further value. For he will find in them models of philosophical composition, fine examples of orderliness in the development of arguments, of care in making them sound and 'water-tight,' besides convincing evidence of the sufficiency of plain English to express difficult conceptions and subtle distinctions. Add to these reasons that the present essays give an admirable conspectus of some central contentions in McTaggart's masterpiece, *The Nature of Existence*, and make a most readable introduction to that difficult work, and the case for their publication is over-established.

I

Of the motives that have led men to the study of philosophy, Mr. Bertrand Russell once distinguished [1] two kinds, those inspired by religion and ethics, and those inspired by the sciences. In Plato, Spinoza, and Hegel he found examples of the former, and in Leibniz, Locke, and Hume instances of the latter ; whilst Aristotle, Descartes, Berkeley, and Kant were thought to have been inspired by motives of both origins. There can be no doubt, if we accept these three divisions, that McTaggart must be placed in the first, in company with Plato, Spinoza, and Hegel. So much Dr. Broad has acknowledged in assigning him to ' the front rank of the great historical philosophers ' [2] and in comparing *The Nature of Existence*, by which McTaggart has ' fully earned his place among the immortals,' with the *Enneads* of Plotinus, the *Ethics* of Spinoza, and the *Encyclopædia* of Hegel.

But though the inspiration of McTaggart's metaphysics is a religious one, it is so only in a universal and philosophical sense of the word. The motive and emotion are not inspired by any particular ' traditional national religion,' such as Christianity or Buddhism, but by what he defines as ' a conviction of a harmony between ourselves and the universe at large.' The conviction, however, is not regarded as a self-sufficient legislative power, authoritative to exact our acceptance of the beliefs it promulgates. Questions of undoubted importance for both feeling and intellect it may ' set,' but it may ' settle ' none for either. The conviction is of a dual character. Its religious and emotional element characterizes a state of the person. But it characterizes him only in relation to some proposition which he believes to be true, e.g. that individuals and the universe are harmoniously related. And this, which is believed and asserted by the convinced person, may be in

---

[1] ' On Scientific Method in Philosophy,' the Herbert Spencer lecture delivered at Oxford in 1914 ; reprinted in *Mysticism and Logic*, 1921, pp. 97–124.
[2] Broad, *John McTaggart Ellis McTaggart, 1866–1925* : Proc. Brit. Academy, vol. XIII.

fact true or false. But the emotion evoked in him on contemplating his belief, the attitudes of hope and aspiration it
inspires, are themselves neither true nor false, but simply
occurrent. And since, *ex hypothesi*, the proposition believed
is one not about the believer's emotion or mental attitudes,
but about a harmony between the universe and all persons,
it could not be the believer's emotion or attitudes that determine the truth or falsity of his belief, but only the fact of such
a harmony obtaining, if there is such a fact. Hence, for the
convinced person to *know* whether his belief is true, he must
first come by knowledge of that which the belief is *prima
facie* about—the universe, persons, and their relations. This
knowledge, not lying ready to hand, must needs be sought,
and, like all knowledge, be sought by intellect. And this
search to discover what is the character of all that exists,
thence, the nature of those existents which are selves, and the
attempt to determine whether the relations between selves
and all other existents are such as to render them harmonious—
such an inquiry is a metaphysical one. So though our problems may originate in emotion, their settlement falls wholly
to reason. Indeed, McTaggart believed that unless feeling,
no less than reason, were permitted to raise its problems, the
aim of philosophy would be limited just as arbitrarily as if
anything other than reason were permitted to solve them.

That metaphysics was of the very greatest practical importance, McTaggart thought evident,[1] for it is on answers it
may return to questions concerning man's place in the universe
and his destiny, that his dearest hopes depend. How serious
are the consequences of answers to these questions, had not,
McTaggart believed, been overlooked by past thinkers,
although the seriousness had not always been sufficiently
recognized. Indeed, during the twenty years in which he

---

[1] 'The practical importance of philosophy consists, not in the
guidance it gives us in life—it gives us, I think, very little—but in
the chance that it may answer this supreme question (whether good
or evil predominates in the universe) in a cheerful manner, that it
may provide some solution which shall be a consolation and an
encouragement.'—p. 151, Essay VI; also, *Some Dogmas of Religion* :
London, Arnold, ch. i.

was working out his own answers to such questions and elaborating a metaphysic which should provide grounds for those answers, Bertrand Russell was advocating an extremely different and antithetical view of the aim, the problems, and the method of philosophy. Among the then younger generation of students at Cambridge the newer view rapidly gained ground over the traditional one. McTaggart too was unquestionably influenced by it in certain minor respects, but what was most distinctive in it he definitely rejected. He confirmed the insistence on the need of submitting to detailed criticism and proof propositions that had become so familiar that they too often passed for truisms.[1] But McTaggart was no party to the extreme curtailments and large assumptions involved in the new programme.

Since the proposals it incorporates are still popular with a large section of the philosophical public in Britain and America, and still often determine both the formulation and the treatment of philosophical problems, McTaggart's conception of the aims and methods of metaphysics may be conveniently elucidated by contrasting certain of his own, with certain of Russell's, declarations on the matter. The difference of their outlook derives for the most part from their dissimilar estimates of the relevance to philosophy of (a) ethics and religion, and (b) the special sciences, and physics in particular.

(a) McTaggart emphasizes the human and practical importance of philosophy, Russell is repeatedly at pains to deny such value of it.[2] What Mr. Russell calls ' ethical meta-

[1] ' The oneness of the world is an almost undiscussed postulate of most metaphysics. " Reality is not merely one and self-consistent, but is a system of reciprocally determinate parts " (Bosanquet, *Logic*, II, p. 211)—such a statement would pass almost unnoticed as a mere truism.'—B. Russell, *Mysticism and Logic*, p. 99. It is a merit in Russell to have persisted in challenging such statements, and not to have let them pass unnoticed ; but it is also an excellence in McTaggart to have tried to demonstrate them in detail.

[2] ' We must renounce the hope,' says Russell, ' that philosophy can promise satisfaction to our mundane desires. What it can do, when it is purified from all practical taint, is to help us to understand the general aspects of the world and the logical analysis of familiar but complex things.'—*Our Knowledge of the External World*, p. 17. And again (*ibid.*, p. 26), ' The hope of satisfaction to our more human

INTRODUCTION

physics' is damned *in limine* by its human, and therefore questionable, origin. For 'ethical metaphysics,' we are told,[1] is 'fundamentally an attempt, however disguised, to give legislative force to our own wishes,' since ethics is 'essentially a product of the gregarious instinct,' and 'is in origin the art of recommending to others the sacrifices required for co-operation with oneself.' From this it follows, for Russell, that 'a philosophy derived from ethical notions is never impartial and therefore never fully scientific,' and his reason for rejecting the standpoint of Plato and Spinoza, of Hegel and McTaggart is, that they have neither sought nor achieved 'ethical neutrality.'

To this objection, I imagine that McTaggart's attitude would be, that 'neutrality' is something the philosopher should *not* seek, though impartiality something that he should. Man's place and prospects in the world, he would feel, are things too important to be set aside on the suggestion that they are 'not sufficiently dry and abstract' to fall within the philosopher's purview. Indeed, McTaggart would object to the whole principle underlying Russell's strictures here, and deny that the proper aim of philosophical inquiry is to be defined in terms of any *method*, however 'scientific.' There is a curious reversal of means and end enshrined in Russell's plea for metaphysics to become 'scientific,' a reversal which seems to be perpetuated in the proposal of current 'logical

desires—the hope of demonstrating that the world has this or that desirable ethical characteristic—is not one which philosophy can do anything whatever to satisfy. The difference between a good world and a bad one is . . . *not a sufficiently abstract difference* to come within the province of philosophy' (my italics). Again, we are later told, 'the philosophy which is to be genuinely inspired by the scientific spirit must deal with somewhat dry and abstract matters, and must not hope to find an answer to the practical problems of life' (*ibid.*, p. 29). 'Whether the universe is progressive, retrograde, or stationary, it is not for the philosopher to say' (*ibid.*, p. 237). 'He is not called upon to tell us anything about the universe as a whole, or to offer grounds either for optimism or pessimism.' Ethical and religious questions, 'such, for example, as the question of a future life, belong, at least in theory, to special sciences' and have no bearing on philosophy.
[1] *Mysticism and Logic*, pp. 107-8 ; 109.

13

positivism,' that metaphysics consists in the *analysis* of certain particular facts, and nothing more. McTaggart never committed his criticisms on these proposals to writing, but I think we can infer what would have been the substance of his objection. The proposal seems to be vitiated precisely in allowing a specialist interest in science, or methodology, to dictate what should and what should not be regarded as the proper problems of philosophy, and to dictate what is and what is not the nature of its subject-matter. Should not the problems and the character of the subject-matter alone be allowed to determine what kind of method is suitable for their treatment ? It seems likely that this was one reason why McTaggart rejected Russell's plea that all reference to ethical and religious notions and values should be excluded *ab initio* from the statement and the study of philosophical problems, and so secure their ' purification from all practical taint.' For to make this exaction is no less than to advance without demonstration what is in fact a far-reaching philosophical dogma, under the thinly disguised pretence that it is an *extra*-philosophical recommendation, whose adoption would in no way prejudice the philosopher's findings, since it is inspired only by a healthy zeal for impartiality. But the ' ethical neutrality ' is itself emphatically partial, and not impartial at all ! That insistence on critical scrutiny of initial assumptions which advocates of a neutral, scientific philosophy enjoin would here seem to have been lulled awhile, and their recommendation of a method whose adoption requires certain major problems of perennial interest and great human importance to be rejected without consideration, seems to be, in the end, purely a piece of special pleading in favour of a particular intellectual attitude congenial to certain temperaments.

McTaggart agrees, however, with the insistence on proof for what is asserted, and readers of these essays have ample occasion to perceive how sincere, strenuous, and ingenious are his efforts to provide it. He regarded the technical study of metaphysics as concerned, at almost every step, with proving or disproving something, and held that proving was an activity which countenanced no appeal whatever to feeling [1] or to anything other than reason and perception. But he would deny that it follows from this, or that good grounds have been offered to show, that some of the things the philosopher is called upon to prove or disprove are connections between certain existents and goodness. To be sure, he does not maintain, but expressly denies, that there is an ' intrinsic *a priori* connection between existence and goodness.' ' The question of the nature of existence,' he says, ' is the one we are setting out to determine, and we have no right to begin by assuming that that nature is good '—nor, he would have agreed, by assuming that it is ' ethically neutral.'

(*b*) The second characteristic difference in philosophical outlook between McTaggart and Russell follows from their views concerning the relevance of the natural sciences to philosophy. Russell maintains that while the general results of the special sciences cannot, their method can, and should, be transferred to philosophy and utilized by it. McTaggart denies that either, results or method, could profitably be transferred to philosophy. No doubt his evaluation of the results attained and attainable in natural science, and his view of their irrelevance to metaphysics, finds most popular speculation, and some philosophical criticism, against him. But his opinion that metaphysics has been dominated in greater or lesser degrees by one or another of the sciences at most periods of its history, and that the domination had been on the whole to its detriment, seems to me both true and insufficiently appreciated.

McTaggart's judgment concerning the relation of the sciences to philosophy is made more plain, again, by contrasting it with that of Mr. Russell, or with the empirical

---

[1] Consider the attitude, where he refers, in a letter, to Tennyson's *In Memoriam* : ' I don't think it's any good appealing, as he is rather fond of doing, to the heart on questions of truth. After all, there is only one way of getting at the truth and that is by proving it. All that talk about the heart only comes to saying, " It must be true because we want it to be." Which is both false and rather cowardly.' —G. Lowes Dickinson, *J. McT. E. McTaggart* : Cambridge, 1931, pp. 38–9. Cf. also, *Some Dogmas of Religion*, ch. i, ii.

temper of present speculation, or, indeed, with the marked empirical tendency of the bulk of British philosophy in the past. McTaggart's readers will find his definite preference for Berkeley among British thinkers very understandable, and will readily discern his affiliation with the Continental, rather than the British, tradition. Though his work plainly reflects the influence of Spinoza, of Leibniz, and, in a lesser degree, of Descartes, McTaggart was no mere eclectic. And though it was his considered opinion, formed from a long and close study of Hegel's writings (on which he ranks as a foremost exponent and critic) that Hegel had penetrated farther into the truth about reality than any of his predecessors, McTaggart was no mere Hegelian. The extent of the influence of great philosophers of the past upon him varied. Probably Hegel influenced him most, Spinoza and Leibniz somewhat less, and Hume least of all, in a positive way. Yet most that he accepted from them was modified, and much that he rejected was used to define positions which he was to undermine in the elaboration of his own doctrine. Of this tendency to make a constructive use of what he rejected, his attitude to Hume is an example.[1] In Hume he found much to admire, much that challenged, but nothing that convinced. His *mot* on Hume—' How very clever but how very wrong ! ' is characteristic ; so, too, the entry in his diary on William James, ' I never realized before how true " Entweder Spinozismus oder keine Philosophie " is, because I never saw how low a clever man could fall for want of Spinozism.' And McTaggart would be of one mind, I imagine, with that contemporary Spinozist, Professor H. F. Hallett, when he declared,[2] ' Though I am an Englishman, my belief in metaphysics as the source of all genuine knowledge of the Real is naked and unashamed,' and would agree with him, as against Hume and modern positivism, that ' a theory which fails to carry its intellectual criticism up to the ultimate analysis of time and temporal productivity cannot rightly be named Metaphysics.' Indeed, McTaggart's whole life's work with its crowning achievement

[1] Cf. Essay III.
[2] Hallett, *Aeternitas* : Oxford, 1930. General Preface.

in *The Nature of Existence*, remains one massive and lasting correction of that ' overweening phenomenalism ' from which the mind either turns to ' the pictorial metaphysics of popular theology and superstition ' or else simply denies (without demonstrating its grounds) the solubility of the great traditional problems.

During the score of years through which *The Nature of Existence* was being patiently elaborated, its detail thought out and re-thought, and its statement being revised four or five times, McTaggart was continually confronted at Cambridge with the piecemeal revision of Humean positivism which issued from applying a scientific method in philosophy. Certain of the logical and epistemological doctrines which Russell and his Cambridge colleagues elaborated and applied to the modification and amplification of Hume's phenomenalism (e.g. knowledge by acquaintance and by description, the theory of descriptions, the logic of relations), McTaggart took over and utilized in his own ways for his own purposes. He saw clearly that what was important in these newer epistemological doctrines was logically independent of the positivistic views of their authors, and independent of their utility for the construction of a positivistic phenomenalism. Accordingly, McTaggart felt himself free to make his own applications of the doctrines and at the same time dissociate himself from the positivist and phenomenalist assumptions. And in this dissociation McTaggart's position seems a strong one. For the advocates of ' scientific method in philosophy ' had offered no philosophical grounds for their proposed curtailment of the objects and problems in philosophy. One sought—and still seeks—in vain for philosophical reasons, as distinct from expressions of personal inclination and promises of good to come. Yet philosophical grounds were fairly to be expected. And there was an impressive historical precedent before their eyes. For Kant—at least the Kant of the ' Transcendental Dialectic ' (from whom the negative restrictions of modern positivism derive)—had himself found it necessary to devote the first half of the *Critique of Pure Reason* to developing the grounds which he used in the second half to *justify* his conclusion that metaphysics as a science of ontology was permanently impossible. Now even though Kant's arguments in the ' Æsthetic ' and ' Analytic ' are inacceptable, it must be admitted that they *do* form a very serious, detailed, and coherent attempt to show *why* such knowledge should not be even theoretically obtainable. Was not an analogous attempt fairly to be expected, is not some such demonstration rightly demanded, from those *épris* for impartiality, before the wholesale proscriptions they require should be conceded ? For the prohibitions and curtailments they seek to introduce into metaphysical research depend not on extra-philosophical pronouncements, but emphatically on philosophical ones. For it would be insufficient that those proscriptions were in fact legitimate, it would also require to be *known* that they were so, in order that we should be justified in assenting to them. It is thus tacitly implied that assured knowledge has already been obtained concerning the character of what exists, the nature and conditions of knowledge itself, and the limitations of our cognitive capacities, and that from that knowledge it can be demonstrated that the traditional problems of metaphysics are either meaningless or such as cannot be answered. If such knowledge has been attained, then it should be communicated ; if it has not, the proscription is wholly arbitrary legislation. ' The problems of philosophy,' Mr. Russell declares, ' have been misconceived by all schools, *many of its traditional problems being insoluble with our means of knowledge.*' [1] This indeed supposes that he has already sufficient knowledge about our means of knowledge to justify the asserted insolubility of those problems, otherwise the declaration is not impartial at all, but grossly prejudicial. Yet Russell attempts no thoroughgoing investigation of our cognitive limitations as Kant did, and rejects the doctrine of the first half of the *Critique*, hence there is no reason to suppose that his declaration expresses more than a bare possibility and a personal preference. Mr. Russell may be right in urging that ' something very different (from the methods hitherto practised) is required if philosophy is to become a science, and to aim at

[1] (My italics), Russell, *Our Knowledge of the External World*, p. 3.

results independent of the tastes and temperament of the philosopher,' but he has shown no reason why his own method should be thought to aim at results which are independent of the tastes and temperament of Mr. Russell.

McTaggart would question, with certain other philosophers, whether indeed, philosophy *is* ' to become a science,' though much naturally depends here on what is meant by ' a science.' At all events, what is meant would not be something other than the results consequent on applying what he calls ' the scientific method,'[1] and alternatively, ' the logical-analytic method.'[2] In proposing that philosophy should ' base itself upon science,' he is, however, careful to emphasize that it is ' by studying the methods of science ' and extending their application that philosophy can be made scientific, not by incorporating its general results and seeking ' to give greater generality and unity ' to them. For the most general results are the least certain and the most liable to be upset by subsequent research.[3] Further, in seeking to give ' greater generality and unity ' to such provisional results, we should be generalizing them beyond experience, but without any assurance that they really do hold of things universally.

McTaggart would agree with Russell that the most general results of science cannot be utilized in metaphysics, and would accept his reasons for the denial. But he supplements those reasons, pointing out (i) that metaphysics treats of certain matters not dealt with at all by any science, and (ii) that science is not interested in the *ultimate* nature of the objects with which it does deal, but ' only in what is apparent or comparatively on the surface.'[4] Further, science assumes certain concepts and propositions as ultimate, and does not

---

[1] Cf. *ibid.*, and art. ' Le Réalisme analytique,' *Bulletin de la Société française de philosophie* (mars, 1911).

[2] Russell speaks of his method as being ' something perfectly definite, capable of embodiment in maxims, and adequate, in all branches of philosophy, to yield whatever objective scientific knowledge it is possible to obtain.' I have failed, however, to find the maxims embodying this method, except that which, in *Mysticism and Logic*, p. 155, he calls ' the supreme maxim,' viz. ' Wherever possible, logical constructions are to be substituted for inferred entities.'

[3] *Mysticism and Logic*, p. 102.   [4] Cf. Essay IX, p. 184.

subject them to a critical examination with a view to eliciting their presuppositions, and showing that those presuppositions are, or are not, founded. Natural science itself has no right to pretend that its laws express the ultimate nature of reality, for it is powerless to justify that claim.[1] So McTaggart would agree with Russell (though, in part, for different reasons) that scientific results cannot be transferred with profit to philosophy. But he would *not* agree with Russell that the *method* of science could be utilized or applied in metaphysics. Hence McTaggart disagrees *in toto* that metaphysics can, and should, ' become a science.' For, since it is of the essence of scientific procedure to furnish results of only a provisional and problematic kind, is this not in itself a sufficient reason for demanding that demonstration be given, or at least an overwhelmingly strong case be made, to show why every method conceivable, other than a scientific one, should be set aside as unsuitable ? To be sure, scientific procedure is in part deductive, but it is also in part ineradicably inductive. Exactly what are the presuppositions of induction logicians are not yet agreed upon, and if they were, neither inductive inference nor the inductive results of empirical science could be used without circularity in attempting to justify those presuppositions. The validity of scientific method, then, not being self-evident, could only be established if we can first of all know, independently of its assumptions, that the universe has a certain kind of ultimate structure, and then show that this structure answers to that presupposed in inductive reasoning. What is indispensable, therefore, is precisely a metaphysic which is *not* obtained by the employment of a scientific method, if ever we are to know that a scientific method is capable of yielding more than hypothetical knowledge even within the sciences.

Again, McTaggart points out, the probability of an inference varies directly as the proportion of the field of observation,

[1] James Ward had also pointed this out : ' Science . . . talks freely of the Universe and of Nature ; but I am at a loss to think of any single *scientific* statement that has been, or can be, made concerning either the one or the other.'—*Naturalism and Agnosticism*, I, p. 26.

inter alia, to the field of inference. Now, on any theory, the number of particulars existent is very great (McTaggart thinks infinite)—so great, indeed, that the number of them in which we could observe any characteristic would be an extremely small proportion of the whole [1] (and in his opinion, an infinitely small proportion). So it follows that any procedure which is inescapably inductive (as every application of scientific method is, in greater or lesser degree) would be useless in metaphysics. And it would be useless for a further reason. Since an inductive method involves generalizing some characteristic that has been found common to several members of the same class, that method cannot be applied to whatever is not a member of some class. But plainly there can be no class each member of which is the totality of existence, i.e. the universe. Hence, characteristics appertaining to the whole of what exists cannot be reached by a scientific method. Nor will it help to deny that there *is* any whole which is the totality of the existent. For the denial would itself be a philosophical assertion requiring proof. And even *were* the denial true, it could never be known and proved to be so by an inductive method. We have no right to rule out in advance the reality of such a whole, for it *may* turn out that existent particulars derive something of their ultimate character precisely from their being parts *of* the whole.[2]

But Russell's account of just what is that ' scientific method ' which should be applied in philosophy is very far from clear. When he contemplates its more empirical and inductive character, he seems to regard it as one with what he calls ' the logical-analytic method ' ; yet some things he says of the latter

[1] Cf. Essay VI, pp. 151, 154 ; also, *Some Dogmas of Religion*, p. 16 : ' It does not seem possible to know empirically anything about the universe as a whole. All we can base such a judgment on is our very imperfect knowledge of what has happened on one planet for a few thousand years. To make an empirical inference from so little to so much would be as wild as to argue that all Chinese were evil because the first one we met turned out to be so.'
[2] Cf. Essay I, p. 37 : ' There is, I think, no question in philosophy—not even among those which border closest on logic or on science—of which we can be sure beforehand that its solution will have no effect on the problems of religion.'

show that it cannot be. For one advantage claimed for the logical-analytic method, accruing from its intimate connection with the newer logic, is, that whilst ' it liberates the imagination as to what the world *may* be, it refuses to legislate what the world *is*.' (And by ' *may* be ' here, Russell means, ' what is logically possible of existence '—not, ' what might chance to occur or come into existence.') Now in this respect, the logical-analytic method is conspicuously different from the method of empirical science. In seeming to allow so much, Russell really allows too little. For scientific method certainly aims at obtaining knowledge of what some part of the world *actually is* (or, at the least, constantly appears as being), and not merely of what the world logically *could* be. So this is a respect, presumably, in which the philosopher should *not* emulate or imitate the empirical temper of the scientist ! And if that is so, it is difficult to see why the philosopher should adopt a scientific method that is inspired by such a temper and aim.

McTaggart therefore maintains that metaphysics cannot become a science, for it can neither utilize the general results of science nor adopt its method. Many of the difficulties that arise in the study of metaphysics, he suggests, are due to the subject not being more abstract than it is : ' if it progresses more slowly than science, it is often because science, by its comparative abstraction,[1] gains in ease and simplicity what it loses in absolute truth.' It is precisely *non*-metaphysical questions that are, in comparison, abstract. But if no alliance is possible between science and metaphysics, neither can there be any conflict between them. This is seen directly the vastly different character of their inquiries and methods is understood. So McTaggart can well agree with Russell when he says ' Philosophy is not a short cut to the same kind of results as those of the (other) sciences ; if it is to be a genuine study, it must have a province of its own, and aim at results which

---

[1] *Some Dogmas of Religion*, p. 33. The point was neatly put by Renan over half a century ago : ' La supériorité de la science moderne consiste en ce que chacun de ses progrès est un degré de plus dans l'ordre des abstractions . . . nous nous éloignons de la nature, à force de la sonder.'—*Souvenirs d'Enfance et de Jeunesse*, Préface, viii.

the other sciences can neither prove nor disprove.' But McTaggart can not agree with Russell on what kind of results are properly to be expected from philosophy, nor on what kind of method should be adopted to secure them.

Lastly, I repeat, Russell has offered no reasons of philosophical importance to show why McTaggart should adopt the method of science in philosophy, and yet this was certainly due from him, having regard to the character of that method and to the inordinate proscriptions its adoption entails. He is too easily content with recommending it for reasons that are at bottom (for all he shows to the contrary) emphatically ' personal,' quasi-æsthetic, and not really impartial at all. For where his recommendation does not rest on an unfavourable estimate of the accomplishments of past thinkers (and too often, in my opinion, on an unwarrantable belittlement of them), he falls back on considerations arising from a ' temperament,' taste or bent, peculiar to himself and his adherents, and so far on something intensely personal. Where his recommendation appeals to something other than personal predilection, it is made to a frankly phenomenalist view of existence, in which all is to be explained in terms of sensa, relations between them, and ' constructions ' out of them. I have stressed how much McTaggart would regard as being at stake on the acceptance of Russell's programme. But lest it be thought I have exaggerated the extent to which Russell neglects the philosophical justification of this programme, I need only say that he himself nowhere claims to justify it, and is content to rest his defence on an *idolum theatri* of the twentieth century, as when he suggests approvingly : ' there is no doubt that what we may call the empirical outlook has become part of most educated people's habit of mind ; and *it is this, rather than any definite argument*, that has diminished the hold of the classical tradition upon students of philosophy and the instructed public generally.' [1] It is, in my opinion, from the uncritical acceptance in philosophy of the dogma underlying this ' habit of mind ' that arises that lack of faith in reason to get us anywhere, so charac-

[1] My italics. Russell, *Our Knowledge of the External World*, p. 8.

teristic of the present. And it is because McTaggart's work eminently expresses so full and strong a confidence in the power of reason to yield us knowledge of the ultimate nature of the existent that the study of his writings is now so valuable and timely a corrective to the ' overweening phenomenalism ' of the present. There is much to support the belief that our present disorders in philosophy are but the farthermost consequences of a positivism whose source must be traced in the phenomenalism of Hume and Kant.

II

It remains to consider the contents of McTaggart's written contributions to metaphysics. These comprise three expository and critical volumes on Hegel's philosophy, a less technical work on religious and ethical subjects, the two volumes in which he presents his own system, and the eleven essays assembled in this book. The whole of this work exhibits a remarkable degree of unity both in aim and treatment. Of the essays collected in the present volume, the earliest (X) was published in 1893, six others (I, II, IV–VI, IX) between 1908 and 1914, two (III, VII) during the period of the War; and the remaining two (VIII, XI) in 1923 and 1924 respectively. That these papers do form a coherent whole, the reader will find on reaching the last essay, in which the main conclusions of the precedent ones are exhibited in systematic connection and related to McTaggart's doctrine of the nature of all existence.

The opening paper indicates the reasons for his estimate of the supreme human importance of philosophical study. He conceived it a momentous matter to discover whether God exists ; whether the self survives bodily death, and if so, to what end ; whether the universe is more good than bad, and whether it becomes better or worse with the passage of time ; whether what exists—the universe and ourself in particular— have any purpose and value. (The last two questions are examined in X and IV, and returned to in XI.) He was convinced that most people do hold beliefs, affirmative or negative, on these questions, with or without explicit awareness

24

of the fact, and that beliefs on them would continue to influence profoundly the happiness of mankind, and determine our practical attitude to reality. ' It will depend on those beliefs, whether we shall consider the universe as determined by forces completely out of relation with the good, or whether, on the contrary, we may trust that the dearest ideals and aspirations of our own nature are realized, and far more than realized, in the ultimate reality. . . . It will depend on them whether our lives seem to us worth living only as desperate efforts to make the best of an incurably bad business, or as the passage to a happiness that it has not entered into our hearts to conceive.' [1]—' Are there any questions which affect our welfare more than these ? It is true that what primarily affects our welfare is the truth on these matters and not our knowledge of the truth. But a belief that things are well with the world brings happiness, a belief that things are ill with the world brings misery. And this involves the intense practical importance of our belief on the problems of religion.' [2]

Religion, which is ' nearly the most important thing in the world,' never remains for long together untouched by mysticism, even though mysticism is not essential to it. And the same is true of philosophy. In II, McTaggart is concerned to distinguish two essential characteristics of mysticism—the assertion of a mystic *unity*, and that of a mystic *intuition* of that unity. The unity is more fundamental than the intuition, for the latter is itself one example of the unity in question, since it consists in the knower and the known being connected in a unity closer than any recognized in ordinary experience or in science. The unity is also the more fundamental because it does not necessarily involve mystic intuition. For it is possible that the unity in question could be proved by discursive thought, and that it is never directly perceived. But assertion of mystic intuition does involve assertion of mystic unity. Any religion or philosophy affirming both these characteristics would be mystical ; any having neither would be non-mystical, and any involving the unity without the intuition would have mystical affinities. McTaggart next

[1] *Some Dogmas of Religion*, pp. 32–3.   [2] Essay I, pp. 39–40.

turns to consider the effects that mysticism tends to produce on the theological and philosophical views of those who hold it. His conception of the scope and character of metaphysical study may be even more definitely fixed by considering his attitude to the traditional types of system and conclusion, inferable from his succinct review of them in the syllabus of his course of public lectures (IX).

It is in the remaining papers, III to XI, which treat of time, eternity, causality, self and value, that we find the substance of McTaggart's answers to the more concrete questions which existence, as it is empirically known, suggests to us. Of these, problems which centre in time are of cardinal importance. In most mysticism, and in much religion and philosophy, time is treated as unreal. That thinkers so different as Spinoza, Kant, Hegel, Schopenhauer, and Bradley should concur in this conclusion, and yet support the denial by such very different arguments, struck McTaggart as 'highly significant.' Yet his own reasons for denying the reality of time are characteristically different from those of any of his predecessors, and his argument to prove its unreality is an extremely original one. Perception, taken at its face value, suggests that what is perceived to exist, exists in time. But what really exists cannot really have incompatible characteristics, even though it appear as having them. Now everything which appears as existing in time, appears as being future and present and past. 'Nothing can really be in time unless it really forms a series of Past, Present, and Future, as well as a series of Earlier and Later.' But to assert any existent really to be a term in the former series is to assert a contradiction, yet, on the other hand, anything really existing in time must have all three determinations. No term would exist in time unless it *were* a term in that series. The position is, then, that no existent can really (as distinct from apparently) be past *and* present *and* future ; yet if it is to exist in time at all it must be all three. And since the *de facto* direction of time and occurrence of change are impossible in an existent unless it have these incompatible characters, it follows that no thing really exists in time or really changes, though most things certainly appear to do both. Thus change and endurance throughout time can be no more than an appearance—whether ' well founded ' as Leibniz held, or, as Hegel conceives, a distorted reflection—of something in the real nature of timeless reality.

And if it were discovered that the contents of this timeless reality were so related as to form a series ordered in one definite direction, then we should be able in some measure to understand how reality *could* appear as it does appear but as it really is not. This, indeed, is the problem of the succeeding essay (VI), and the answer put briefly is, that a timeless existence is possible, and may rightly be regarded as future, if the series which appears as a time-series really is a series of perceptions ordered according to adequacy, so that the highest of the series differs only by an infinitesimal amount from the reality represented, and so that the more adequate perceptions appear as latest in the series. Thus, the terms which, *sub specie temporis, appear* related as earlier to later, are *really* related by the relations of ' included in ' and ' including '—the last term of the series including all the others. McTaggart shows in this essay, more arrestingly than has ever been shown before, how desperately important is the view which is taken—whether as the result of argument or not—of time and its relation to the existent. For that view will determine much in the account eventually given of the nature of existence in general, of the nature and destiny of individuals in particular, and of the place of error in the world.

But substances, direct objects of perception, stand in other relations than those of inclusion. Another that determines them is the relation of causality. So much, however, is not established in essay VII.[1] There, McTaggart does not discuss whether causality applies to what really exists, or only to its appearances, but limits himself to considering what is meant, and what should be meant, by the word Causality. He first distinguishes seven characteristics that have been ascribed to causality by various thinkers. Of these, he retains two, which he maintains has been ascribed by everyone, and

[1] But consult, *The Nature of Existence*, i, xxv.

suggests that his consequent definition is more convenient and in closer accordance with common usage. Thus, he defines causality as a relation of determination (of the kind called implication), which holds only between realities that are substances, though it ' rests on ' (i.e. requires, in order to hold between them) a relation between certain of their characteristics. To appreciate its full significance, this definition requires to be taken with McTaggart's doctrine of Substance.[1] Though he defines Substance in an unusual way, so that many things come to be called substances that are not usually so called,[2] Substance is not so defined as to leave it uncertain whether the term has application to what exists.

Of the existence of substances in his sense, we are assured by direct perception. And, McTaggart agrees with Descartes, perception assures us each of the existence of one particular substance, or persistent, which is our self. That is to say, McTaggart agrees with Descartes, *that* each self knows itself by direct perception, or ' acquaintance,' though he does not think the fact that the self *is* so known is so obvious a fact as Descartes supposed. And McTaggart had good grounds for thinking it not so obvious, for in the century following Descartes's, Hume was to deny that there *is* an existent self perceptually knowable at all. Descartes found it sufficient to record the empirical fact, and left it to each person to satisfy himself about it by his own perception. McTaggart, while agreeing that the self's existence *is* an empirical fact certified by perception, also gives reasons (in III) why the self *must* be known by perception. Indeed, the argument of III should be read as being directed, not merely against Hume's position that what we call the self is ' nothing but a bundle or collection of different perceptions,' but equally against all revisions of the Humean hypothesis, such as those of William James and Russell. For, it follows for the three alike, that all self-knowledge would have to be wholly ' knowledge by description.' McTaggart's answer and argument seem absolutely conclusive and to dispose finally of this part

[1] Cf. *The Nature of Existence*, I, Bk. II, also Essay XI, p. 275.
[2] Cf. my footnote to p. 85.

of positivistic phenomenalism. To Russell's question,[1] ' Why should not the thinker be simply a series of thoughts, connected with each other by a causal law ? ', Descartes would reply, because I directly perceive that the thinker is not any or many thoughts, but precisely that which is perceived to be thinking them. What I am aware of on self-inspection is not merely my present *thought*, but *myself-thinking-that-thought*. In agreeing with this, however, McTaggart contends that not only as matter of fact are there occasions on which I directly so perceive myself, but also that there *must* be some occasions on which I do so. To deny there is any occasion on which I directly perceive myself is to maintain that all self-knowledge is obtained discursively, and that the self is known only by description. True, much self-knowledge is descriptive, and is expressed in statements of which ' I ' is the grammatical subject. And we cannot, to be sure, infer the existence of a persisting self from the fact that I understand and know to be true many statements about ' I.' Yet not all the knowing which is knowing of myself could consist in knowing only those true descriptions in which ' I ' occurs.

So, McTaggart starts from the fact that I do know the meaning of many descriptions in which ' I ' occurs, and also know many of them to be true. Now, in order to know the meaning and truth of such statements, I must know their constituents. These constituents must be known either by direct perception, or by means of descriptions. He then proceeds by a *reductio ad absurdum* argument to show that in the end I could know *who it is* that the descriptions describe only if I already know myself not descriptively but perceptually. For, to illustrate, in asserting myself to be now having some certain experience, two descriptions would be involved : viz. ' the person who is now having the experience *x* ' *and* ' the person who is now asserting that he has the experience *x*.' But how could I know from these two descriptions *alone* that it is *I* and no one else, who am the person in question ? Though, in fact, it *is* I who am both having that experience now and judging now, I could never *know* that

[1] B. Russell, *An Outline of Philosophy* : London, 1927, p. 171.

fact if the hypothesis that self-knowledge is wholly by description were true. The most that the hypothesis allows for is
the *possibility* of the two descriptions being known to refer
to one and the same person, and not each to a different person.
But it does not make possible knowledge of *who that person is*.
It does not enable me to identify that one and the same person
with myself, and justify me in refusing to identify that person
with everyone other than myself. I can know that one and
the same person to be the very person he is in fact, if, and
only if, I know *myself* to be that person. And if I perceive
myself directly, then I *can* know this, if I do not perceive
myself directly, I cannot ; thus in this way alone can I know
that the two descriptions are both descriptive of me. Since,
therefore, as a matter of empirical fact, I *do* understand the
unique reference of descriptions which are, in fact, descriptive
of me, and *can* understand that reference only because I directly
perceive myself, any theory to the effect that the self is ' a
bundle or collection of perceptions,' or is ' the passing thought,'
or is ' a logical construction ' out of sensa, is thereby disproved. For, from all such theories it would follow that I
can never know what it is that is described by statements in
which the term ' I ' occurs, and therefore that I can never
understand those statements or know any of them to be true.
But this is plainly false. For I *do* know what they describe,
and I *do* know some of them to be true.

In the remainder of III, McTaggart treats of the persistence
of the self so perceived, declares personality to be a simple and
indefinable quality which I perceive in ' I ' when I perceive
myself and which is perceived in nothing else that I perceive.
Lastly, he argues that it is possible for a self not to be self-
conscious, but impossible for one self to be part of another
self, or for any two selves to have a part in common.

Early on in the course of public lectures which McTaggart
delivered annually at Cambridge he would treat of Scepticism
and Agnosticism. To the assertion that there is, and can be,
no knowledge, McTaggart would point out that the assertor
does not deny, but asserts, the truth of his own position, and
would then propose a dilemma designed to show that extreme

scepticism is logically untenable, hence, if we have *some* knowledge, it is possible to get more. To the argument : ' " all propositions are false " is a contradictory assertion, because this is itself a proposition, and therefore its truth would imply its falsity,' it had been frequently objected that a proposition ' cannot be about itself ' and that therefore extreme scepticism, though ' logically barren,' is not self-refuting. In essay VIII, McTaggart examines whether propositions can be ' about themselves,' shows that they cannot, and draws a distinction between propositions being ' about,' and ' being applicable to,' themselves. From this, he shows that propositions *can* ' apply ' to themselves, and in some cases to themselves alone. He points out too, that it is not strictly correct to say that the proposition, ' there is no knowledge,' *contradicts itself.* It would do so only if it involved its own assertion, but it does not. There is, however, a contradiction involved in *asserting* it. So it is as impossible to maintain it as if it were self-contradictory.

The essays numbered X and XI are respectively the earliest and the latest of McTaggart's writings to be published during his lifetime. The former, composed at the age of twenty-seven, and the latter, written a year before his death, have been placed together at the end of the volume in the belief that if they are read in that order, the character of the modification his thinking underwent in those thirty years will be seized more readily, freshly and completely, than it could be from a summary account. The reader will notice that during those years no one of the essential conclusions reached in X is set aside ; all reappear in XI. Yet they reappear in a form noticeably transfigured. In the early paper, trace of F. H. Bradley's influence is inescapable ; in the last paper it is wholly absent. Yet the ultimate conclusions are the same in both, and McTaggart remained convinced of their substantial correctness to the day of his death. Where, then, lies the modification ? Not, to be sure, in the content of the conclusions he was convinced of, but in his manner of establishing and presenting those conclusions. Later, McTaggart resolved to forgo the use of a dialectical method of the Hegelian type—for which the argumentation of essay X indeed cries out—and to adopt a plain deductive argument from definitions, axioms, and existential premises perceptually certified. This change of method is manifest in essay XI. It is by this method he proceeded throughout *The Nature of Existence* (of which XI states the bare results, without their demonstrations), much in the manner of the Scholastics, but with the difference—which lends a nuance of modernity to the work—that he employs certain logical conceptions, taken from the theory of descriptions and the logic of relations, that Russell and Moore had meanwhile been elaborating and perfecting. In a word, then, the last paper shows unmistakably that he finally sought to establish the conclusions of his early essay by a method significantly different from that which he had intended to use in 1893, and which has little in common with Hegel's, except that it is not inductive.

These last two essays supplement each other to great effect. The former conveys brilliantly the essence and spirit of McTaggart's philosophy ; the last exhibits its whole groundwork—proposes a plan of the ultimate structure of the universe —and shows *how* its parts should appear, as they do appear, to percipient selves. An idealist philosophy, McTaggart conceives, has three stages. It is concerned to demonstrate that reality is *not* exclusively material, but that it *is* exclusively spiritual, and thence to determine what is the fundamental nature of spirit. Ultimate reality cannot be an undifferentiated unity. It consists in a plurality of individual selves and their parts. Hence, arises the principal question of essay X, ' How can individuals express completely and at once, both their own individuality and the unity of absolute reality ? ' They could not express them by either knowledge or volition alone. So much can be seen from considering what would be the nature of perfected knowledge and perfected volition, for each postulates a perfection to which it is inherently impossible that it should attain. The perfected existence of selves could, however, express both the individuality and the unity demanded, through love. This indicates the essential character of our experience at the ultimate stage of our existence.

The universe is a community of eternal selves. Each self contains parts which are its perceptions, and each perception will have the quality of being an emotion. Every emotion is directed towards something, and ' the cogitation of that towards which the emotion is directed, and the emotion towards it, are the same mental state,' being both a perceiving and a loving of that which is perceived. A direct perception of another self will therefore be a loving of that self, and an indirect perception of other selves will be qualified by a feeling of affection for them. Love in ultimate reality will be intenser than now, and felt for more persons than now. And since it will not, as at present, be accompanied by unsatisfied volition, it will yield intenser pleasure. Thus, the value of our existence in this ultimate stage will be infinitely greater than the aggregate of values in our antecedent stages, for the love in it will be unbounded. Our condition will be one of supreme good. ' In timeless reality there is no change and no weariness, and that which is highest can exist without ceasing.' Of the nature of that good, McTaggart thinks we can infer something :

' We know that it is a timeless and endless state of love— love so direct, so intimate, and so powerful that even the deepest mystic rapture gives us but the slightest foretaste of its perfection. We know that we shall know nothing but our beloved, and those they love, and ourselves as loving them, and that only in this shall we seek and find satisfaction. Between the present and that fruition there stretches a future which may well need courage. For, while there will be in it much good, and increasing good, there must await us evils which we can now measure only by their infinite insignificance as compared with the final reward.' [1]

S. V. KEELING.

[1] The closing paragraph of *The Nature of Existence*, II, p. 479.

JOHN McTAGGART ELLIS McTAGGART, born in London, September 3rd 1866 ; eldest son of Francis Ellis McTaggart, and Caroline Ellis, his cousin ; Educated at Clifton and Trinity College in Cambridge. Entered Clifton, January 1882, and Trinity, October 1885 ; placed in the first class of the Mental and Moral Sciences Tripos, with distinction in Metaphysics, 1888 ; elected a Fellow of Trinity, 1891 ; visited New Zealand, 1892 ; returned to Cambridge, 1893 ; published ' Studies in Hegelian Dialectic,' 1896 ; appointed to a lectureship at Trinity, 1897 ; revisited New Zealand, married Miss Margaret Elizabeth Bird of Taranaki, 1899 ; published ' Studies in Hegelian Cosmology,' 1901 ; created Litt.D. of the University of Cambridge, 1902 ; elected a Fellow of the British Academy, 1906 ; published ' Some Dogmas of Religion,' 1906 ; published ' A Commentary on Hegel's Logic,' 1910 ; created LL.D., honoris causa, of the University of St. Andrews, 1911 ; appointed Henry Sidgwick Lecturer, 1914 ; published ' The Nature of Existence,' Volume I, 1921 ; retired from his lectureship at Trinity, but continued to lecture on the history of philosophy and on special problems, by arrangement with his successor ; died, January 18th 1925 ; ' The Nature of Existence,' Volume II, was edited and published by Dr. C. D. Broad in 1927.

PHILOSOPHICAL STUDIES

I

'DARE TO BE WISE'

At the other end of the world is a University [1] which has adopted for its own the motto which best expresses the nature of a University : *Sapere aude*. It is of the duty laid on our Society [2] to follow this injunction that I wish to speak.

Our object is to promote discussion upon religion, philosophy, and art. And in discussing religion and philosophy there is a special significance in the command, Dare to be wise. In seeking truth of all sorts many virtues are needed, industry, patience, humility, magnanimity. And courage also is often needed in the search, since the observer of nature must often risk his life in his observations. But there is another need for courage when we approach religion and philosophy.

And this need comes from the tremendous effect on our own welfare, and the welfare of our fellow beings, of those aspects of reality with which religion and philosophy are concerned. This effect is, in the first place, a characteristic of that reality, the problems about which would usually be called religious. But it spreads to all philosophy, for there is, I think, no question in philosophy—not even among those which border closest on logic or on science—of which we can be sure beforehand that its solution will have no effect on the problems of religion.

The profound importance to our welfare of the truth on

---

[1] The University of New Zealand.

[2] [An address delivered before the ' Heretics ' Society in Cambridge, on the 8th December, 1909, and published by the Rationalist Press Association Ltd.—*Ed.*]

these questions involves that our beliefs about those truths will also have a great importance for our welfare. If our lives would gain enormously in value if a certain doctrine were true, and would lose enormously in value if it were false, then a belief that it *is* true will naturally make us happy, and a belief that it *is* false make us miserable. And happiness and misery have much to do with welfare.

The practical importance to our lives of these matters has not always been sufficiently recognized of late years. This error is due, I think, to excessive reaction from two errors on the other side.

The first of these errors is the assertion that, if certain views on religious matters were true, all morality would lose its validity. From this, of course, it would follow that all persons who believed those views and yet accepted morality would be acting illogically and foolishly. That this view is erroneous seems to me quite clear. Our views on religious questions may affect some of the details of morality—the observance of a particular day of rest, or the use of wine or of beef, for example. But they are quite powerless either to obliterate the difference between right and wrong, or to change our views on much of the content of morality. At least, I do not know of any view maintained by anyone on any religious question which would, if I held it, alter my present belief that it is right to give water to a thirsty dog, and wrong to commit piracy or to cheat at cards.

Another form of this same error is the assertion that certain beliefs on religious matters, though they might not render morality absurd, would in practice prevent those who accepted them from pursuing virtue persistently and enthusiastically. This view seems refuted by experience, which, I think, tells us that the zeal for virtue shown by various men, while it varies much, and for many causes, does not vary according to their views on religious matters. The men who believe, for example, in God, or immortality, or optimism, seem to be neither better nor worse morally than those who disbelieve in them.

The second error is the view that certain beliefs on religious

38

matters would destroy the value, for those who accepted the beliefs, of many of those parts of experience which would otherwise have the highest value. Tennyson, for example, maintained that disbelief in immortality would destroy the value of love, even while life lasted :

> And love would answer with a sigh,
> The sound of that forgetful shore
> Will change my sweetness more and more,
> Half-dead to know that I shall die.[1]

Here, again, it seems to me, there is certainly error. Our views as to the ultimate nature and destiny of the universe may affect our judgments as to the generality of certain forms of good, or as to their duration, or as to the possibility of their increase in intensity hereafter. But I do not see how they can affect our judgment of the goodness of these good things, as we find them here and now. Indeed, if we do not start with the certainty that love for an hour on earth is unconditionally good, I do not see what ground we should have for believing that it would be good for an eternity in heaven.

These views, then, I admit to be errors, and those do well who reject them as errors. But the reaction from them, as I said, goes sometimes too far, and leads to a denial of the practical importance of the problems of religion. And this is, again, a great mistake. Whatever may be the true answer to the problems of religion, good will be different from bad, and right from wrong, and much of what we do and feel in this present life will be good, and much will be bad. But if we ask how much good exists in the universe and how much bad ; if we ask if the main current of the universe is for right, or for wrong, or indifferent to both ; if we ask what is the eventual destiny of the universe or of ourselves—all these questions must be answered one way or the other according to the solution we adopt of religious problems, and of those problems of philosophy which bear on religion. Are there any questions which affect our welfare more than these ? It is true that what primarily affects our welfare is the truth on these matters, and not our knowledge of the truth. But a

[1] *In Memoriam.*

39

belief that things are well with the world brings happiness, a belief that things are ill with the world brings misery. And this involves the intense practical importance of our beliefs on the problems of religion.

Let us consider what some of these problems are which we call religious. In the first place, there is the general question of optimism or pessimism. Is the universe as a whole more good than bad ? It is, of course, possible to maintain that it is impossible for us to answer this question. But some systems maintain that it can be answered, and some of them answer that the good prevails, and some of them hold that it is outbalanced by the evil. The practical importance of the truth on this question does not require to be enforced. For the goodness or badness of the universe is the whole of which every other matter of practical importance is a part.

Our belief on the subject, therefore, must have great influence on our happiness. So far, indeed, as I am only concerned with my welfare in this life, or with that of my friends, the more general question will have little influence, for in these limited fields we have empirical means of judging the present or inferring the immediate future, which are more certain than inferences from the general nature of the universe. But few people limit their interests entirely to those whom they know personally. And then there is always the question whether my own life, and those of my friends, may not, perhaps, extend indefinitely farther than that short period in our present bodies which is all that we can now know by observation.

And there is another question, equally important. Does the universe become better or worse as time goes on, and, if it becomes either, which does it become ? This is of equal importance, because it is a disposition of our nature—apparently a fundamental and inevitable disposition—to regard good and evil in the future with very different feelings from those with which we regard good and evil in the past. If the world were known to be more evil than good on the whole, we should still regard it cheerfully, if we believed that most of the evil lay in the past, and that the future was predominantly good. And, though the world as a whole were known to be more good than evil, that would afford us but little comfort if that part of its course which still lay in the future were more evil than good.

Then, to come to less general questions, there is the question of immortality. Our beliefs on this subject, also, will profoundly affect our happiness. Some desire annihilation, some shrink from it, but very few are indifferent. And even of these, I suppose, none would be indifferent as to the further question of what kind the future life would be, if there were a future life at all.

Then there is the existence of God. The importance of this question for our welfare has, no doubt, been exaggerated, through a failure to comprehend the alternatives. It has been supposed that the only alternative to a belief in God is a belief in some Scepticism or Materialism which would be incompatible with any hope that the universe as a whole was coherent, orderly, or good. But this is a mistake. There are systems which hold the universe to be all this, although they deny the existence of God. And, on the other hand, the existence of God would certainly not be by itself a guarantee that the universe was good. That there is some evil in the universe is beyond doubt. If it is there because God did not object to it, how do we know how much evil he may tolerate, or even welcome ? If it is there—as most reasonable Theists would say now—because God could not help it, how do we know how much evil it may be beyond his power to prevent ? Theism may possibly form a link in a chain of argument leading to Optimism, but it is far indeed from being a complete proof of Optimism.

But in spite of all this it cannot be denied that to many people the belief that there is or is not a God is most intimately connected with their happiness. And even those who are indifferent on this point would certainly not be indifferent on the question whether, if there is a God, he is such as he was supposed to be by the early Jews, or, again, by the Jesuits or the Calvinists of the sixteenth century.

Our beliefs on religious questions, then, do profoundly

affect our happiness. We can conceive—indeed, we know in history, and in the thought of the present day—beliefs the acceptance of which would make life almost intolerably miserable to anyone whose interests reached beyond the immediate present and his immediate environment. And here we find the need of courage. For, if we are to think on these matters at all, we must accept the belief for which we have evidence, and we must reject the belief for which we have no evidence, however much the first may repel or the second allure us. And, sometimes, this is not easy.

When we deal with the knowledge of science, or every-day life, we have no similar struggle. In the first place, it is here often very indifferent to us *what* the true solution of a problem may be, provided that, whatever it is, we can know it. It may be of great importance to us to know what sort of building will best stand the shock of an earthquake, but comparatively unimportant what sort it is, since, whichever it may be, we can build in that manner in earthquake districts. It may be very important to know which of two medicines will cure a disease, but quite unimportant which it is, so long as we know it and can use it.

If, indeed, we have to put the question, Is there *any* medicine which can cure this disease ? then, indeed, it may matter very much to us what the answer is. And in such a case we may be tempted, for a short time, to believe that a cure has been found, when in point of fact it has not. But the temptation does not last for long. When the medicine is tried, and fails to cure, then conviction comes to all except the weakest. But there is no corresponding help in religion and philosophy. For, if there is ever to be any experimental verification of our beliefs on such subjects, at least it will not be on this side of death. If through cowardice we depart from the right path, we must not hope for experience to take us back.

The strain is so hard that often and often in the history of thought men have tried to justify their weakness by asserting that we were entitled to believe a proposition if its truth would be very good, or at any rate if its falsity would be very bad. Over and over, in different forms, this demand meets us—not infrequently in the work of the men of whom we should least expect it. But, whenever we find it, we must, I maintain, reject it. It may well be that the universe, if this or that belief were false, would be very bad. But how do we know that the universe is *not* very bad ? There is no intrinsic *à priori* connection between existence and goodness. If we can show that the nature of existence is such that it *is* good, so much the better. But then the question of the nature of existence is the one which we are setting out to determine, and we have no right to begin by assuming that that nature is good.

Nor can we fall back on the argument, which is often used, that our desires for the good—those desires the thwarting of which produce the misery we are avoiding—are as real as anything else in the universe, and form as sound a basis for an argument as anything else. Unquestionably they are real, and form a basis for an argument ; but the question remains, What argument can be based on them ? If they were to be any good here, the argument would have to be that, because they really exist as desires in us, therefore the universe must be such as will gratify them. And this is invalid. The existence of a desire does not involve the existence of its gratification. Each of us has had many desires which were not satisfied, and which can now never be satisfied.

We cannot argue, then, from the pain that a belief gives us to the falsity of that belief. And, if we decide to think freely on these subjects, we run the risk of arriving, as others have arrived before us, at conclusions the pain of which may be very great. It is true that, so far as I know, no person who has thought freely on these subjects has arrived at conclusions so maddening as those of some traditional theologies now fading into the past. The ideas of an endless hell, of an unjust God, are fruits of ancient tradition, or of interpretation of alleged revelations—never, I believe, of independent reasoning. But to find no more hope, no more purpose, no more value in the universe than was found by Hobbes, by Hume, or by Schopenhauer—the pain of this, especially to one who has hoped for better results, or, perhaps,

43

has once held them gained—the pain of this is sometimes not trifling.

Why should we not endeavour to escape it ? Why should we not accept, without inquiry, some traditional faith ? There may be arguments for it, there may be arguments against it. But others have accepted it without inquiry into these arguments. Why should not we ?

Such a suggestion has greater attractions than it would have had two generations ago. In Europe, in the present age, a man is not likely to accept any religion in this way, except some form of Christianity. And the Christianity of sixty years ago, while no doubt such that many men could honestly *believe* it to be true, was such that no man could *wish* it to be true, unless he was devoid either of imagination or of humanity. Much Christianity of the present day is still of this type. But it would be most absurd and unjust to deny that the type of Christianity which becomes every year relatively more powerful is very different. Its view of the universe is one which might well entitle us to call the universe good. Why should we not accept it without the risks of inquiry ?

Or, if we cannot do that, why trouble about these problems at all ? Is not the world we see big enough to occupy lives so short as ours ? Shall we not enjoy the good, strive to increase it and to share it, and ask no questions about what is behind, beyond, and—perhaps—above ?

Yet some follow after truth. And what shall be their reward ? May we answer, in words which were written about Spinoza, and which are worthy to have been written by him : ' Even that which true and fearless men have preached through all the generations to unheeding ears. Seek the truth, fear not and spare not : this first, this for its own sake, this only ; and the truth itself is your reward—a reward not measured by length of days nor by any reckoning of men ' ? [1]

It is most beautiful and most true, but it is not the whole truth. For knowledge of the truth, though a great good, is not the only good, nor perhaps the highest good. If my friend is in pain or estranged from me, if the universe is

[1] Sir Frederick Pollock, *Spinoza : His Life and Philosophy*, ch. ix.

44

worthless or worse than worthless, it is no adequate consolation to know that at least I see the evil clearly.

And then, is truth always the reward for seeking the truth ? Always it cannot be, for if some have attained, the others must have failed who disagreed with them. The reward of the search—are we sure that it will be anything but the search ?

Can we give any other bidding than that which was once given to a search yet more sacred ?

> Come—pain ye shall have, and be blind to the ending !
> Come—fear ye shall have, mid the sky's overcasting !
> Come—change ye shall have, for far are ye wending !
> Come—no crown ye shall have for your thirst and your fasting,
> But——[1]

And here we must stop, before the promise that follows. The crown of our thirst and our fasting may be the opened heavens and the Beatific Vision. It may be nothing but the thirst and the fasting itself.

No great inducement, perhaps, all this ? And no inducement is needed. There are those who long for truth with a longing as simple, as ultimate, as powerful as the drunkard's longing for his wine and the lover's longing for his beloved. They will search, because they must. Our search has begun.

[1] William Morris, *Love is Enough*.

II

MYSTICISM

Mysticism is one of the great forces of the world's history. For religion is nearly the most important thing in the world, and religion never remains for long together untouched by mysticism. It is not, indeed, the case that mysticism is essential to religion. Nor is it essential to any of the great forces of religion except, perhaps, Brahminism. It is possible to hold the Jewish, the Christian, or the Mahometan religions without being in the least mystical. Even of Buddhism, I suppose the same might be said. But, on the other hand, each of these religions can be, and often is, held in a mystical form. Islam, which, as it came from its founder, was absolutely unmystical, has been the home of some of the most daring mystical thought. Since mysticism is so closely connected with religion, it will inevitably be closely connected with philosophy in those countries and epochs in which religion and philosophy are closely united. Thus the philosophies of the East have always been very largely mystical. And in mediæval Europe we find a constant conflict among the Schoolmen between mysticism and orthodoxy—for mysticism, when carried far, has, as we shall see, a tendency adverse to theistic orthodoxy.

In the more modern philosophy of Europe mysticism is also powerful. Not many philosophers have had more influence—none have had more fascination—than Spinoza. And Spinoza's system is the supreme example of philosophic mysticism. In later times there is Hegel, whose fundamental mysticism has not been adequately recognized. This is probably due to the fact that it is to be found chiefly in the *Logic* and the *Philosophy of Religion*, which are at once the most important and the least known of his works. And, again, the most important of living philosophers, Mr. Bradley, has distinct tendencies to mysticism, though it is not the mysticism of Spinoza or of Hegel.

Many definitions of mysticism have been suggested. They have varied considerably, and none have gained universal acceptance. But, while there has been much difference as to the meaning of the word, there is but little difference as to its application. There is a very general agreement as to whom we should call mystics, and whom we should not. All that is doubtful is the nature of the quality which is essential in order that a man should be classed among mystics.

It seems to me that the essential characteristics of mysticism are two in number. In the first place it is essential to mysticism that it asserts a greater unity in the universe than that which is recognized in ordinary experience, or in science. How complete this unity is, how far it excludes differentiation, are questions which would be answered differently by different mystics. What is essential is the affirmation of a unity greater than that which is usually acknowledged.

The second essential characteristic of mysticism is the affirmation that it is possible to be conscious of this unity in some manner which brings the knower into closer and more direct relation with what is known than can be done in ordinary discursive thought. It is possible, it is said, to be conscious of the truth of abstract propositions, or be in conscious relation with spiritual reality, in a manner so direct and immediate that it may be compared to the perception of matter by our senses.[1]

Thus what is asserted by mysticism is firstly, a *mystic unity* ; and secondly, a *mystic intuition* of that unity. The mystic intuition would, of course, be one example of the unity which

[1] Compared, that is to say, as to directness and immediacy. In respect of truth, many mystics would assert that the perceptions of the senses were either entirely delusive, or, at least, much more delusive than the direct spiritual intuition of which they speak.
[In McTaggart's copy of this essay, the following marginal note appears in his handwriting : ' M Ba Han holds that neither of these is true of Buddhism. But, *inter alia*, he holds that Buddhism does not deny the reality of the universe.'—*Ed.*]

47

it perceives, since the knower and the known would be connected by such a unity.

Of these two characteristics the mystic unity is the more fundamental. It is possible to assert it without asserting any mystic intuition—to hold that the existence of the unity can be proved by ordinary discursive thought, and can never be directly perceived. On the other hand, the mystic intuition cannot be asserted without the mystic unity, for such an intuition would be, as has just been pointed out, an example of the mystic unity. For this reason I shall devote more space in this paper to the consideration of the unity, although most accounts of mysticism give greater attention to the intuition.

I consider that any system which had both these characteristics would be generally classed as mystical, that any system which had neither would be generally classed as non-mystical, and that any system which had one without the other would be recognized as having, at least, some mystical affinities. If this is the case, my definition will have some claim to be considered correct.

Dr. Inge, in his admirable Bampton Lectures on Christian Mysticism, gives a definition which we may briefly consider. ' As a type of religion,' he says, in the first lecture, ' mysticism seems to rest on the following propositions, or articles of faith : First, the soul (as well as the body) can see and perceive. . . . The second proposition is that, since we can only know what is clear to ourselves, man, in order to know God, must be a partaker of the divine nature.' Thirdly, ' without holiness no man may see the Lord . . . Sensuality and selfishness are absolute disqualifications for knowing " the things of the Spirit of God." ' Further, ' there is one more fundamental doctrine . . . our guide on the upward path, the true hierophant of the mysteries of God is love.'

The second of my essential propositions is, it will be seen, almost identical with Dr. Inge's first. His second—the divine nature of man—is the affirmation, in a particular case of that mystic unity which was affirmed in my first proposition. The fact that Dr. Inge takes only a particular case is explained by the explicit limitation of his definition to religious mysticism, and the further tacit limitation to theistic religion. In this case the unity between God and man, if not the only unity of this sort, will certainly be the most important. Dr. Inge's third and fourth propositions, while true of many mystical religious systems, cannot, I think, apply to all. The fourth, for example, independently of its theistic form, would not be unreservedly true of Buddhism.

Dr. Royce, again, in the first volume of *The World and the Individual*, has a discussion of mysticism which is of the highest importance. His definition, in his second lecture, is that mysticism is the position for which ' that is real which is absolutely and finally *immediate*, so that when it is found, i.e. felt, it altogether ends any effort at ideal definition, and in this source *satisfies* idea as well as constitutes the fact.' To this, as will be seen, there is a strong resemblance in my second essential proposition—that which asserts the mystic intuition. The reality is to be *felt*. But I cannot agree with Dr. Royce in eliciting this to be sufficient by itself. Besides the immediacy of apprehension, mysticism seems to me to involve the unity— closer than appears on the surface—of the reality which is apprehended.

Thus I may claim for my definition of mysticism some support from both of these high authorities, though I do not find myself in complete agreement with either.

If we wish to classify mystical systems, we shall do so most conveniently by reference to the first of the essential characteristics—the assertion of the mystical unity. This unity may be asserted to a greater or less extent, and on this the other peculiarities of each system will be found to depend very largely.

In the first place, then, it may be held that the mystical unity extends over the whole universe, or it may be held that it extends over part of it only. The latter view gives us the conception of a universe in which certain portions form an inner system, more closely united than the whole is.

It would be difficult to find any reason for believing in such a special unity, except in the case of spirits, nor would such unity, in any other case, have sufficient practical interest to induce us to develop the conception. And thus we find that when such a special and exclusive unity is maintained, finite spirits like ourselves are at any rate one side of the unity. The unity is generally held to exist between God and other spirits—either all other spirits, or those who are specially distinguished by wisdom, virtue, or divine favour. With the rest of the universe—whether that be only matter, or whether it also includes less happy spirits—God is believed to be in a less intimate relation. Sometimes, again, the unity is conceived, without reference to theism, as a unity between all or some finite spirits, in the midst of a universe whose other parts are less closely connected.

Passing to the more developed form which asserts the unity to exist between all the parts of the universe, we find first that such a unity may be regarded not as present, but as future—as a goal which the universe must or may reach, and in which it will find the culmination of its whole process. Or, again, the unity may not be regarded as future—either because it is looked on as persistent throughout time, or because time is regarded as unreal. (The unreality of time is frequently, though not always, a part of mystical belief, that which appears as successive being regarded as really included in the deeper unity of an eternal co-existence.)

This conception of the mystic unity as omnipresent, and as dominating the whole universe without exception, is, of course, a more extreme form of mysticism than those which we have previously considered. But a difference may be found among those who regard the unity as omnipresent. The unity may be regarded as only one aspect of the universe, and as combined with diversity. Or it may be said that, in reality, there is no diversity at all, but only unity.

The difference between the two views is very great. The first, while asserting that there is a deeper unity between the parts of the universe than is generally recognized, does not deny that those parts are really different from each other.[1] Indeed, it is possible to hold, with Hegel, that this deeper

---

[1] [This is McTaggart's own position. Cf. Essays X and XI.—*Ed.*]

unity, so far from making them less differentiated than they are commonly supposed to be, actually makes them more differentiated. Hegel maintained—and there is much to be said in support of his theory—that finite existences can only be really individual and differentiated in proportion as they are united between themselves in a close unity. The organs of a human body are contained in a closer unity than the stones in a heap, and at the same time those organs have each a more individual nature, and are more clearly differentiated from one another than the stones of a heap. Hegel says that this coincidence of greater unity of the whole with greater differentiation of the parts is not accidental but necessary, and that it is a general law true of all that exists.

If this principle of Hegel's should be true, it is clear that the doctrine of a mystic unity would carry very important consequences as to the differentiation of the parts of the universe, and that the bearing of these on the reality of human personality, and on human immortality, will also be very important. But, apart from any theory that a closer unity *involves* greater differentiation, still, if the closer unity is *compatible* with differentiation, it will be possible to regard the different parts of the universe—including ourselves—as possessing reality.

But the aspect is very different when we come to the final form of mysticism—that which asserts that the mystic unity is the only reality, and denies that there is any differentiation at all. It is comparatively but little that space and matter and time must on this view be pronounced unreal. All finite persons must be pronounced equally unreal, since each such person is less than the whole universe, and would, if real, involve a real differentiation in it. Nor is this all. Not only men, but God—in any ordinary sense of the word ' God '— must go also. For a God who was not the whole universe would also introduce differentiation—differentiation between God and the rest of the universe. Again, if there is no differentiation anywhere, there can be none within God. And all knowledge, all willing, all loving, involve some differentiation within the being that experiences them. These

51

also, then, can have no reality. And a Being which neither knew, willed nor loved would certainly not be God in any ordinary sense of the word. Neither God, nor man, nor anything else definite would be left. The one reality would be a perfectly simple Being—difficult, if not impossible, to distinguish from Nothing.

Paradoxical as this view may seem, it has had much fascination for great thinkers. Much of the philosophy and much of the religion of India is based upon it. And it was one of the two influences whose conflict in Spinoza produced the system elaborated in his *Ethics*.

A system of this sort must treat all differentiation and plurality as mere illusion. And, going farther, it has to treat even the existence of illusions as illusion. For if the illusions existed, then there would really be something finite and differentiated, which would be incompatible with the doctrine that nothing but the mystic unity exists. Oriental philosophers have not hesitated to draw this conclusion ; but their treatment of the problem would require a discussion too lengthy and technical to be suitable here.

The belief in the mystic intuition is found in company with every form of the belief in the mystic unity, although, as was said above, it would be possible to believe in the mystic unity without accepting the mystic intuition. It should be noticed that the belief in such a state of mystic intuition does not necessarily involve the rejection of efforts to justify mysticism by arguments. A person who enjoyed the mystic intuition, indeed, would need no proof. What he perceived would all appear to him as immediately certain. But a system which holds that a state may exist when proof is superfluous, may yet offer a proof of its doctrines for the benefit of those who have not reached that intuitive state. Spinoza, for example, undertakes, in his *Ethics*, to prove the existence of that unity of the universe which, according to him, would be perceived directly, and without proof, by those who attained to the Third Species of knowledge.

There is, of course, no doubt that men have repeatedly attained to a state of consciousness which appeared to themselves to be that of mystic intuition. This is not a problem of philosophy, but an undisputed psychological fact. The philosophical problem is whether they are really in more direct communication with reality than is possible under other circumstances, or whether they are mistaken in supposing that this is the case.

Before passing from this account of the nature of mysticism to the consideration of certain results which flow from it, I will give two examples of mystical teaching—one theistic, where the union is between God and man ; the second pantheistic, where God is only the name for the unity of which all finite things are illusive emanations.

The first is from the *Diary* of Jonathan Edwards.

' After this my sense of divine things gradually increased, and became more and more lively, and had more of that inward sweetness. The appearance of everything was altered : there seemed to be, as it were, a calm sweet ease, or appearance of divine glory, in almost everything. God's excellency, his wisdom, his purity and love, seemed to appear in everything : in the sun, moon and stars ; in the clouds and the blue sky ; in the grass, flowers, trees : in the water, and all nature : which used greatly to fix my mind. . . . Holiness, as I then wrote down some of my contemplations on it, appeared to me to be of a sweet, pleasant, charming, serene, calm nature : which brought an inexpressible purity, brightness, peacefulness and nourishment to the soul. In other words, that it made the soul like a field or garden of God, with all manner of pleasant flowers : all pleasant, delightful and undisturbed : enjoying a sweet calm and the gentle vivifying beams of the sun. The soul of a true Christian, as I then wrote my meditations, appeared like such a little white flower as we see in the spring of the year ; low, and humble on the ground, opening its bosom, to receive the pleasant beams of the sun's glory : rejoicing, as it were, in a calm rapture ; diffusing around a sweet fragrancy ; standing peacefully and lovingly, in the midst of other flowers round about ; all in like manner opening their bosoms, to drink in the light of the sun. There was no part of creature-holiness, that I had so great a sense of its loveliness, as humility, brokenness of heart, and poverty of spirit; and there was nothing that I so earnestly longed for. My heart panted after this,—to lie low before God, as in the dust; that I might be nothing, and that God might be *all*.'[1]

The other is from the *Mantik-ut-tair* of Faríd-Uddín Attar, translated by Edward Fitzgerald under the title of the *Bird Parliament*. The birds, so runs the story, set forth to seek their king, and a few of them, overcoming all obstacles, reached the mountain on which he dwelt. And then—

> . . . They ventured from the Dust to raise
> Their Eyes—up to the Throne—into the Blaze,
> And in the Centre of the Glory there
> Behold the figure of—*Themselves*—as 'twere
> Transfigured—looking to Themselves, behold
> The Figure on the Throne en-miracled,
> Until their Eyes themselves and *That* between
> Did hesitate which Seer was, which Seen;
> They That, That They: Another, yet the Same;
> Dividual, yet One: from whom there came
> A voice of awful Answer, scarce discern'd
> From *which* to aspiration *whose* return'd
> They scarcely knew; as when some Man apart
> Answers aloud the Question in his Heart—
> ' The Sun of my perfection is a glass
> Wherein from *Seeing* into *Being* pass
> All who, reflecting as reflected see
> Themselves in Me, and Me in Them: not *Me*,
> But all of Me that a contracted Eye
> Is comprehensive of Infinity:
> Nor yet *Themselves*: no Selves, but of The All
> Fractions, from which they split and whither fall.
> As water lifted from the Deep, again
> Falls back in individual Drops of Rain
> Then melts into the Universal Main.
> All you have been, and seen, and done, and thought,
> Not *you* but *I*, have seen and been and wrought:
> I was the Sin that from Myself rebell'd:
> I the Remorse that tow'rd Myself compell'd:
> I was the Tajidar who led the Track:
> I was the little Briar that pull'd you back:
> Sin and Contrition—Retribution owed,
> And cancell'd—Pilgrim, Pilgrimage, and Road,
> Was but Myself toward Myself: and your
> Arrival but *Myself* at my own Door:

---

[1] *Diary*, p. 55. Cp. *American Philosophy—the Early Schools*, by I. Woodbridge Riley, p. 156.

MYSTICISM

Who in your Fraction of Myself behold
Myself within the Mirror Myself hold
To see Myself in, and each part of Me
That sees himself, though drown'd, shall ever see.
Come you lost Atoms to your Centre draw,
And *be* the Eternal Mirror that you saw:
Rays that have wander'd into Darkness wide
Return, and back into your Sun subside.' [1]

I shall now consider the effect which mysticism tends to produce on the theological and philosophical views of those who hold it. But it is only of tendencies that we can speak. For we find that mysticism has, in point of fact, been held in conjunction with every variety of theological and philosophical belief. All that is essential to it is the belief in the mystic unity and the mystic intuition. There are mystics in whose creed the existence of a God is a fundamental element, and others with whom the non-existence of God is equally fundamental. Human immortality is for some mystics the greatest of all truths, for others the most dangerous of all errors. Free will is essential to some mystics, determinism to others. A mystic can accept or reject the existence of matter, of space, of time. In ethics he can be as strong a hedonist as Bentham, or as strong a rigorist as Fichte. Only one thing is necessary—that he should see unity when the rest of the world does not see it.

Even the general rationality of the universe need not be accepted by him. A complete sceptic, indeed, he cannot be, since he accepts certain propositions as true.[2] But it would be possible for him to hold that much of the detail of the universe was a mere irrational chaos, in which, or in part of which, the element of unity exists as rational.

Neither is it necessary for the mystic to hold that the universe is completely good, or even that it is more good than bad. It is, indeed, generally the case that mystics regard the truth of mysticism as good. But they may hold that the truth, or the knowledge of their doctrine makes the universe

[1] *Letters and Literary Remains of Edward Fitzgerald*, edited by William Aldis Wright, ii, 481.
[2] [Cf. my Introduction, p. 30-1, and Essay VIII.—*Ed.*]

55

better than it would otherwise have been, and yet hold that the universe as a whole is bad. They may hold that, along with the element of unity in the universe, there is also differentiation, and the differentiation may be so bad as to render the universe as a whole more bad than good. And, while the mystic intuition may be a perfectly good state, it may be attained so rarely as to have but little effect on the total sum of values in existence.

But while all this is true, it is true also that a belief in mysticism does tend to draw a man towards certain theological and philosophical opinions, and away from others. It is clear that such an extreme mysticism as the last form which we considered must have a great effect on such opinions. For, as we have seen, it is incompatible with either the reality of God or the reality of man. But it is incompatible also with the reality of virtue and vice, since these only occur in finite beings, and are themselves finite and differentiated.

This, indeed, is only one form of mysticism, and a form so extreme that it seldom arises in the West. But its importance in this connection lies in the fact that all enthusiastic mysticism tends to develop in this direction, unless the holder is prepared to accept Hegel's principle that greater unity is not only compatible with greater differentiation, but actually involves it.

If a thinker does not realize this principle, it will seem to him to be a certain disloyalty to the mystic unity to admit any reality in the differentiations—which include, it must be remembered, all finite things and people. And, therefore, in proportion as he is enthusiastic about the mystic unity—and most mystics are enthusiastic about it—he will continually diminish, perhaps unconsciously, the reality he allows to finite things, until he finds himself on the brink of the extreme mysticism which denies all reality to the finite. There he may stop, either because the result seems too paradoxical, or because it is incompatible with the religious opinions which he finds himself unable to surrender. But in this case his position will not be restful. For while these motives may prevent him from advancing, his mysticism will continually urge him to advance.

It is for this reason that the course of mysticism has been so troubled in the three great monotheistic religions, Judaism, Christianity, and Islam. Mysticism arose in each of these in the minds of men who were theists of more than usual devoutness, whose desire after God was such that they desired a union with Him more close than that recognized by ordinary thought. But the fascination of the unity was such that mystic after mystic emphasized the bond till he denied, or all but denied, the beings whom the bond united. The Churches, which saw God, immortality, sin, disappearing, naturally interfered by condemnation and persecution. But, against so fundamental a tendency in human nature, their success was never permanent.

We can thus see why mysticism in the West has been judged sometimes to be especially theistic, and sometimes to be fatal to theism. In theistic societies the chief attraction of mysticism was the closer union of man to God, whether it is asserted as present, or promised in the future. Hence it arose most among those who were most passionately theistic. But its further development tended to merge God, man, and all else in one undifferentiated unity. And in this it has proved itself an enemy to theism, more dangerous than others better recognized.

There are only two ways of avoiding this. One is to stop the emphasis on the unity at such a point as may yet leave room for the reality of differentiation. The other is to accept Hegel's principle that the greater closeness of the unity involves the greater individuality of the parts. In this case, in proportion as the mystic unity is conceived as more intense, the more real will the beings be who are united by it.

With this principle, therefore, the most enthusiastic mysticism need not involve the denial either of God or man. At the same time, while in this case mysticism would have no tendency to incompatibility with theism, it would not involve theism. For it would be possible to conceive the mystic unity as existing only between spirits like ourselves, without a God at all. It is this view which, I believe, Hegel took himself, since, in his *Philosophy of Religion*, he asserts that God, when

57

seen adequately, is seen to be a community (*Gemeinde*) of finite spirits, which leaves no room for a God in the ordinary sense of the word.

And while, on this principle, enthusiastic mysticism is compatible with theism, it has a tendency to lead to conclusions which history shows us are not usually accepted willingly by theists. If such a mystic unity does exist between God and man, it is difficult to refrain from an assertion that the nature of God and man are fundamentally similar. This, one might think, should not be inacceptable to any of the three theistic Churches, since they all accept the statement that man was made in the image of God. Yet, in point of fact, any emphasis on that similarity has often been distasteful to them.

A more serious difficulty, perhaps, lies in the fact that if such emphasis is laid on the mystic unity we soon come to the conclusion that nothing is real except in so far as it is in this unity. No difficulty would be caused by the view that man can only exist in so far as he is united to God, but the correlative statement, that God can only exist in so far as He is united with man, is one which, though it has always found supporters, has not generally recommended itself to theists.

And, again, theistic orthodoxy usually tends—though not always—to emphasize the reality of sin, and to reject any theory which regards sin as merely negative, or as a lower stage of virtue. When Kant said that virtue and sin differed, not as heaven and earth, but as heaven and hell, he expressed the general—though not the universal—opinion of the theistic religions.

Now, there are many forms of mysticism which can scarcely take sin seriously, and which have no desire to do so. If the mystic union is regarded as something which men may succeed in reaching, or which they may fail to reach, then, indeed, sin can be given unlimited reality. But this is not the most usual form of mysticism. The mystical unity is generally considered either to be eternally present, or to be a goal which, while it is at present in the far future, must be inevitably reached some day. And, since that unity is generally held to be incompatible with sin, the result would be that sin would be looked at, either as an illusion, or, at most, as something which was, intrinsically and of its own nature, ephemeral and self-destructive. This is a conclusion which, whether true or false, and whether good or bad, certainly prevents us from taking sin seriously, when we consider it from the point of view of absolute reality.

Thus, within Judaism, Christianity, and Islam, while mysticism continually springs up, it is continually checked again. In the religions of India the situation is different. There the conviction of the mystical unity might, I suppose, be regarded as the fundamental religious force, and to mould the whole fabric of the religion. It does not conflict with orthodoxy, for it has made orthodoxy.

Let us now inquire what constitutes the charm of mysticism. For, to many people—to many who believe it, and to many others who cannot believe it, though they wish to do so— mysticism is most profoundly attractive, while to many others, again, it is profoundly repugnant.

When mysticism is welcomed as something good, three different things may be meant. It may mean that it is good that the universe is joined in a mystic unity, whether the fact that it is so joined is known to any person or not. It may mean that the explicit recognition of this unity by mystics is good. Or it may mean that the immediate perception of this unity in the mystic intuition is good.

Of course, all these three assertions are compatible, and they are generally held together. Those who find good in mysticism would usually say that the mystic unity of the universe is itself a good thing, irrespective of any knowledge of it, that a further good is produced in proportion as conscious beings become aware of this unity, and that yet a further good is produced in proportion as conscious beings pass into a state of mystic intuition, and exchange their abstract and discursive conviction that this *must be* the nature of the universe, for the direct and immediate perception that this *is* the nature of the universe.

Mankind in general, as I have said, are divided as to whether such a mystic unity would be good. But of those whom the world knows as mystics—that is, as believing that the mystic unity is real—all, as far as I know, also hold that it is good. It is, of course, possible that a man should hold it real and yet hold it bad. That none of those who are known as mystics do hold this position is due, I think, to two causes. In the case of all but the strongest minds our judgments of what is are apt to be swayed by our wishes as to what should be. And among these weaker thinkers, therefore, mysticism will tend to be accepted only if it is welcome. And with those who do not yield to this temptation, it will still be the case that, if a man *has* arrived at the conclusion that what is real is not desirable, he will not be specially anxious to publish his belief—still less to preach it with fervour and passion. And thus a believer in mysticism who did not welcome his belief is less likely to become known to the world.

In considering the attraction of mysticism we must deal separately with the extreme form which denies human personality and with those milder forms which accept it. In the first place, let us ask what is the fascination of the first, which is experienced by so many Orientals, if by comparatively few Europeans.

It is evident, to begin with, that this will be attractive to any person whose view of the world is inherently pessimistic. If all life, all consciousness, is inevitably evil, because it is life, and because it is consciousness, then there is comfort in a creed which teaches, either that all life and consciousness is an illusion, or that we may hope to attain a point at which they, with all the torture that they bring, will vanish for ever. The view that life and consciousness will vanish like this is not, of course, exclusively mystical. It is held, in various forms, without the least connection with mysticism. But it is held also by mysticism of the type which we are now considering, and for this reason such mysticism will be welcomed by those of its adherents who are also pessimists.

This boon, however, as I have said, might be also offered by any non-mystical system which looked on personality as unreal or transient. But there is another, which only mysticism can give. There are, we find, many people in the world

60

to whom their existence is distasteful, not simply as existence, nor, on the other hand, on account of any particular evils in it, but on account of its finitude. Such people, like the pessimists, would, if they could, reject their personality, but not, like the pessimists, merely in order to lose it. They would reject it because it involves finitude and discrimination from other reality. To lose their personality by simple annihilation would not content them. They do not wish to be annihilated, but to be swallowed up and merged in the one Infinite Being.

And this is offered them by mysticism of the extreme form, whether it holds that all personality and finitude are an illusion, and that nothing ever exists but the Infinite Being, or whether it only looks on personality and finitude as something destined to pass away, leaving the Infinite Being alone.

It may be objected that such a being without finitude must be a being without determination, and so without any nature of any sort, and that, therefore, it is really Nothing—for what else can that be which has no nature ? In that case, to be absorbed into such a Nothing would be simple annihilation, and could only be attractive, like annihilation, to the pessimist.

This argument may be correct—I believe that it is. But it is irrelevant for our present object, which was to inquire in what the fascination of the extreme form of mysticism consists. For that inquiry the important point is not what the Infinite Being would logically be, on the mystic's premises, but what it is thought to be. Now, it is certain that, whether rightly or wrongly, many people who hold this view of the Infinite Being, do regard it as being very different from Nothing, and so regard absorption into it as very different from annihilation.

We pass to the forms of mysticism which do not reject human personality. Here the attraction of the doctrine seems to depend on three causes. In the first place, the recognition of oneself as a part of a larger whole, the parts of which are closely connected, is for many people a source of intense happiness. It is not necessary for this that the whole should be conceived as of a definitely good nature, though no doubt its recognition as definitely bad would be destructive of the happiness. But so long as it is not conceived as definitely bad, the consciousness of membership of it gives happiness. It is not our business here to attempt to account for this disposition; all that concerns us is the undoubted fact that it is found in many people, though by no means in all.

Everyone, except an absolute sceptic, must recognize himself as in some unity with the rest of the universe, for he is connected with it by reciprocal causation, if in no other way. And the consciousness even of this comparatively external connection has been a source, to some people, of great happiness. But the closer connection which is involved by the mystic unity, if that is believed to exist, is obviously calculated to give such happiness in more cases, and to a greater extent.

In the second place, this mystic unity will connect us with other persons—with God, or with other men, or with both. A close relation may be found in hatred as well as in love; but most mystical systems hold that, so far as this unity between persons enters into consciousness, it takes the form of love.

This is an important point. The belief that love is the supreme good is not uncommon. A man who holds it will think better of the universe if he regards love, not as an isolated event in the middle of others, but as the principle of unity by which the universe is constituted. He will think better, in particular, of himself and other conscious beings, since his doctrine will assign to love a more constant and fundamental place in their nature than appears in ordinary life. And he will look forward with more confidence to the continuation in the unknown future of that love which he now feels for particular persons, since in it he will regard himself as having reached more nearly to the true nature of reality than in the other offices of life.[1]

In the third place, much of the trouble of life for each of us comes from the attitude of opposition to other men into which he is forced—by their faults, or by his own, or by the general course of events. To many men this is one of the greatest burdens of life. And they will find comfort if they

[1] [Essay X is an amplification of the theme of this paragraph.—Ed.]

see reason to believe that the unity between us is deeper—not, indeed, than the differentiation, but than the opposition. In that case, the judgment, suggested by the apparent state of our relations that I am fundamentally opposed to any other man will be an illusion—an illusion which, according to some forms of mysticism, we may be confident will some day vanish. And even if it does not vanish, still, the knowledge that it is an illusion brings comfort.

I have not been attempting to demonstrate that mysticism must be, or ought to be, attractive to all people. I am only pointing out the reasons why it is attractive to some people. Its attraction depends on a judgment of value which is ultimate and does not allow of argument.

If, to speak once more of the extreme form of mysticism, one man says that it is good to know that all finitude, including our own personality, is unreal, and another man says that it is bad to know it, and a third that it seems to him to be quite indifferent—and all these views are maintained—it is useless for them to dispute. It may be possible to prove or disprove the theory that finitude is unreal, but whether this finitude would be good or bad comes very rapidly to an ultimate judgment, incapable of proof or disproof.

And it is not only as to the extreme form of mysticism that our judgments of value differ. They differ also as to the milder form which admits that personality can be real. As there are many people to whom the belief in the mystic unity is the greatest consolation in life, so there are many to whom the mystic unity, in any form, is repugnant. There are many even to whom the chief value of their personality lies—not in entire isolation, since that would destroy all content—but in predominant isolation, in being more fundamentally separated from other men than united to them. To those who felt in this way the existence of the mystic unity would appear a great calamity.

But when—which is generally the case—the mystic unity is held to be universal, and not shared only by a few favoured beings, certain consequences are involved as to the goodness of which opinions would differ profoundly. There are men to whom the absolute reality of sin seems essential for the absolute reality of virtue, and even—a different matter and much more important—for the absolute reality of good. Such men may recoil from the treatment of sin as ephemeral or unreal, which is characteristic of so many mystical systems, and in which others find so great a fascination. And, again, it is sometimes felt that conflict and strife—for worthy ends and by honourable means—are an ultimate good, and not merely a necessity under present circumstances. And those who feel this will find repugnant to them that feature of mysticism which to others seems its chief good—the assertion that our harmony with our fellow-beings is more fundamentally real than our opposition to them.

Once more, the closer the connection of the universe, the more impossible—or, at any rate, the more obviously impossible—is any contingency or chance. And the existence of contingency and chance as absolutely real seems to be regarded by some people as very good, as it is certainly regarded by some others as very bad. This is largely connected with the question of undetermined free will in human beings, which is often regarded as essential to a satisfactory universe.[1] It is not, however, exclusively connected with this. It would seem as if there were people to whom heaven would have no attractions—or, at any rate, much diminished attractions— unless those who reached it had been in some danger of going to hell.[2]

Thus mankind are divided—and, for the present at least, irreconcilably divided—on the goodness or badness of the view of the universe which mystics hold to be true. This, of course, has no bearing on the question of its truth. It might be that all men should think such a bond to be evil—it might be even, that they were right in thinking it evil—and yet they might be bound by it. Here, as elsewhere, the duty of the thinker—

---

[1] [For a full discussion of this view, see McTaggart, *Some Dogmas of Religion* (London, Edward Arnold, 1930), ch. v, especially sections D and E.—*Ed.*]

[2] This point of view is described with great vivacity and, apparently, with considerable sympathy by Dr. James, in his *Pragmatism* (cp. especially, p. 296).

often his hardest, and often his most neglected, duty—is to avoid confusing the two great questions : Is this real ? and Would this be good ?

Those who do hold that the mystic view of the world is true, and that the nature of the world revealed by this view is good, will naturally take pleasure in dwelling on their consciousness that this is so. They may be able to pass into what they recognize as the state of mystic intuition. Or, if they cannot do this, yet they may, in the ordinary course of ordinary thought, fix their attention on their belief that the universe does form such a mystic unity. And in doing this— whether by mystic intuition or by ordinary thought—they often experience happiness more exquisite than any that they can enjoy by any other means.

It does not lie within every man's power to attain this happiness, but those who can attain it can likewise, if they choose, refrain. For it is possible to turn our thoughts away so that they shall not dwell on the mystic element in the universe sufficiently to produce this pleasure ; while with regard to a state of mystic intuition the difficulty, by all accounts, is to reach it, not to abstain from reaching it. And thus the question will arise whether it is well to enjoy this happiness, or whether those who can enjoy it will do well if they refuse to do so.

I am not asking whether it would be right, if it were possible, to give oneself up entirely to the pleasures of such contem- plation, neglecting entirely all the interests and duties which arise out of the finite. The question is whether it would be right to indulge in such contemplation habitually, though not uninterruptedly.

Nor am I speaking of those who, by some half-conscious self-sophistication, cheat themselves by enjoying visions of that in whose reality they do not believe. I speak of those who believe that the mystic unity is real and is good. Even if they are right in believing it to be real and in believing it to be good, we can still ask if its contemplation is beneficial, or whether the pleasure that it brings is analogous to the pleasures of morphia and chloral. The latter view has been maintained.

The chief reason, as I understand, which is given for condemning the pleasures of mystical contemplation, when they are confined within the limits mentioned above, is that they arise from looking only at one side of the truth about the universe, while the other side is ignored.

Thus this condemnation would not apply with regard to the extreme form of mysticism. For if that is true, then the *only* reality in the universe is the mystic unity. All plurality, all differentiation, whether of things and persons, or of parts of space and time, is mere illusion. And thus no aspect of the universe could be ignored when it is contemplated solely as a mystic unity. On the contrary, it is then only that it would be truly contemplated.

And, again, this condemnation would not be always applicable, even with that form of mysticism which holds that there is real differentiation in the universe. For it is not necessary that, in contemplating the unity, we should ignore the differentiation, or that, in contemplating them both, we should find our happiness only in one of them. It may well be that it is just the balance of the two which brings happiness in contemplation—just the fact that perfect individuals are united in a perfect unity, or (to put the same fact from the other side) that the perfect unity expresses itself in perfect individuals. Here, again, no aspect of the reality is ignored.

But there certainly are cases in which the happiness derived from mysticism arises from fixing the attention exclusively on the element of unity, and from ignoring the element of differentiation, though it is admitted to be real. This may happen in two ways. The mystic in question may, in the first place, hold that the unity is the only element in the universe which is uniformly and necessarily good. Of the other element—the differentiation—he may hold that it is completely evil, or, at any rate, more bad than good. In this case he will find happiness by ignoring in his contemplation, as much as possible, all but the element of unity.

Or it may happen for more subjective and variable reasons. A mystic may hold that the differentiation in the universe is good—he may even hold that the opposition, conflict, enmity

66

in the universe are also good, in that subordinate place which is all that mysticism can allow them. But there may be times and circumstances in which he can find no delight in contemplating what he thus judges good. He may be ill; he may be tired out, physically or spiritually; he may be crushed by recent defeat, or by reaction from recent victory. And so all differentiation, with all that it brings with it, may be repulsive for a time, and he may find happiness only in the consciousness of the unity and its peace.

> I am tired of tears and laughter,
> And men that laugh and weep;
> Of what may come hereafter
> For men that sow to reap:
> I am weary of days and hours,
> Blown buds of barren flowers
> Desires and dreams and powers
> And everything but sleep.[1]

This, though the last line is, perhaps, a shade too negative, expresses the mood in which only the unity of all things brings comfort.

Now, when a man who admits differentiation to be real turns his attention only to the other side of the reality—the unity—and so gains happiness, he certainly gains his happiness by ignoring one side of the reality. Is there anything wrong in this?

I do not see that there is. To ignore one side of the reality is an ambiguous phrase. It may mean that we judge it not to be there. In this sense we undoubtedly do wrong when we ignore anything because it is bad. The object of judgments is to express the truth, and if we judge anything to be unreal, when in fact it is real, we are acting wrongly, whatever may be the cause of our judgment.

But when the mystic finds his happiness in contemplating one side of reality, he does not necessarily deny the existence of the other side. He may judge both sides to exist; but, since the contemplation of the unity brings happiness, and the contemplation of the differentiation does not, he directs his

[1] 'The Garden of Proserpine,' A. C. Swinburne, *Poems and Ballads*, first series.

subsequent attention to the unity and away from the differentiation.

I can see no reason why a man should not act in this way. And, if happiness is good, there is a very obvious reason why he should act in this way, since it will increase his happiness. In the ordinary affairs of life, action on such a principle would be generally approved. Suppose that the view from the eastern windows of my house is beautiful, while the view from the western windows is ugly. I shall act very absurdly if I assert that I have no western windows, or if I assert that the view is beautiful. And I shall act wrongly if I refuse to look out from them when there is any practical advantage in doing so—if, for example, I could form and carry out a scheme for improving the prospect. But when I have recognized the ugliness, and if I cannot improve it, shall I be doing wrong if I look by preference eastward to beauty? Should I not rather be doing wrong if I acted in any other way?

In like manner the mystic whom we are now considering turns his attention from that which he judges to be evil, or which he temporarily finds distasteful, to that which gives him happiness. He will be less fortunate than that other mystic who finds all reality good—the differentiation as well as the unity. But he will act rightly. For he will gain happiness—and happiness is good. And, if happiness differs in quality, his is of no ignoble kind.

III

PERSONALITY

What is a self, and how are we conscious of it ? The words ' self ' and ' person ' may be taken as equivalent, and, as ' personality ' is a more familiar term than ' selfness,' we may put our question in this form, What is personality, and how do we know it ?

The quality of personality [1] is known to me because I have perception—in the strict sense of the word—of one being which possesses the quality, namely, myself. The view that I perceive myself is not a very common one, especially in recent philosophic thought, but a discussion of it is absolutely essential for the comprehension of the nature of spirit.

In this article the word perception is used to denote that species of awareness which we have of the existent—awareness being a mental state which is not a belief, though it is knowledge. It is of great importance to be clear as to what is meant by ' awareness ' and ' perception.' The present writer uses both terms in the manner introduced by B. Russell, and explained by him in his paper on *Knowledge by Acquaintance and Knowledge by Description.*

I am aware of an object, or am acquainted with an object—the phrases are used as synonymous—when ' I have a direct

[1] [In the *Nature of Existence*, II, p. 62, McTaggart calls this quality ' the quality of being a self,' and defines ' spirituality ' by means of ' the quality of being a self.' Spirituality is ' the quality of having content, all of which is the content of one or more selves,' and is possessed by parts of selves, selves and groups of selves (cf. also this article, p. 90). All these are ' substances.' Only certain of them, however, have ' the quality of being a self ' (viz. those that are individual selves), and this quality is declared to be a ' simple ' one. What McTaggart refers to above as ' the quality of personality ' is that which, in the *Nature of Existence*, he calls ' the quality of being a self,' not the quality he there names ' spirituality.'—*Ed.*]

cognitive relation to that object. . . . In fact, I think the relation of subject and object which I call acquaintance is simply the converse of the relation of object and subject which constitutes presentation. That is, to say that S has acquaintance with O is essentially the same thing as to say that O is presented to S. . . . When we ask what are the kinds of objects with which we are acquainted, the first and most obvious example is *sense-data*. When I see a colour or hear a noise I have direct acquaintance with the colour or the noise.' We are also acquainted, in introspection, with ' objects in various cognitive and conative relations to ourselves. When I see the sun, it often happens that I am aware of my seeing the sun, in addition to my being aware of the sun, and when I desire food, it often happens that I am aware of my desire for food . . . The awarenesses we have considered so far have all been awarenesses of particular existents, might all in a larger sense be called sense-data. For, from the point of view of theory of knowledge, introspective knowledge is exactly on a level with knowledge derived from sight or hearing. But, in addition to awareness of the above kind of objects, which may be called awareness of *particulars*, we have also what may be called awareness of *universals*. . . . Not only are we aware of particular yellows, but if we have seen a sufficient number of yellows, and have sufficient intelligence, we are aware of the universal *yellow* ; this universal is the subject in such judgments as " Yellow differs from blue," or " Yellow resembles blue less than green does." And the universal yellow is a predicate in such judgments as " this is yellow," when " this " is a particular sense-datum. And universal relations, too, are objects of awarenesses ; up and down, before and after, resemblance, desire, awareness itself, and so on, would seem to be all of them objects of which we can be aware.' [1]

This, then, is what ' awareness ' means. By ' perception '

[1] Russell, pp. 1–4. The present writer cannot accept, without some reservation, the account of what objects it is that we are aware of by introspection, but this does not affect the meaning of aware-ness. [The article cited appears in the *Proceedings of the Aristotelian Society* for 1910–11, and is largely reproduced in Russell's *Mysticism and Logic*, pp. 209–32. London, 1921.—*Ed.*]

is meant the awareness of what Russell calls ' particulars,' ' or sense-data in a large sense.' All of these are substances and we can, of course, be aware of them only when they exist. Perception, therefore, is always awareness of the existent. But awareness which is not perception need not be of the existent. If I know what any simple characteristic means, I am aware of it, but my awareness, e.g. of yellow, does not prove that there is any existent thing which has the characteristic of yellow.

Perception, however, is not limited to the perception of substances. There is, indeed, no perception except when a substance is perceived, but, along with the substance, we are able to perceive some particular characteristic of the substance. This is proved by the fact that we make judgments which no one would assert were in all cases incorrect, that a substance has certain characteristics, for which our only evidence is our awareness. And, since the judgment is that a particular existent substance has the characteristic, the awareness on which it is based must be perception. Since the characteristic and the existent themselves exist, the best definition of perception will be that it is awareness of the existent.

What existent things do we perceive ? It is clear that I do not perceive physical objects (as opposed to sense-data) or other people's minds. My only ground for believing in them is by an inference from the sense-data which I do perceive. This does not mean that every belief in them is a deliberate and conscious inference from a premiss about sense-data. On the contrary, I often judge that there is a table in the room, or that I have met a friend, without making any judgment whatever that I have perceived any sense-data. But, although my judgment that there is a table in the room is not an inference from sense-data, it will not be a judgment which I have any right to make unless I have experienced sense-data such that the existence of the table in the room could be legitimately inferred from them. And, if any doubt is thrown, by myself or others, upon the correctness of my judgment as to the table, the only way in which it can be justified is by an inference from sense-data.[1]

[1] In the same way the only way of justifying my belief that another person exists will be by an inference from sense-data which (except for

We do perceive, then, sense-data (using this word in the larger sense, to include our perception of mental events by introspection). We do not perceive physical objects or other people's minds. But one question still remains. Does each of us perceive himself?

The present writer believes that this is the case. The reasons which have led him to this view were suggested by a passage in Russell's paper already quoted above.[1]

I am certainly aware of certain characteristics—e.g. the characteristic of equality. I know, then, the proposition, ' I am aware of equality.' If I know this proposition, I must know each constituent of it. I must therefore know ' I '. Whatever we know must be known by acquaintance or description. If, therefore, ' I ' cannot be known by description, it must be known by acquaintance, and I must be aware of it.

Now, how can ' I ' be described in this case? The description must be an exclusive description, i.e. one which applies to nothing but ' I ', since I do not know what ' I ' means unless I know enough about it to distinguish it from everything else. I am aware, as already said, of equality, and I am aware, by introspection, that there is an awareness of equality. Can I by means of these, describe ' I ' as that which is aware of equality? But it is obvious that this is not an exclusive description of ' I ', for it could not be that unless it were certain that I was the only person who ever possessed awareness of equality. It is obvious that this is not certain, and that it is possible that someone else besides me was, is, or will be, aware of equality. (In point of fact, I have overwhelming empirical evidence for the conclusion that some other persons

a Berkeleyan) will lead first to a belief in his body (or a reality appearing as his body) and then to himself. Of course the sense-data which are the basis of such an inference need not be as closely connected with the object inferred as to be a case of what is commonly called seeing, touching, etc. the object itself.' I never saw the Andes or the death of Cæsar, but my belief in them is an inference from visual sense-data in reading books about them.

[1] Russell did not, however, work out his contention in detail which was not essential for the main design of his paper.

are 'aware of equality.') Thus we cannot get an exclusive description of ' I ' in this way.

It may be thought that an exclusive description could be reached by going a step farther. I am not only aware, it may be said, that there is an awareness of equality, but I am also aware that there is *this* awareness of equality, the particular mental act which is my awareness of equality here and now. Now, if ' I ' were described as that which is aware of *this* awareness of equality, should we not have reached an exclusive description ? For no one else, it may be argued, could be aware of *this* awareness of equality except ' I ' myself who have it. Of course, in order that this may be an exclusive description of ' I ', I must know what I mean by *this* awareness of equality. But this would be a case of knowledge by awareness. This awareness of equality would be a sense-datum, of which we could be aware by introspection, since no one denies that sense-data can be known by awareness. Thus, it is said, we can dispense with the necessity for awareness of self, and hold that the only awareness of the existent—the only perception—is of sense-data.

This argument, as has been seen, has, as one of its steps, the assertion that no one can be aware of an awareness of equality except the person who has that awareness. To this point we shall return later. But first we must point out that, even if this step were correct, the argument would not be valid.

The judgment which we are now considering is the judgment, ' I am aware of *this* awareness.' Now this is not merely a judgment that some person, however identified, is aware of the awareness. It also asserts that the person who is aware of the awareness is the person who is making the judgment. And how can I be entitled to assert this identity if ' I ' can be known only by description ? In that case I am aware of this awareness, and of making a judgment, and I may be entitled to conclude that there is someone who is aware of the awareness, and that someone is making the judgment, since both awarenesses and judgments require persons to make them. And it may be the case that ' the person who is aware

73

of this awareness ' is an exclusive description of the person to whom it applies. But how do I know that the person thus described is the person who makes the judgment ? If I am not aware of my self, the only thing I know about the person who makes the judgment is just the description ' the person who makes this judgment.' And, granting that this is an exclusive description, I am still not entitled to say, ' *I* am aware of this awareness,' unless I know that the two exclusive descriptions apply to the same person. If the person is known only by these descriptions, or by other descriptions, it does not seem to me possible to know anything of the sort. Thus, if ' I ' can be known only by description, it seems impossible that we can know that I am aware of this awareness, or of anything else, since the judgment, ' I am aware of X,' always means that the person who is aware of X is also the person who is making the judgment.

On the other hand, if I do perceive my self, there is no difficulty in justifying either the judgment, ' I am aware of this awareness,' or the judgment, ' I am aware of equality.' There is no need now to find an exclusive description of ' I ', because I am aware of it, i.e. know it by acquaintance, and therefore do not require to know it by description. And I can now justify the assertion, implied in the use of ' I ', that the person who is aware (whether of *this* awareness or of equality) is the person who makes the judgment. For in perceiving my self I perceive also, as was said above, some of the characteristics of my self. And, if I perceive it to have the character of being aware, of equality, or of an awareness, and also perceive it to have the characteristic of making this judgment, I am justified in holding that it is the same person who is aware and who makes the judgment.[1]

We have thus good reason to assert that I can perceive

[1] It may possibly be said that the awareness is never simultaneous with the judgment asserting the awareness. The present writer would be inclined to doubt this. But at any rate it is clear that the judgment can succeed the awareness very rapidly, and in that case we are probably justified in asserting that the self which is aware and the self which judges the awareness are the same self. This point will be discussed later.

my self—i.e., if I can know my self at all. For it would be impossible for anyone who believed that the self could be known to deny the truth of some proposition which takes the form ' I am aware of X.' And we have seen that such propositions cannot be justifiably accepted unless we can be aware of— i.e. perceive—my self.

Thus the attempt to describe the self which is aware of equality by its identity with the self which is aware of *this* awareness of equality has broken down, even if we grant the premiss which it assured—that ' that which is aware of *this* awareness of equality ' is an exclusive description of the substance to which it applies. But we must now examine into the truth of this premiss, for, although the argument would not hold even if it were valid, the question of its validity is important in itself.

It is very commonly held that it is impossible for any person to be aware of any mental state except the person who has the state, and, therefore, that only one person can be aware of it. With regard to awareness which is not perception, it is universally admitted that more than one person can be aware of the same thing. It is only by awareness that we can know what any simple characteristic means—since, being simple, it cannot be defined—and the meaning of compound characteristics depends on the meaning of simple characteristics. If, therefore, two people could not be aware of the same simple characteristic, it would be impossible for one person ever to communicate his thoughts to another.

Opinions differ with regard to sense-data in the narrower sense of the word—excluding those admittedly gained by introspection, and including only those which come, or appear to come, from the external senses. Some thinkers regard them as such that two people can perceive the same sense-datum. Others, however, hold that each sense-datum can be perceived only by one person, although sense-data perceived by different people may be caused by the same object and may justify inferences as to the existence of that object.

But that which falls wholly within a mind is usually denied to be perceptible by any mind except that in which it falls,

75

whether it be a state of the mind, a relation between two states of the mind, or a relation between the mind and one of its own states. Thus those thinkers who hold, as some do, that sense-data in the narrower sense are states of the mind are invariably to be found among those who hold that each sense-datum can be perceived only by one person—who is, of course, the person of whom they are states. And, in the case of the remainder of sense-data in the wider sense—those which are admittedly mental, and reached by introspection—it is generally held, or, rather, tacitly assumed, that they can have no other percipient than the mind within which they fall. Among these, of course, are all awarenesses.

Now it does not seem that we are justified in asserting this as an absolute necessity. No doubt it is the case that I do not perceive any state of mind of any person but myself. I have good reason to believe that none of the persons whom I know, or who have recorded their experience in any way which is accessible to me, has ever perceived the states of mind of any other person than himself. Nor have I any reason to believe that any other self in the universe has done so.[1] But the fact that there is no reason to suppose that it does happen is very far from being a proof that it could not happen. Is there any reason for supposing that it could not happen? Even if it is asserted that we have no reason to suppose that any self does perceive anything but its own states (a view

[1] [On this point, McTaggart inserted the following footnote in *The Nature of Existence*, II, p. 66 : ' The statements in this paragraph refer only to our present experience. I shall endeavour to show later that metaphysical considerations lead us to the conclusion that, in absolute reality, selves perceive each other, and the parts of each other. It may be said that the statement in the text is not true, even as to present experience, since we know that various persons have mystical experiences in which they claim to have direct experience of other selves. It would take us too far to endeavour to interpret the significance of mystical experiences in this respect. But I do not think that any of the accounts known to me lead to the conclusion that one self does really perceive another and still less that he perceives parts of another. If, however, I should be wrong in this, such a result would strengthen my argument in the text, that there is nothing intrinsically impossible in the perception by one self of the states of another self.'—*Ed.*]

which involves that sense-data in the narrower sense are states of the self), there is no impossibility in its doing so. That relative isolation of a self (of course it is not complete isolation) which would prevent it from entering into a relation of perception with anything outside itself need not be essential to the self because it is true of it throughout our experience. If, on the other hand, sense-data in the narrower sense are not parts of the self, then I can perceive something which is outside me, which is one step towards perceiving what is inside another self. The fact that in our experience this second step is never taken does not prove that it is impossible.

It must be remembered that, if A should perceive a state of B's, that would not make it a state of A's or any less exclusively a state of B's. To have a state and to perceive it are two utterly different things. In our present experience, as we have just said, no one does the second who does not do the first. But the first often occurs without the second. I often have a state, even a conscious state, without being aware of that state,[1] and this does not make it any the less my state. Since the two are so distinct, A might perceive a state of B's, which perhaps B himself did not perceive, and yet it would be B's state and not A's. Confusion on this point has had a good deal to do with the prevailing belief that one self cannot perceive a state of another self.

It is, therefore, not intrinsically impossible that one self should be aware of a state of another self (or that more than one self should be so), and, as a self can be aware of its own state, it is not intrinsically impossible that two selves should be aware of the same awareness. We cannot, therefore, be certain that ' the person who is aware of *this* awareness ' is an exclusive description of a person of whom it is true. And, if ' I ' can be known only by means of this description, I

---

[1] If this were not so, every conscious state would start an infinite series of perceptions, since a perception is itself a state, and I should have to be again aware of that, and so on. We know that this is not the case. We do not very often perceive a perception, and perception of a perception of a perception scarcely ever happens except when we are engaged on an epistemological or psychological investigation.

cannot be certain who ' I ' is, and cannot be certain that I know the meaning of the proposition, ' I am aware of *this* awareness,' or of the proposition, ' I am aware of equality ' (since the ' I ' in the latter was to be described by means of the former). But it is certain that I know the meaning of these propositions, and it is certain that I am certain of their truth. Thus, for a second reason, the attempt to show that ' I ' can be known by description in this manner, has broken down.

An attempt might be made to know ' I ' by description which would not be liable to the second objection. For it might be said—and truly—that, while it is not impossible for more than one self to be aware of a particular awareness, it is impossible for more than one self to *have* the same particular awareness. If I am aware of X, it is not impossible that you, as well as I, should be aware of my awareness of X, but it is impossible that my particular awareness of X should also be your awareness of X, or anybody else's, since what is a state—i.e. a part—of one self can in no case be a state of another self.

This view the present writer believes to be correct. It has been denied, both on the ground that my awareness of X is not a part of me and on the ground that two selves might possibly have a common part. But it is not necessary to decide these points here, as it can be shown that, even if the view is correct and no two selves can have the same awareness, it will still be impossible to know ' I ' by description.

The attempt to know it by description on this basis would be as follows. If we start from ' I am aware of equality,' and wish to describe the ' I ', we must proceed to the further proposition, ' I have *this* acquaintance with equality,' which will always be true if the other is. Then the ' I ' in the latter proposition can be described as the self which has *this* acquaintance with equality. This description cannot apply to more than one thing, and is therefore an exclusive description of it. And the thing so described is the ' I ' in both propositions. And in this way we do avoid the second objection. But our new attempt is still open to the first objection—that it involves that two descriptions apply to the same self, and that we have no right to make this assumption. For, when I assert the proposition, ' I have this awareness,' it means that the self who has this awareness is the same as the self who asserts the proposition. Now, I can only describe the one—if it is to be described at all—as the self which has this awareness, and the second as the self which makes this judgment. Both of these are exclusive descriptions. (Of course, by ' this judgment ' is meant the psychical fact of judgment, not the proposition which is asserted.) But I have no reason to suppose that they refer to the same self, and therefore I am not entitled to say, ' I have this awareness,' or, consequently, ' I am aware of equality.'

If, on the other hand, I am aware of my self, I am entitled to say, ' I have this awareness,' because I am aware of my self with the two characteristics of having the awareness and of making the judgment. Once more, then, we are brought back to the conclusion that, if I am entitled to make any assertion about my awareness of any thing, I must be aware of my self.

Nor is this all. The same line of argument will show that, unless ' I ' is known by awareness, I am not justified in making *any* statement about my self, whether it deals with awareness or not. If I start with the proposition, ' I am angry,' and then, on the same principle as before, describe ' I ' as that which has *this* state of anger, my assertion will involve the assertion that it is the same self which has this state of anger and which is making this proposition. And, if ' I ' can be known only by description, there is no reason to hold that it is the same self which both has the state and makes the assertion.

It is not, of course, impossible for us to have good reasons for believing that two descriptions both apply to some substance which we know only by description. I know other people only by description, but I may have good reason to believe of my friend X that he is both a socialist and a post-impressionist. But the case now before us is not analogous to this. My beliefs about X depend for their correctness on the correctness of various inferences from sense-data of which I am aware—perhaps auditory sense-data which I hear, and which I infer to be due to his desire to communicate his opinions to me. But, when I judge that I am angry, the conclusion that it is I who am angry is not an inference from my awareness of a state of anger whose characteristics are such that it can only belong to a particular person. I am as directly certain that it is I who am angry as I am that the state of anger exists. And, if ' I ' is not known by awareness, the only alternative is that ' I ' should be described as that which is involved in the simple fact of the existence of the state of anger—the only element in the proposition of which, on this hypothesis, we are aware. That is, it must be described simply as the self which has this state of anger. And in this description there is nothing from which we can legitimately conclude that this is the same self as that which makes the assertion.

Our conclusion, then, is that, if ' I ' can be known at all, it must be known by awareness, and that, if it cannot be known by awareness, we are not justified in asserting any proposition in which the term ' I ' occurs. Unless we take this extremely sceptical alternative, we must admit that ' I ' is known by awareness.

It may be asked why this result has not been accepted by so many—perhaps most—recent philosophers. The explanation may be partly that they saw that ' the self which has this state ' is an exclusive description of a self, when this state is known by awareness, and that they did not see the further point that this description gave us no ground to identify the self which has the state with the self making the assertion, and that this identity is implied in the use of ' I '. But probably the chief reason is that they looked for the awareness of the self in the wrong way. They tried to find a consciousness of self which had the same *positive* evidence for being an awareness as is found in an awareness of equality or in an awareness of some particular sense-datum. And this attempt failed. For the ' I ' is much more elusive than the other realities of which we are aware. It is divided into parts which are not themselves selves (unlike the parts of sense-data, which, if perceptible, are also sense-data) ; and of these parts we can be aware, and generally are, or can be, when we are aware of the ' I '. It is easy, therefore, to suppose that it is only the parts—the actual states, of which we are aware, while the ' I ' is known only by description, and the belief in it can be justified only by inference from the states. This view also gains plausibility from the fact that ' I ' has no content except parts of this sort. For it is natural, though erroneous, to argue that, if all the parts of the ' I ' can be perceived separately, it is impossible to perceive the ' I ' as a whole except by perceiving all those parts. And, of course, in perceiving the ' I ' we do not perceive all its parts.

Thus, if we merely inspect our experience, the awareness of the ' I ' is far from obvious. The only way of making it obvious is that suggested by Russell and employed in this article. We must take propositions containing the ' I ', and, to test the view that ' I ' is known by description, endeavour to replace ' I ' with its description. Only then does the impossibility of knowing ' I ' except by awareness become clear.

Our conclusion is that ' I ' must be known by awareness, if it is to be known at all. The alternative remains that it is not known at all, and that no statements which contain ' I ' as a constituent are justifiable.

Of those philosophies which, without falling into complete scepticism, deny the reality of the self, the two most important are Hume's and Bradley's. Hume (*Treatise of Human Nature*, I, iv, 6, ed. T. H. Green and T. H. Grose, 2 vols. London, 1909, I, 533 ff.), seems to take the view that we must be aware of the self if we know it at all, since he contents himself with proving to his own satisfaction that we can have no ' impression ' of it, and does not discuss the possibility that I might have a ' compound idea ' of it, as I have of the death of Cæsar, which I did not see. He offers two arguments against the possibility of an impression of the self. The first is that the impression, if there were one, must be the same throughout life.

' But there is no impression constant and invariable. Pain and pleasure, grief and joy, passions and sensations succeed each other, and never all exist at the same time. It cannot, therefore, be from any of these impressions, or from any other, that the idea of self is deriv'd ; and consequently there is no such idea.'

In answer to this we may say, in the first place, that it is not necessary that the impression should be the same throughout life. If I had it for a minute, it would be enough ground to believe in the self then. Whether there was any reason to suppose that the same self existed before and afterwards would be a matter for further argument. But whether it did or did not, a self that lasted for a minute would still be a self. As for the passage quoted, no one would deny that no impression of ' pain and pleasure, grief and joy, passions and sensations ' could be an impression of the self. But to conclude at once, as he does, that no other impression can be an impression of self is entirely unjustified.

His grounds for making this illegitimate step are probably the fact that, if there is a self, it has parts, all of which are pains, pleasures, griefs, joys, passions, sensations, or something else which is not a self, and his supposition that, in that case, there can be no impression of the self which is not an aggregate of these. And this becomes explicit in his second argument.

Mankind, he says, ' are nothing but a bundle or collection of different perceptions, which succeed each other with an inconceivable rapidity, and are in a perpetual flux and movement.'

Without accepting the detail of this, we may agree that all the content of a self falls within various mental states, not selves, and that—at any rate, within certain limits—these change while the self remains the same self. But it does not follow from this that the self is not an existent reality, any more than it follows that a college is not an existent reality, because it is made up of men who are not colleges, and who join and leave the college while it remains the same college.

Moreover, Hume's attempt to account for the arrangement

of the mental states without accepting the reality of the self, when looked at more closely, seems to involve the very reality that it was meant to exclude. For what is meant by saying that the perceptions which exist form different ' bundles or collections ' ? It does not mean that those which form the same bundle are connected in space with one another more closely than they are with those in other bundles, for Hume does not regard the perceptions as being in space. Nor can it be that they are connected more closely in time, or by resemblance. For, if there is really a bundle wherever there is, on the ordinary theory, a self, then similar and simultaneous perceptions are found in different bundles, and dissimilar and non-simultaneous sensations in the same bundle. It seems impossible to avoid the conclusion that the contents of each bundle must be determined to be parts of that bundle by their relation to, or inclusion in, some reality which is not any one of the contents, nor the aggregate of these taken as a plurality, but is something as ultimate as, say, one of the contents. If we reach this, we have reached the self.

It is not necessary to consider in detail all the stages in Bradley's searching and brilliant analysis of the various possible meanings of the self, on which he founds his conclusion that the self is not absolutely real. It is clear that, if the view which we have taken is to be refuted in consequence of any of his criticisms, it will be by those he offers in respect of the sixth sense of the word which he discusses—that in which the self is a subject which becomes an object (*Appearance and Reality*, London, 1908, ch. ix). For the self which, as we have decided, each of us knows by awareness as his ' I ' is, as we saw, that which is the subject which perceives and judges. We do not say that it is only that, that it does nothing else. On the contrary, it is that which loves when my judgment, ' I love ', is true, and which is angry when my judgment, ' I am angry ', is true. But it is also that which is the subject in all knowledge. If Bradley has succeeded in disproving the reality of a self which is the subject of knowledge, he has disproved our conclusion. But, if he has not done this, he has not weakened our conclusion at all, since none of the

other senses of self which he discusses is such that its validity
is involved in the validity of self in our sense.

The self, Bradley says, is a concrete group. With this we
may agree, since Bradley apparently means by it only that
there is a plurality of parts in the self. He then points out
that most, if not all, of the content of the self, can become an
object, and from this he concludes that very little, if any, of
the content of the self can belong to it essentially. His view
is that what becomes an object becomes *ipso facto* part of the
not-self, and what is not-self cannot be the self, or part of it.
If Bradley is right in holding that whatever becomes an object
must be removed from the self, then it is clear that no self
can know its own existence. For no self could know its
own existence without being an object of knowledge to itself,
and a self cannot be its own object if the object *ipso facto*
ceases to be self. Thus not only must we abandon the view
that I know my self by awareness—which we had found
reason to think was the only way in which I could know
myself—but, more generally, all knowledge of my self by my
self is directly shown to be impossible.

But what reason is there for holding that a self cannot be
its own object, remaining all the time the self which has the
object ? There appears to be no reason whatever. The presumption is certainly that it can be its own object, for, if it
could not, I could never know myself (whether by awareness
or by description), and consequently could never know any
proposition in which ' I ' occurs. Now, there are propositions
in which ' I ' occurs which I do assert, and which are *prima
facie* true. The present writer can see no ground why this
presumption should be rejected. It cannot be denied that
there are certain relations in which a substance can stand to
itself, and what is there in the case of the relation of knowledge
which should make us reject the *prima facie* view that this is
one of them ? So far from that being the case, the more we
contemplate our experience, the more reason we find that it
is impossible to reject knowledge of self. If we are right in
this, Bradley's objection to the reality of the self, in the sense
in which we have taken self, falls to the ground.

I am, then, aware of my own self. We now pass to a question of considerable importance—the relation of the self to time, or to that real series which appears as a time—series. It is a common view that the definition of substance should include permanence in time, or, at least, persistence through a certain amount of time.[1] But it is better to adopt a different definition, by which that which existed at a single and indivisible point of time would also be a substance.[2] With regard to selves the view that nothing is a self unless it is persistent through time, is still stronger. Indeed, many refutations of the reality of selves confine themselves to showing, or attempting to show, that a self, defined in whatever way is being criticized, could not persist for the period covered by the life of a human body.

What can we say, on our theory, as to the persistence of the self? I know my self by awareness, and I can therefore be certain only of those of its characteristics of which I am aware, or which are involved in those of which I am aware. Am I aware of the persistence of my self through time? It seems to me that I am. For awareness lasts through the specious present. At any point of time, then, I may perceive myself at that point of time, and also my self at any previous

---

[1] For the sake of brevity, ' time ' is used as an equivalent to ' time, or that real series which appears as a time-series,' whenever the context removes any danger of ambiguity. [For elucidation of the phrase ' that real series which appears as a time-series,' cf. Essay V.—Ed.]

[2] [Cf. p. 275. This definition of substance is the one adopted in, and regarded as ' of cardinal importance throughout,' *The Nature of Existence* (viz. a substance is that which exists ' and has qualities and is related, without being itself either a quality or a relation '). But see footnote to XI, p. 275. McTaggart considered this to be the traditional definition of substance, but its adoption leads us to call ' substances ' very many things that were certainly not traditionally so called. In reading McTaggart, confusion may easily arise from failing to bear in mind the very wide sense in which he uses the word ; for by it ' many things are classed as substances which would not usually be called so,' (e.g. ' a sneeze,' ' a party at whist,' ' all red-haired archdeacons ' are each a single substance). In this wide sense, ' a substance ' seems indistinguishable from what is now often indicated by the phrase ' a particular ' (when this is distinguished from phrases of the form ' a particular *x* ').—*Ed.*]

point of time within the limits of a specious present. And if, between these points, I begin or cease to perceive something else, I shall, if I attend to the relation between the two perceptions, be aware of my self as persisting while other things change, and so as persisting in time.[1]

This period of time is, of course, very short relatively to the life of a human body. Have we any reason to suppose that the self which we perceive through a specious present persists itself through any longer time ? It has been held by some writers that, for past periods which are earlier than any part of the specious present, but yet relatively near, our memory gives us absolute certainty that the things which we remember did occur. If that is the case—it is not necessary for us to discuss whether it is or not—I can have absolute certainty that I existed at a time which falls within the limits where memory is absolutely trustworthy. If, at the present moment, I remember that I was aware of myself in the past, then the ' I ' who now remembers and the ' I ' who was then aware must be the same ' I ', unless the memory is erroneous— which it cannot be, by the hypothesis, within these limits— and therefore the same ' I ' must have persisted from the moment of the remembered awareness to the moment of the remembrance.

Beyond this, there is no *certainty* of the persistence of self. If, outside the limits of certain memory, I remember that I did or was certain things in the past, that professed memory may be deceptive in two ways. It may, in the ordinary sense, be false, as when, in a dream, I remember that I committed a murder ten years ago. In the second place, even if the events which I now remember did happen to someone in my body, I may be in error in thinking that ' I ' experienced them.

---

[1] It does not, of course, follow that a thing begins or ceases to exist because I begin or cease to perceive it, but at any rate the perceptions will begin and cease. Since the perceptions are parts of the self, it follows that the same self can contain parts which exist at different times. It is also obvious that it can contain parts which exist simultaneously. If I know that I am angry, my self contains simultaneously a state of anger and a state of awareness (of the anger). Again, I am sometimes aware that I am both hot and happy.

There may then have been another self related to my body, whose experience I now know and mistakenly judge to have been my own. The latter alternative is not at all probable, but it is not impossible. But, although there is no absolute certainty that my present self has lasted longer than the specious present and the short preceding period of certain memory—if there is such a period—yet there may be very good reason for holding that it is extremely probable that it has done so. There is very little reason to doubt that the feelings with which I now remember that I saw Benares really did occur more than twenty years ago, and the self which experienced them was the same one which is now remembering them. And there is very little reason to doubt that the same ' I ' of which I am now aware did have various experiences ever since the birth of my present body, although I have no memory whatever of most of them. On similar grounds there is very little reason to doubt that, unless my body dies within the next week, the ' I ' of which I am now aware will still exist at the end of this week.

The grounds on which we come to such conclusions will, of course, be empirical. But the results which we have reached as to the nature of the self, and as to my absolute certainty of my own existence within certain temporal limits, will have an important bearing on the validity of the conclusions as to further persistence.[1] For, when objections have been offered to the common-sense view that each self—at any rate under usual circumstances—persists through the whole life of a living body, they have generally been made on the ground either that we do not know what the self is which is said to persist or that its persistence is incompatible

---

[1] [By a simple extension of this line of thought there arises naturally the question whether the self which we know to exist now will also exist after the death of our present body, and whether it existed before the birth of that body. But, though intimately connected with the problem of the self's ultimate reality and its perceptible character, discussion of the self's pre-existence and immortality is logically distinct from it, and calls for separate treatment. This it receives in McTaggart's *Some Dogmas of Religion*, chaps. iii and iv ; also in his *Studies in Hegelian Cosmology*, ch. ii.—*Ed.*]

with the changes in the ' bundle ' of mental events. But we are now able to say that by the self we mean something of which the ' I ' of which I am aware is an example. And so the question of any self existing to-day, whether it existed twenty years ago, is a perfectly definite question, whatever may be held about the true answer. We are also now able to say that, within the specious present, we are aware of a self which remains the same while changes occur among the mental events.

We have thus justified the statement at the beginning of this article. The quality of being a person is known to me because I perceive one being which possesses the quality, namely, myself. To be a person is a quality which I perceive in ' I ', when I perceive ' I ', and which I do not perceive in anything else which I do perceive, though I believe, rightly or wrongly, that it is possessed by other substances which I do not perceive. But is it a compound of various other qualities, or is it simple and indefinable ? It would appear that it is the latter. There is a quality of personality, which, like redness, is made known to us by our perception of substances which have it, and, like redness, is simple and indefinable.

What is the relation of consciousness to personality ? When we say that a self is conscious, we mean that it is conscious of something, i.e. it knows something. It would be a difficult question to decide whether the possession of personality necessarily involved the possession of consciousness, and, if so, whether a self had to be conscious at all times when it was a self, or whether its personality could continue during intervals when it had not consciousness.

A self-conscious self is one which knows itself, which, by our previous results, involves that it is aware of itself. Must a self be self-conscious ? It has been maintained that it must be so. Sometimes it is said that consciousness is essential to the self, and that no being could be conscious unless it were self-conscious. Sometimes it is admitted that a being might be conscious without being self-conscious, but then, it is said, it ought not to be called a self. The present writer disagrees with both these views. It seems to him quite possible for a being to be conscious without being self-conscious. It is true that the only conscious being of whom I am ever aware is necessarily self-conscious, since it is myself. But I am not always self-conscious when I am conscious. Memory gives me positive reason to believe in states when I am not aware of myself at all—not states that are either abnormal, on the one hand, or mystic, on the other, nor states in which in any sense I am not a self, or am less a self than at other times, but a perfectly normal and frequent state in which I am conscious of other objects, and am not conscious of myself, because my attention does not happen to be turned that way. I seem to remember such states. And, even if I did not remember them, it would still be perfectly possible that there should be such states, though there might be no reason for supposing that there were. And there is no reason why there should not be beings who are always in the condition in which I am sometimes, of being conscious without being self-conscious.

In answer to such considerations as these, it is sometimes said that self-consciousness is always found when consciousness is found, but that the self-consciousness is so faint that it escapes observation when we try to describe the experience which we remember. If there were any impossibility in the existence of consciousness without self-consciousness, it is doubtless to this hypothesis that we should be driven. But there seems no reason whatever why I should not be conscious of something else without being conscious of myself, and therefore no reason why we should conclude to the existence of this faint self-consciousness, of which, by the hypothesis, we can have no direct evidence.

Again, it is said that there is always implicit or potential self-consciousness. By this is meant that a conscious self could always be self-conscious if circumstances turned its attention to itself, instead of away from itself, that there is no intrinsic impossibility of self-consciousness. This is doubtless the case with me, and selves like me, at the times when we are not self-conscious. But it does not alter the fact that, at those times, we are just as really not self-conscious as at other times we are really self-conscious. Why should there not be beings who were conscious but whose nature was such that they could never be self-conscious ?

It has also been maintained, as we said above, that, even if there could be beings who were conscious without being self-conscious, the name of self should be reserved for those who are self-conscious. This usage, it seems, would not be so convenient as the one which we have adopted. To call a conscious being a self only when it was self-conscious would involve that each of us would gain and lose the right to the name many times a day. It would be less inconvenient if the name of self were given to those conscious beings which are ever self-conscious, even at the times when they were not so. But there is a more serious difficulty. We are invited to define personality as being conscious of self. And consciousness of self is a complex characteristic which can be defined only when it is known what we mean by a self. Therefore, if self means the same on the two occasions when it enters into the statement, ' a self is that which is self-conscious,' we have a circular and unmeaning definition of selfness. But, if we avoid this by self not meaning the same on each occasion, it is obvious that we are using the word in a very inconvenient manner. On the whole, therefore, it seems better to say that selfness does not involve self-consciousness.

We have now determined what is meant by self, and how it is that we have the characteristic of personality. Spirituality may be defined as the quality of having substantial content all of which is the content of one or more selves. From this it follows that all selves are spiritual substances,[1] but that they are not the only spiritual substances. Parts of selves, such as thoughts and volitions, or the parts of thoughts and volitions, would be spiritual. And so would groups of selves, whether those groups are important, such as a nation, or

---

[1] [The two possibilities of the self being an activity of its body, or of it being of such a nature that it cannot exist without a body, are discussed separately in *Some Dogmas of Religion*, sections 62–82.— *Ed.*]

trivial, such as a bridge-party, or purely arbitrary, such as the group made up of Louis XIV, Sir Nathaniel Wraxall, and Sir Isaac Newton. (So, also, we may note for the sake of completeness, would be a group made up of some selves and some parts of selves. But this has no practical importance.) These are all spiritual substances, but they would not all be called spirits, since usage confines the phrase ' a spirit ' to what is also called a self.

It would sometimes be maintained that our definition of spirit is too narrow. Whatever falls within the substantial content of any self, it would be said, is certainly spiritual, but spirit also includes content which is not part of any self. There is, or may be, knowledge, volition, emotion—in a word, experience—which does not fall within any self, and is not the experience of any self, and all this, it would be said, falls within spirit.

It might perhaps be admitted that if there were such non-personal experience, it would have a good claim to be called spiritual. But the present writer submits that it is impossible that there should be. This is not a question about names. The assertion is that we mean the same thing by the names ' knowledge,' ' volition,' and ' experience ' as is meant by the advocates of this view, and that we mean the same thing by the term ' self.' (At any rate, any slight difference that there might be in the meanings of the words would not account for the difference of opinion about impersonal experience.) The assertion is that there cannot be experience which is not experienced by a self, because it seems evident, not as part of the meaning of the terms, but as a synthetic truth about experience. This truth is ultimate. It cannot be defended against attacks, but it seems beyond doubt. The more clearly we realize the nature of experience, or of knowledge, volition, and emotion, the more clearly, it is submitted, does it appear that any of them is impossible except as the experience of a self.

Nor are we led to doubt this conclusion by finding that it leads us into any difficulties. For nothing that we know suggests to us in the least the existence of impersonal experience. We never perceive it, since each of us perceives only himself and his own sense-data—and none of the facts that we do perceive is better explained on the hypothesis that there is non-personal experience than on the hypothesis that there is not.

All substantial content of spirit, then, must fall within some self. But now another point arises. Can any substantial content fall within more than one self ? In that case, either one self would form part of another or two selves would overlap, having a part common to both. Is this possible ? It seems impossible that any part should be common to two or more selves. When I contemplate, to begin with, what is meant by an act of knowledge, a volition, or any other part of my experience, it seems as impossible to me that such a state should belong to more than one self as it is that it should not belong to a self at all. It may be said that this still leaves open the possibility that there should be parts of a self of which that self is not and cannot be aware—which are, in the ordinary phrase, unconscious parts of the self—and that these may be common to more than one self, though conscious parts could not be.

It is doubtful whether this view, that unconscious parts can be common to two selves though conscious parts cannot, has ever been maintained. Whenever it has been held that two selves could have a common part, it has always been held that one self could be part of another. And, since all selves are always held to have some conscious parts, this would involve that some conscious parts were parts of two selves. But, whether the view has been maintained or not, it seems false. From the nature of the case I cannot observe an unconscious state of a self, and all that I could know about it would be that it was a state of a self, and an unconscious state. But this is enough. For, when I consider what is meant by a self, it seems to me clear that a self is something which cannot have a part in common with another self. The peculiar unity which a self has puts it into a relation with its parts which is such that a part could not have it to two selves. Or, to put it the other way round, any relation which a substance could have to two wholes, of each of which it is a part, cannot be the relation of the state of a self to the self.

Since selves persist through time, each self is divided into parts persisting through the parts of the self's persistence. (And these parts, it would have, even if we were wrong in our view that acts, of knowledge, volition, and the like, are parts of the self who knows and wills.) It seems equally impossible that any part in this dimension should be common to two or more selves.

The impossibility of any part of any self belonging also to any other self is, we may say, an ultimate truth, and cannot be proved. But it can be indirectly supported by discussing various ways in which it has been said that it is possible that one part should belong to more than one self. In the first place, it is often said that one self (and so the parts of it) can be part of another, if the included self is a manifestation of the inclusive self. This view has always been popular, because one of the chief grounds for wishing to show that one part can be part of another has been to make it possible for man to be part of God. For various religious motives, many people have been anxious that a personal God—a God who is a self—should be the whole of what exists, or the whole in which all spiritual life falls. And, if man is to be part of God, it is a natural and attractive view to regard man as manifesting God's nature. If a self could be part of another on condition of its being its manifestation, it would cover those cases in which people are generally most desirous to show that one self is part of another. Now, it is no doubt true that a self can manifest the nature of a whole of which it is a part. Thus we may say that Dante manifested the nature of the society of the Middle Ages, and that Chatham manifested the nature of England. But England and the Society of the Middle Ages are not selves. Again, one self can manifest the nature of another. Thus a theist, who is not a pantheist, might say of a good man that he manifested the nature of God. But the manifestant is not part of the self whose nature he manifests. It seems that in many cases in which it is said that one self can be part of another the assertion is based on

93

a confusion about manifestation. It is said that the inclusion can take place if the included self manifests the other. And, because a self can be conceived to manifest the nature of a whole of which it is a part, and can be conceived to manifest the nature of another self, it is confusedly held that it can be conceived to manifest the nature of something which is *both* a whole of which it is a part and another self. But this, of course, is an illogical inference.

In the second place, it is suggested that if a self A perceived a self B, and all its parts, and had other contents besides those perceptions, then B would be a part of A, and the parts of B would also be parts of A. This suggestion also applies chiefly to the inclusion of man in God. For we know of no case where a man can perceive another man, or his parts, and it is generally said (though, as said above, probably erroneously) that this would be impossible. But in the case of God it is often thought that this limitation need not apply. It is possible, no doubt, that B and its parts might be perceived by A, whether A was God or not. But this will not make B and its parts into parts of A. B perceives its own parts, or some of them, but the relation of having them as parts and the relation of perceiving them are quite different relations, and, if A should have the second, it does not follow that it will have the first. The confusion is probably due to the fact that, in our ordinary experience, no one perceives the part of a self except the self of which it is a part, and it is therefore mistakenly assumed that anything which did perceive it must be a self of which it is a part.

These considerations diminish any doubt which might fall on the truth of our position that the inclusion in selves of other selves or their parts is impossible. If it really is an ultimate truth, it may be said, why have so many thinkers believed that it is not true at all ? But any force that there might be in this objection is diminished when we see that many of the people who asserted that the inclusion was not impossible had confused it with one of various other things which are quite possible, but are not the inclusion in question.

It is sometimes asserted, not only that such an inclusion

is possible, but that we have empirical evidence that it does occur in those comparatively rare instances usually known as cases of ' multiple personality.' The most striking of these, and the one best adapted to prove the contention, if any of them could do so, is the case recorded by Morton Prince in his well-known work, *The Dissociation of a Personality* (New York, 1906). It does not seem to the present writer that any of the most interesting facts recorded in this book, or any other facts of the same class of which he has read, are incompatible with the view that only one self is, in each case, concerned with all the events happening in connection with any one body, the characters, and the events remembered by that self, suffering rapid oscillations due to causes not completely ascertained. That such oscillations do take place has been certain since the time of the first man who became quarrelsome or maudlin when drunk, and reverted to his ordinary character when sober. The oscillations in such a case as we are now considering differ in degree, no doubt, from those seen in everyday life, but they introduce no qualitative difference.

Whether all the facts recorded of multiple personality can be explained in this way is a question into which we cannot now enter. But, if there were any of such a nature as to be incompatible with the theory that a single self was concerned in them, they would necessarily be of such a nature as to be compatible with the theory that they were caused by two selves, neither of them including the other, or any part of the other, which happened to be connected with the same body—a connection which we do not come across in any other part of our experience, but which has no intrinsic impossibility.[1] Thus any fact of multiple personality, whether the divergence of personality were slight or great, could be accounted for without requiring the hypothesis of inclusion,

---

[1] No great difficulty is represented by the fact that, on this theory, one self would sometimes ' remember ' what had happened to the other. Two such selves would have an important and unusual connection, in the occupation of the same body, which might well be sufficient to account for this.

and no doubt can arise from these facts as to the correctness of our view that the impossibility of the hypothesis of inclusion is an ultimate truth.

Since such inclusion is an impossibility, it follows that, unless I am the whole universe, the universe cannot be a self. For I am aware of myself as a self, and, if I am not the whole universe, I am part of it. And the whole of which a self is part cannot be a self. This result is the same whether, of that part of the universe which is not me, all, some, or none consists of other selves.

IV

THE INDIVIDUALISM OF VALUE

In this paper I shall endeavour to show that goodness and badness are individualistic in a way in which the existent reality which is good or bad need not be individualistic. In other words, even if, as I believe to be the case, all existent reality forms a single unity, in which the unity is as real and important as its differentiations—even in that case the goodness or badness to be found in that whole would not be a unity. It would be a multiplicity of separate values—positive or negative—which would indeed be added together as respects their quantity, but which, when added, would only be a mere aggregate, not a unity like the unity of existence. In other words, again, the universe as a whole is neither good nor bad. I do not mean by this that it is equally good and bad, but that the terms, in their strict sense, have no application to the universe as a whole. (This last statement of my position will require, as we proceed, a verbal modification, which need not concern us at present.)

It is generally, though not universally, admitted that nothing is ultimately good or bad except conscious beings and their conscious states. Other things and events may be good or bad as means in so far as they tend to produce goodness or badness in conscious beings, but they cannot be held to be so ultimately, and in their own right.

It is to be expected that this view will be generally accepted. For almost all people who try to formulate the good at all find it in one or more of three things—pleasure, virtue, and self-realization.

Now if a person finds the good only in pleasure, or only in virtue, or—like Kant—places the perfect good in virtue combined with as much pleasure as it deserves, it is clear that he must hold that only conscious beings and their states can be good. For happiness and virtue, and their contraries, pain and vice, are all states of consciousness. The same result would almost certainly follow if the good is found in self-realization, or in harmonious self-development, or some similar notion. Whether it would be possible or not, it would certainly be difficult to attach any meaning to such notions except in the case of a conscious being. And, in point of fact, the supporters of such theories do always, so far as I know, find good and evil exclusively in conscious beings, and their states.

Thus, rightly or wrongly, there is a large consensus of opinion in favour of this view. And it is a view which seems to me to be obviously correct. I shall therefore assume its correctness in this paper, and my results will entirely depend upon it, since, if anything else could have moral value for its own sake, there would be no reason to regard the good as specially individualistic.

When a judgment of value is asserted to be ultimately true, it is, of course, useless to seek for a proof, or to demand one. It must be either accepted or left alone. This particular judgment is, as I have said, one which I feel myself compelled to accept, and the fact that so many other people accept it may be taken as evidence that an argument based on this premiss will not necessarily be useless.

Mr. Moore, indeed, holds that other things may have value besides conscious beings and their states. His discussion of the subject is of the greatest interest, but it has not diminished the certainty which I feel, whether rightly or wrongly, that none of these other things can possess value.

There are two points on which we must guard against misconception. In the first place, if I say that only conscious beings and their states have value, I do not mean that they cannot have value unless the conscious being knows them to have value. He might not know that the state in which he was conscious of being had value, and yet it might have it. He might not know that his life and character as a whole had value, and yet it might have it. If, in making a certain decision, I acted in a selfish manner, my state of consciousness might have considerable negative value, even if I did not recognize that selfishness was a vice. In the same way, the happiness of a kitten or a young child may be good, although they do not judge themselves to be happy, and do not recognize that happiness is a good.

We may, indeed, go further, and add that there is no necessity, in order that a state should have value, that it should be recognized by *anyone* as having value. If there is no omniscient being—a hypothesis which is at any rate possible—many men must have acted generously or selfishly on occasions when neither they nor anyone else recognized the generosity or the selfishness. But the acts would, all the same, be generous or selfish, and would be good or evil accordingly.

In the second place, we must remember that among the states of consciousness which may be good or bad are included, not only those which give us direct perception of external objects, but those which give us knowledge of them in any other way. This point is important, because Mr. Moore, in criticizing Sidgwick's argument, takes Sidgwick's example as his text, and so—as it seems to me—-rather obscures the main issue.

Sidgwick had said (*Methods of Ethics*, I, ix, 4) that ' no one would consider it rational to aim at the production of beauty in external nature apart from a possible contemplation of it by human beings.' To this Mr. Moore replies (*Principia Ethica*, Sec. 50) :

' I, for one, do consider this rational ; [and] let us see if I can now get anyone to agree with me. Consider what this admission really means. It entitles us to put the following case : Let us imagine one world exceeding beautiful. Imagine it as beautiful as you can ; put into it whatever on this earth you most admire—mountains, rivers, the sea ; trees and sunsets, stars and moon. Imagine all these combined in the most exquisite proportions, so that no one thing jars against another, but each contributes to the beauty of the whole. And then imagine the ugliest world you can possibly conceive. Imagine it simply one heap of filth, containing everything that is most disgusting to us for whatever reason, and the whole, as far as may be, without one redeeming feature. . . . The only thing we are not entitled to imagine is that any human being ever has, or ever, by any possibility, *can*, live in either— can ever see and enjoy the beauty of the one or hate the foulness of the other. Well, even so, supposing them quite apart from any possible contemplation of human beings ; still is it irrational to hold that it is better that the beautiful world should exist, than the one which is ugly ? Would it not be well, in any case, to do what we could to produce it rather than the other ? Certainly I cannot help thinking that it would ; and I hope that some may agree with me in this extreme instance.'

Now such words as ' contemplation ', ' live in ', ' see ', suggest the direct perception—by sight or in some equally immediate manner—of the world and its beauty or ugliness. And this leaves the possibility open that a world not ' contemplated ' in this way may still be known—by inference, or revelation— to exist. Indeed, Sidgwick's suggestion, adopted by Mr. Moore, that we should consider if it would be rational to aim at the production of it, implies that its existence, or at any rate the possibility of its existence, may be known. For it would not be rational to aim at the production of any result unless we knew that it was possible to produce it.

Now I should admit that there might be some value in a beautiful world which was known to exist, or even which was only known to be possible, although no conscious being ever directly perceived its beauty. The value would not, I think, be great, but, I think, the value would exist. But in this case I should say that what had value for its own sake was the knowledge which some conscious being had that the world existed, or was possible, and that the existence or possibility of the world was only valuable as a means to that knowledge.

I do not suggest that Mr. Moore has confused the two questions—direct perception on the one hand and knowledge of any sort on the other. I am confident that he has not confused them, but I think that, by taking the rather unfortunate example that Sidgwick gives, he has unintentionally given an undue plausibility to his contention by making it easy for his readers to suppose that the only question is whether value would arise from the beauty of a world not directly perceived, when the real question is whether value could arise from the beauty of a world not known in any way.

On this question I have, as I have said, a conviction that there would be no such value. Let us suppose that a beautiful world arises somewhere of which no conscious being has had or ever will have any knowledge of any sort—nor the knowledge that it exists or might exist. Such a supposition can never, *ex hypothesi*, be verified, but we can intelligibly make it. Then it seems certain to me that the beauty of that world would have no value whatever. Of course I am as unable to give any arguments for my view as Mr. Moore is to give any arguments for his contrary view.

On this basis, then, that nothing has value but conscious beings and their states, it will follow that, unless the universe as a whole is a conscious being, the universe as a whole can have no value, positive or negative. It is neither good nor bad. As the belief that the universe as a whole is a conscious being—i.e. a single person—is a very rare one, I shall leave it out of account for the present, though I shall return to it. And, leaving it out of account, it is impossible that the universe as a whole can be good or bad. Parts of the universe are conscious beings—indeed, according to one theory, all parts of the universe are conscious beings. And so parts of the universe and their states may have value. But this cannot be said of the universe as a whole.

This result may be unexpected, but I think it is inevitable. It will perhaps appear less paradoxical if we remember that we are speaking only of ultimate value—value as an end, not value as a means. Value as a means may be possessed by other things than conscious selves and their states. Thus a beautiful material world, though devoid of value as an end, may have value as a means if it produces in conscious beings a state of knowledge, or of æsthetic pleasure, which has value as an end. And things which are unknown to any conscious being may also have value as means, if they are the causes of desirable states in conscious beings. If a volcanic eruption, whose occurrence was unknown to any conscious being, had fitted a certain district for vine-growing, it would be of value as a means to the desirable state of consciousness of the conscious beings who, in subsequent centuries, drank the wine.

Now the universe as a whole can be of value as a means. The fact that the universe is a unity, and that it is this particular sort of unity, may be known to conscious beings, and this knowledge of it may increase their happiness, or stimulate their virtue, or may in some other way change their conscious states so as to affect the value of those states. Then their knowledge and virtue may have ultimate value. And so the universe as a whole may have value as a means of providing this knowledge or virtue.

(It may be said that the belief would have the same value if it were a false belief, for the existence of which it would not be necessary that the universe should be the unity it is believed to be. But, if the truth of a belief makes it more valuable, this would not be the case. And in the case of a man who has too much penetration to be deceived on a particular subject the existence of such a unity would be an essential condition of the belief in it.)

Again, the unity of the universe, and the fact that it is a particular sort of unity, will certainly influence all conscious beings, whether it is known to them or not. They would be different from what they are if the unity of the universe were different, or if they themselves were not parts of a universe. (In the latter case, indeed, it might be maintained that they would not exist at all.) And so it will affect their natures, and therefore their values, and will itself have value as a means.

There is, once more, a sense in which a predicate may be used of a whole which is really applicable only to the parts, and to use it in this sense is quite legitimate, if only the distinction is clearly made. It is quite legitimate to say that one town is more drunken than another, although it is impossible for a town to get drunk at all. What is meant is either that the aggregate drunkenness, or the average drunkenness, of the inhabitants is greater in one town than in another. In the same way, if we came to the conclusion that the average conscious being in the world was in a good state, or was becoming better, we could say that the universe as a whole was in a good state or was becoming better. But we should not be speaking of any value belonging to the universe as a whole, but of the average value of its conscious parts.

Our conclusion, if valid, is of very general importance, for, as I said before, the opinion that the universe as a whole is not a conscious being is by far the most generally accepted. It accompanies all theories of the universe which may be called atheistic, since a person who was also the universe would naturally be held to be God, except in the improbable event of his being considered wicked. And most forms of theism also hold that the universe is not a conscious being. They generally hold that all non-divine conscious beings were created by God, but they do not hold that they form part of God. Thus the universe, in the widest sense, includes both God and his creatures, but is not identical with God, and is not personal.

The belief that the universe is a person is not always found even in systems which would be classed as pantheistic. For the name of pantheism is generally given to any system which, while it denies the existence of a God other than the universe, holds that we are entitled to regard the universe more or less in the same way as theists regard God. If we can trust to its workings, approve the necessary results of its character, feel admiration, reverence or love for it, the system would be called pantheism. Now, rightly or wrongly, many philosophers have thought that the universe could be regarded in one or more of these ways without being looked on as a person, or as the work of a person. Thus Spinoza is usually classed among pantheists, although he certainly did not regard the universe as a person. And Hegel's philosophy would be called pantheistic, even by those who deny that he regarded the universe as personal.

No doubt there are to be found, among pantheistic systems,

some which regard the universe as a whole as being a single person. Lotze unquestionably accepted this view, and some Hegelians do the same. (It has been maintained that Hegel himself did so, but this I believe to be erroneous.) Those who accept such systems, and those only, would be entitled to hold that the universe as a whole had value otherwise than as a means.

But even in this case judgments of value will be found, I think, to be more individualistic than other judgments as to the fundamental characteristics of existence. If such theories as Lotze's are true, I shall be part of another person, and my state at that moment will be part of his state at that moment. But I submit that the value of myself will not be part of the value of him, but will be a separate amount which must, together with the value of all other finite individuals, be *added* to the good or evil of the personal whole, if we wish to estimate the total of the values in the universe. And, in the same way, the value of my state, which is a part of the state of the personal whole at any moment, is not included in the value of that state but must be added to it as a separate item.

The reason of this is, it seems to me, that there are certain qualities which, whenever they are found in a conscious being, possess positive value—that is, are good. There are others which, whenever they are found in a conscious being, possess negative value and are bad. Now if the view of Lotze and some of the Hegelians of the Right should be correct—a view which to me, I must confess, appears patently false—my consciousness is part of God's consciousness, but is also a finite consciousness. Hence, if within God's consciousness there are x finite consciousnesses, the total number of consciousnesses is neither one nor x. It is $x +$ one.

Let us suppose that righteousness is good for its own sake. Then, if God is righteous, and I also am righteous, it will follow, even if I am part of God, that there are here two separate goods—one of them presumably much greater than the other. But the point comes out more clearly with a different case. Let us suppose that God is righteous, but that I am unrighteous, and that unrighteousness is bad for its own sake. Then it seems clear to me that God's righteousness is good and that my unrighteousness is evil. And it also seems clear to me that, in any attempt to estimate all existent value, these two values, in spite of my being part of God, must be placed side by side with one another, in the same way that my unrighteousness must be placed side by side with the righteousness of Socrates.

If I am right, the conclusion will be that, whether the universe is a single person or not, there are a plurality of beings who have value, and whose states have value, and that all these must be taken into account when we attempt to estimate all existent values. The value of a universe in which there is more than one consciousness, is only one value in the second sense spoken of above—as an aggregate of separate values.

I do not think that the truth of this has been sufficiently realized. We often find that philosophers, and philosophers of very different schools, have argued from the unity of the universe to a corresponding unity of value. Even in philosophies of a materialistic type, which do not regard the unity of the universe as more than a unity of reciprocal causality, we sometimes find the tacit supposition that the value of individuals is merged in the value of the whole in the same way that, according to these philosophies, the individual itself is a transitory and unimportant episode in the whole. But this is inconsistent. If, as most of the supporters of these philosophies would admit, value can only be found in consciousness, then in all questions of value consciousness is the only matter of importance, however dependent, ephemeral or limited its existence may be. These characteristics may assist in making consciousness bad rather than good, but cannot make it less important, in the true sense of important, which always, I conceive, involves the question of value.

But it is more relevant to our present purpose to recall that idealists have failed, more frequently than philosophers of other schools, to recognize this individualism of value, even when they have held that the universe is not a conscious being, and that only conscious beings and their states have value. The failure has been partly due to the error mentioned above—the assumption that the value to be found in a whole must have as much unity as the whole itself has. But there is another ground of error which, as a matter of historic fact, seems to have influenced idealists more than other philosophers. This ground is a misapprehension of the sense in which almost all good—and especially almost all of the highest good—is social in its character.

In any case, good is so far social that it depends largely on other men whether the state of a particular man is good. It depends largely on the action of other men, in the present or the past, whether a particular man is now learned or ignorant, virtuous or vicious, healthy or diseased, happy or miserable. But, in addition to this, the good is largely social in a deeper sense—the sense that not only are my relations to other men the essential conditions of a good state of myself, but the consciousness of those relations *is* the good in question. In patriotism, geniality, love, for example, my relation to other men is not a mere means to the good, as my relation to my wine merchant is the means by which I procure the good of wine drinking. Patriotism, geniality, love, it would be said, are themselves goods.

That there are goods of this sort would be very generally admitted (though not universally) by others besides idealists. But the idealists have emphasized these particular goods, and their superiority to others. Some of them have gone as far as to assert that among them is to be found the only true good, in which all others are summed up and transcended. And thus the social character of good has been more prominent in idealistic systems than in others.

This has, on the whole, been a distinctly valuable part of the influence of idealism. But idealism, I think, has often gone farther, and, in going farther, has gone too far. Because it has value for A to be in a relation with B, it has been argued that the relation has value in itself, and that the whole which is constituted by A and B in relation with one another has also value. Since all things in the universe stand in relation to one another, the conclusion is reached that the whole

106

which is constituted by all these beings in relation—that is, the universe itself—may have value in itself.

This, I submit, is erroneous. To love may be good in itself. And to love is to be in a relation with another person. But if A loves B, what is good is not the relation between them, but the state of A in being one of the terms of that relation. If to be loved is good in itself, as well as to love, then the state of B is also good in being the other term of the relation. (And if the relation is one of reciprocal love, then, certainly, B's state is good.) But the relation is not good, though both of the terms are good because they have this relation. And, though there is only one relation, there are two goods. It is good that A should love. It is good that B should be loved. And these goods are two and not one, though they are causally connected.

This is inevitable on the hypothesis, on which we are proceeding, that only conscious beings and their states have value. For a relation between two beings is neither a conscious being nor a state of one. If A and B love one another, then the relation which connects them cannot be a state of one of them only, for then it would not unite the two of them. Nor can it be a state of both of them jointly, for two conscious beings cannot have the same state, though they may have similar states. Nor is it a state of each of them separately, for then you would have two states—one in each and no relation. And it is certainly not a state of any third conscious being.

It is of course true that a relation of love between A and B implies that each of them is in a state of love—each, that is, is in a state of having the relation. And these states have value. But then they are two, not one—and one of them is in A and the other in B. The relation united A and B, but it is not a state of consciousness, and has no value. The state of A and the state of B have value, but they do not unite A and B.

Of course when I say that what has value is not the relation but the conscious state in each related being which the relation implies, I do not mean that the value lies in a conscious recognition or classification of that state. If A is related to B by the relation of love, he must be in the conscious state toward B of loving him, and this has value. It is not necessary for this state to have value that A should know it to have value, or even that he should know it to be love.

Let us pass to a few corollaries of this position. If it is true, Mr. Moore's principle of organic value will only have a limited application. It may be true that two characteristics, x and y, of a particular state of A may have a different value when together than the sum of the values they would have had separately. But a state of A and a state of B cannot (as ends) have a different value together than the sum of the values they would have had separately. For A and B are not a conscious being, but an aggregate of conscious beings, and a state of A and B has therefore no value except in the sense in which an aggregate of values may be described as one value. And a value in this sense is simply the sum of the constituent values.

Again, the individualism of Hedonism is frequently made a reproach against it, even by those who hold that value depends on consciousness. But, if our result is right, it follows that any theory of value which confined it to consciousness must be, if it is to be consistent, as individualistic as Hedonism. Individualism is indeed more evident in the case of Hedonism. It is more *obvious* that the happiness of a country is the sum of the happiness of the citizens, than that the same is true of virtue or of other excellences. But it would not form a solid ground of reproach to Hedonism that it was more difficult to go wrong about it than about other theories.

Again, if this principle is true, it will not be true to say— as is so often said—that the individual and society are recip-rocally means and end. On the contrary, while the individual is an end, the society is only a means.[1] It will remain true, even on this theory, that the individual ought, in certain cases, to sacrifice himself to the society, but this will only be because the resulting effect on society will be a means to

[1] [Cf. McTaggart, *Studies in Hegelian Cosmology*, ch. vii on ' The Conception of Society as an Organism ' ; especially sections 197–202. —*Ed.*]

the creation, in other individuals, of value exceeding that which is lost in the self-sacrifice. It is really for the welfare of other individuals that the sacrifice of one's own welfare is made in any cases where it is justifiable at all.

Once more, the truth of this principle may have some bearing on socialism. There is indeed nothing actually inconsistent with ethical individualism in the advocacy of any development, however great, of the functions of the State. For such a development is generally recommended by arguments which profess to show that the welfare of individual citizens would be greater under such a system. Thus we could logically combine an ethical individualism as thorough as Mill's with a socialism as extreme as Fourier's.

But socialism derives much of its support from other arguments, rather implied, perhaps, than distinctly expressed. It is often held that to substitute collective action for individual action must be right because the State is intrinsically higher than the individuals, and stands towards them as a body does to its parts, or even as a cathedral does to its stones, which have no value except as contributing to the beauty of the whole. Socialism owes, I think, a good deal of the support of its adherents, and still more of their enthusiasm, to this view. It is, indeed, only on this view that the phrase ' the religion of socialism ' can be anything but a foolish exaggeration, since religion concerns itself with ultimate values.

But if what I have said is true, it will follow that, whatever activity it is desirable for the State to have, it will only be desirable as a means, and that the activity, and the State itself, can have no value but as a means. And a religion which fastens itself on a means has not risen above fetish-worship. Compared with worship of the State, zoolatry is rational and dignified. A bull or a crocodile may not have great intrinsic value, but it has some, for it is a conscious being. The State has none. It would be as reasonable to worship a sewage pipe, which also possesses considerable value as a means.

V

THE UNREALITY OF TIME

It doubtless seems highly paradoxical to assert that Time is unreal, and that all statements which involve its reality are erroneous. Such an assertion involves a far greater departure from the natural position of mankind than is involved in the assertion of the unreality of Space or of the unreality of Matter. So decisive a breach with that natural position is not to be lightly accepted. And yet in all ages the belief in the unreality of time has proved singularly attractive.

In the philosophy and religion of the East we find that this doctrine is of cardinal importance. And in the West, where philosophy and religion are less closely connected, we find that the same doctrine continually recurs, both among philosophers and among theologians. Theology never holds itself apart from mysticism for any long period, and almost all mysticism denies the reality of time. In philosophy, again, time is treated as unreal by Spinoza, by Kant, by Hegel, and by Schopenhauer. In the philosophy of the present day the two most important movements (excluding those which are as yet merely critical) are those which look to Hegel and to Mr. Bradley. And both of these schools deny the reality of time. Such a concurrence of opinion cannot be denied to be highly significant—and is not the less significant because the doctrine takes such different forms, and is supported by such different arguments.

I believe that time is unreal. But I do so for reasons which are not, I think, employed by any of the philosophers whom I have mentioned, and I propose to explain my reasons in this paper.

Positions in time, as time appears to us *prima facie*, are distinguished in two ways. Each position is Earlier than

some, and Later than some, of the other positions. And
each position is either Past, Present, or Future. The distinctions of the former class are permanent, while those of the
latter are not. If M is ever earlier than N, it is always earlier.
But an event, which is now present, was future and will be
past.

Since distinctions of the first class are permanent, they
might be held to be more objective, and to be more essential
to the nature of time. I believe, however, that this would be
a mistake, and that the distinction of past, present, and future
is as *essential* to time as the distinction of earlier and later,
while in a certain sense, as we shall see, it may be regarded
as more *fundamental* than the distinction of earlier and later.
And it is because the distinctions of past, present, and future
seem to me to be essential for time, that I regard time as
unreal.

For the sake of brevity I shall speak of the series of positions
running from the far past through the near past to the present,
and then from the present to the near future and the far
future, as the A series. The series of positions which runs
from earlier to later I shall call the B series. The contents
of a position in time are called events. The contents of a
single position are admitted to be properly called a plurality
of events. (I believe, however, that they can *as* truly, though
not *more* truly, be called a single event. This view is not
universally accepted, and it is not necessary for my argument.)[1]
A position in time is called a moment.

[1] [The argument of this paper is substantially reproduced in the
Nature of Existence, II, ch. xxxiii, though the above observation in
parenthesis is expressed rather differently. McTaggart writes (*ibid.*,
p. 10) : ' The contents of any position in time form an event. The
varied simultaneous contents of a single position are, of course, a
plurality of events ' though these may be properly spoken of as an
event. To this he adds the following footnote : ' It is very usual
to contemplate time by the help of a metaphor of spatial movement.
But spatial movement in which direction ? The movement of time
consists in the fact that later and later terms pass into the present,
or—which is the same fact expressed in another way—that presentness passes to later and later terms. If we take it the first way, we
are taking the B series as sliding along a fixed A series. If we take
it the second way, we are taking the A series as sliding along a fixed

The first question which we must consider is whether it is essential to the reality of time that its events should form an A series as well as a B series. And it is clear, to begin with, that we never *observe* time except as forming both these series. We perceive events in time as being present, and those are the only events which we perceive directly. And all other events in time which, by memory or inference, we believe to be real, are regarded as past or future—those earlier than the present being past, and those later than the present being future. Thus the events of time, as observed by us, form an A series as well as a B series.

It is possible, however, that this is merely subjective. It may be the case that the distinction introduced among positions in time by the A series—the distinction of past, present, and future—is simply a constant illusion of our minds, and that the real nature of time only contains the distinction of the B series—the distinction of earlier and later. In that case we could not *perceive* time as it really is, but we might be able to *think* of it as it really is.

This is not a very common view, but it has found able supporters. I believe it to be untenable, because, as I said above, it seems to me that the A series is essential to the nature of time, and that any difficulty in the way of regarding the A series as real is equally a difficulty in the way of regarding time as real.

It would, I suppose, be universally admitted that time involves change. A particular thing, indeed, may exist un-

B series. In the first case time presents itself as a movement from future to past. In the second case it presents itself as a movement from earlier to later. And this explains why we say that events come out of the future, while we say that we ourselves move towards the future. For each man identifies himself especially with his present state, as against his future or his past, since it is the only one which he is directly perceiving. And this leads him to say that he is moving with the present towards later events. And as those events are now future, he says that he is moving towards the future. Thus the question as to the movement of time is ambiguous. But if we ask what is the movement of either series, the question is not ambiguous. The movement of the *A* series along the *B* series is from earlier to later. The movement of the *B* series along the *A* series is from future to past.'—*Ed.*]

changed through any amount of time. But when we ask what we mean by saying that there were different moments of time, or a certain duration of time, through which the thing was the same, we find that we mean that it remained the same while other things were changing. A universe in which nothing whatever changed (including the thoughts of the conscious beings in it) would be a timeless universe.

If, then, a B series without an A series can constitute time, change must be possible without an A series. Let us suppose that the distinction of past, present, and future does not apply to reality. Can change apply to reality? What is it that changes?

Could we say that, in a time which formed a B series but not an A series, the change consisted in the fact that an event ceased to be an event, while another event began to be an event? If this were the case, we should certainly have got a change.

But this is impossible. An event can never cease to be an event. It can never get out of any time series in which it once is. If N is ever earlier than O and later than M, it will always be, and has always been, earlier than O and later than M, since the relations of earlier and later are permanent. And as, by our present hypothesis, time is constituted by a B series alone, N will always have a position in a time series, and has always had one.[1] That is, it will always be, and has always been, an event, and cannot begin or cease to be an event.

Or shall we say that one event M merges itself into another event N, while preserving a certain identity by means of an unchanged element, so that we can say, not merely that M has ceased and N begun, but that it is M which has become N? Still the same difficulty recurs. M and N may have a common element, but they are not the same event, or there

---

[1] It is equally true, though it does not concern us on the hypothesis which we are now considering, that whatever is once in an A series is always in one. If one of the determinations past, present, and future can ever be applied to N, then one of them always has been and always will be applicable, though of course not always the same one.

H

would be no change. If therefore M changes into N at a certain moment, then, at that moment, M has ceased to be M, and N has begun to be N. But we have seen that no event can cease to be, or begin to be, itself, since it never ceases to have a place as itself in the B series. Thus one event cannot change into another.

Neither can the change be looked for in the numerically different moments of absolute time, supposing such moments to exist. For the same arguments will apply here. Each such moment would have its own place in the B series, since each would be earlier or later than each of the others. And as the B series indicate permanent relations, no moment could ever cease to be, nor could it become another moment.

Since, therefore, what occurs in time never begins or ceases to be, or to be itself, and since, again, if there is to be change it must be change of what occurs in time (for the timeless never changes), I submit that only one alternative remains. Changes must happen to the events of such a nature that the occurrence of these changes does not hinder the events from being events, and the same events, both before and after the change.

Now what characteristics of an event are there which can change and yet leave the event the same event ? (I use the word characteristic as a general term to include both the qualities which the event possesses, and the relations of which it is a term—or rather the fact that the event is a term of these relations.) It seems to me that there is only one class of such characteristics—namely, the determination of the event in question by the terms of the A series.

Take any event—the death of Queen Anne, for example— and consider what change can take place in its characteristics. That it is a death, that it is the death of Anne Stuart, that it has such causes, that it has such effects—every characteristic of this sort never changes. ' Before the stars saw one another plain ' the event in question was the death of an English Queen. At the last moment of time—if time has a last moment—the event in question will still be a death of an English Queen. And in every respect but one it is equally devoid of change. But in one respect it does change. It began by being a future event. It became every moment an event in the nearer future. At last it was present. Then it became past, and will always remain so, though every moment it becomes farther and farther past.[1]

Thus we seem forced to the conclusion that all change is only a change of the characteristics imparted to events by their presence in the A series, whether those characteristics are qualities or relations.

If these characteristics are qualities, then the events, we must admit, would not be always the same, since an event whose qualities alter is, of course, not completely the same. And, even if the characteristics are relations, the events would not be completely the same, if—as I believe to be the case— the relation of X to Y involves the existence in X of a quality of relationship to Y.[2] Then there would be two alternatives before us. We might admit that events did really change their nature, in respect of these characteristics, though not in respect of any others. I see no difficulty in admitting this. It would place the determinations of the A series in a very unique position among the characteristics of the event, but on any theory they would be very unique characteristics. It is usual, for example, to say that a past event never changes, but I do not see why we should not say, instead of this, ' a

---

[1] [To this statement, repeated in *The Nature of Existence*, II, p. 13, McTaggart appends the footnote : ' The past, therefore, is always changing, since at each moment a past event is farther in the past than it was before. This result follows from the reality of the A series, and is independent of the truth of our view that all change depends exclusively on the A series. It is worth while to notice this, since most people combine the view that the A series is real with the view that the past cannot change—a combination which is inconsistent.'—*Ed.*]

[2] I am not asserting, as Lotze did, that a relation between X and Y *consists* of a quality in X and a quality in Y—a view which I regard as quite indefensible. I assert that a relation Z between X and Y *involves* the existence in X of the quality ' having the relation Z to Y ' so that a difference of relations always involves a difference in quality, and a change of relations always involves a change of quality. [This doctrine is fully expounded in *The Nature of Existence*, I, ch. ix, ' Derivative Characteristics.'—*Ed.*]

past event changes only in one respect—that every moment it is farther from the present than it was before.' But although I see no intrinsic difficulty in this view, it is not the alternative I regard as ultimately true. For if, as I believe, time is unreal, the admission that an event in time would change in respect of its position in the A series would not involve that anything really did change.

Without the A series, then, there would be no change, and consequently the B series by itself is not sufficient for time, since time involves change.

The B series, however, cannot exist except as temporal, since earlier and later, which are the distinctions of which it consists, are clearly time-determinations. So it follows that there can be no B series where there is no A series, since where there is no A series there is no time.

But it does not follow that, if we subtract the determinations of the A series from time, we shall have no series left at all. There is a series—a series of the permanent relations to one another of those realities which in time are events—and it is the combination of this series with the A determinations which gives time. But this other series—let us call it the C series—is not temporal, for it involves no change, but only an order. Events have an order. They are, let us say, in the order M, N, O, P. And they are therefore *not* in the order M, O, N, P, or O, N, M, P, or in any other possible order. But that they have this order no more implies that there is any change than the order of the letters of the alphabet, or of the Peers on the Parliament Roll, implies any change. And thus those realities which appear to us as events might form such a series without being entitled to the name of events, since that name is only given to realities which are in a time-series. It is only when change and time come in that the relations of this C series become relations of earlier and later, and so it becomes a B series.

More is wanted, however, for the genesis of a B series and of time than simply the C series and the fact of change. For the change must be in a particular direction. And the C series, while it determines the order, does not determine the direction. If the C series runs M, N, O, P, then the B series from earlier to later cannot run M, O, N, P, or M, P, O, N, or in any way but two. But it can run either M, N, O, P (so that M is earliest and P latest) or else P, O, N, M (so that P is earliest and M latest). And there is nothing either in the C series or in the fact of change to determine which it will be.

A series which is not temporal has no direction of its own, though it has an order. If we keep to the series of the natural numbers, we cannot put 17 between 21 and 26. But we keep to the series, whether we go from 17, through 21, to 26, or whether we go from 26, through 21, to 17. The first direction seems the more natural to us, because this series has only one end, and it is generally more convenient to have that end as a beginning than as a termination. But we equally keep to the series in counting backward.

Again, in the series of categories in Hegel's dialectic, the series prevents us from putting the Absolute Idea between Being and Causality. But it permits us either to go from Being, through Causality, to the Absolute Idea, or from the Absolute Idea, through Causality, to Being. The first is, according to Hegel, the direction of proof, and is thus generally the most convenient order of enumeration. But if we found it convenient to enumerate in the reverse direction, we should still be observing the series.

A non-temporal series, then, has no direction in itself, though a person considering it may *take* the terms in one direction or in the other, according to his own convenience. And in the same way a person who contemplates a time-order may contemplate it in either direction. I may trace the order of events from the Great Charter to the Reform Bill, or from the Reform Bill to the Great Charter. But in dealing with the time-series we have not to do merely with a change in an external contemplation of it, but with a change which belongs to the series itself. And this change has a direction of its own. The Great Charter came before the Reform Bill, and the Reform Bill did not come before the Great Charter.

Therefore, besides the C series and the fact of change there must be given—in order to get time—the fact that the change is in one direction and not in the other. We can now see that the A series, together with the C series, is sufficient to give us time. For in order to get change, and change in a given direction, it is sufficient that one position in the C series should be Present, to the exclusion of all others, and that this characteristic of presentness should pass along the series in such a way that all positions on the one side of the Present have been present, and all positions on the other side of it will be present. That which has been present is Past, that which will be present is Future.[1] Thus to our previous conclusion that there can be no time unless the A series is true of reality, we can add the further conclusion that no other elements are required to constitute a time-series except an A series and a C series.

We may sum up the relations of the three series to time as follows : The A and B series are equally essential to time, which must be distinguished as past, present, and future, and must likewise be distinguished as earlier and later. But the two series are not equally fundamental. The distinctions of the A series are ultimate. We cannot explain what is meant by past, present, and future. We can, to some extent, describe them, but they cannot be defined. We can only show their meaning by examples. ' Your breakfast this morning,' we can say to an inquirer, ' is past ; this conversation is present ; your dinner this evening is future.' We can do no more.

The B series, on the other hand, is not ultimate. For, given a C series of permanent relations of terms, which is not in itself temporal, and therefore is not a B series, and given the further fact that the terms of this C series also form an A series, and it results that the terms of the C series become a B series, those which are placed first, in the direction from past to future, being earlier than those whose places are farther in the direction of the future.

---

[1] This account of the nature of the A series is not valid, for it involves a vicious circle, since it uses ' has been ' and ' will be ' to explain Past and Future. But, as I shall endeavour to show later on, this vicious circle is inevitable when we deal with the A series, and forms the ground on which we must reject it.

The C series, however, is as ultimate as the A series. We cannot get it out of anything else. That the units of time do form a series, the relations of which are permanent, is as ultimate as the fact that each of them is present, past, or future. And this ultimate fact is essential to time. For it is admitted that it is essential to time that each moment of it shall either be earlier or later than any other moment ; and these relations are permanent. And this—the B series— cannot be got out of the A series alone. It is only when the A series, which gives change and direction, is combined with the C series, which gives permanence, that the B series can arise.

Only part of the conclusion which I have now reached is required for the general purpose of this paper. I am endeavouring to base the unreality of time, not on the fact that the A series is more fundamental than the B series, but on the fact that it is as essential as the B series—that the distinctions of past, present, and future are essential to time, and that, if the distinctions are never true of reality, then no reality is in time.

This view, whether it is true or false, has nothing surprising in it. It was pointed out above that time, as we perceive it, always presents these distinctions. And it has generally been held that this is a real characteristic of time, and not an illusion due to the way in which we perceive it. Most philosophers, whether they did or did not believe time to be true of reality, have regarded the distinctions of the A series as essential to time.

When the opposite view has been maintained, it has generally been, I believe, because it was held (rightly, as I shall try to show later on) that the distinctions of present, past, and future cannot be true of reality, and that consequently, if the reality of time is to be saved, the distinction in question must be shown to be unessential to time. The presumption, it was held, was for the reality of time, and this would give us a reason for rejecting the A series as unessential to time. But of course this could only give a presumption. If the analysis of the notion of time showed that, by removing the A series, time was destroyed, this line of argument would be no longer open, and the unreality of the A series would involve the unreality of time.

I have endeavoured to show that the removal of the A series *does* destroy time. But there are two objections to this theory, which we must now consider.[1]

The first deals with those time-series which are not really existent, but which are falsely believed to be existent, or which are imagined as existent. Take, for example, the adventures of Don Quixote. This series, it is said, is not an A series. I cannot at this moment judge it to be either past, present, or future. Indeed I know that it is none of the three. Yet, it is said, it is certainly a B series. The adventure of the galley-slaves, for example, is later than the adventure of the windmills. And a B series involves time. The conclusion drawn is that an A series is not essential to time.

The answer to this objection I hold to be as follows. Time only belongs to the existent. If any reality is in time, that involves that the reality in question exists. This, I imagine, would be universally admitted. It may be questioned whether all of what exists is in time, or even whether anything really existent is in time, but it would not be denied that, if anything is in time, it must exist.

Now what is existent in the adventures of Don Quixote ? Nothing. For the story is imaginary. The acts of Cervantes' mind when he invented the story, the acts of my mind when I think of the story—these exist. But then these form part of an A series. Cervantes' invention of the story is in the past. My thought of the story is in the past, the present, and—I trust—the future.

But the adventures of Don Quixote may be believed by a child to be historical. And in reading them I may by an effort of the imagination contemplate them as if they really

[1] [McTaggart considers a third objection in *The Nature of Existence*, II, sections 313–18, involved in Russell's view that past, present, and future belong not to time *per se* but only in relation to a knowing subject. In sections 334–41 he gives three reasons for rejecting the theory of time elaborated by Dr. C. D. Broad in *Scientific Thought*, London, 1923 ; ch. ii, especially pp. 79–82.—*Ed.*]

happened. In this case, the adventures are believed to be existent or imagined as existent. But then they are believed to be in the A series, or imagined as in the A series. The child who believes them historical will believe that they happened in the past. If I imagine them as existent, I shall imagine them as happening in the past. In the same way, if anyone believed the events recorded in Morris's *News from Nowhere* to exist, or imagined them as existent, he would believe them to exist in the future or imagine them as existent in the future. Whether we place the object of our belief or our imagination in the present, the past, or the future, will depend upon the characteristics of that object. But somewhere in our A series it will be placed.

Thus the answer to the objection is that, just as a thing is in time, it is in the A series. If it is really in time, it is really in the A series. If it is believed to be in time, it is believed to be in the A series. If it is imagined as in time, it is imagined as in the A series.

The second objection is based on the possibility, discussed by Mr. Bradley, that there might be several independent time-series in reality. For Mr. Bradley, indeed, time is only appearance. There is no real time at all, and therefore there are not several real series of time. But the hypothesis here is that there should be within reality several real and independent time-series.

The objection, I imagine, is that the time-series would be all real, while the distinction of past, present, and future would only have meaning within each series, and could not, therefore, be taken as ultimately real. There would be, for example, many presents. Now, of course, many points of time can be present (each point in each time-series is a present once), but they must be present successively. And the presents of the different time-series would not be successive, since they are not in the same time. (Neither would they be simultaneous, since that equally involves being in the same time. They would have no time-relation whatever.) And different presents, unless they are successive, cannot be real. So the different time-series, which are real, must be able to exist independently of the distinction between past, present, and future.

I cannot, however, regard this objection as valid. No doubt, in such a case, no present would be *the* present—it would only be the present of a certain aspect of the universe. But then no time would be *the* time—it would only be the time of a certain aspect of the universe. It would, no doubt, be a real time-series, but I do not see that the present would be less real than the time.

I am not, of course, asserting that there is no contradiction in the existence of several distinct A series. My main thesis is that the existence of *any* A series involves a contradiction. What I assert here is merely that, supposing that there could be any A series, I see no extra difficulty involved in there being several such series independent of one another, and that therefore there is no incompatibility between the essentiality of an A series for time and the existence of several distinct times.

Moreover, we must remember that the theory of a plurality of time-series is a mere hypothesis. No reason has ever been given why we should believe in their existence. It has only been said that there is no reason why we should disbelieve in their existence, and that therefore they may exist. But if their existence should be incompatible with something else, for which there is positive evidence, then there would be a reason why we should disbelieve in their existence. Now there is, as I have tried to show, positive evidence for believing that an A series is essential to time. Supposing therefore that it were the case (which, for the reasons given above, I deny) that the existence of a plurality of time-series was incompatible with the essentiality for time of the A series, it would be the hypothesis of a plurality of times which should be rejected, and not our conclusion as to the A series.

I now pass to the second part of my task. Having, as it seems to me, succeeded in proving that there can be no time without an A series, it remains to prove that an A series cannot exist, and that therefore time cannot exist. This would involve that time is not real at all, since it is admitted that the only way in which time can be real is by existing.

THE UNREALITY OF TIME

The terms of the A series are characteristics of events. We say of events that they are either past, present, or future. If moments of time are taken as separate realities, we say of them also that they are past, present, or future. A characteristic may be either a relation or a quality. Whether we take the terms of the A series as relations of events (which seems the more reasonable view) or whether we take them as qualities of events, it seems to me that they involve a contradiction.

Let us first examine the supposition that they are relations. In that case only one term of each relation can be an event or a moment. The other term must be something outside the time-series.[1] For the relations of the A series are changing relations, and the relation of terms of the time-series to one another do not change. Two events are exactly in the same places in the time-series, relatively to one another, a million years before they take place, while each of them is taking place, and when they are a million years in the past. The same is true of the relation of moments to each other. Again, if the moments of time are to be distinguished as separate realities from the events which happen in them, the relation between an event and a moment is unvarying. Each event is in the same moment in the future, in the present, and in the past.

The relations which form the A series, then, must be relations of events and moments to something not itself in the time-series. What this something is might be difficult to say. But, waiving this point, a more positive difficulty presents itself.

Past, present, and future are incompatible determinations. Every event must be one or the other, but no event can be more than one. This is essential to the meaning of the terms. And, if it were not so, the A series would be insufficient to give us, in combination with the C series, the result of time.

[1] It has been maintained that the present is whatever is simultaneous with the assertion of its presentness, the future whatever is later than the assertion of its futurity, and the past whatever is earlier than the assertion of its pastness. But this theory involves that time exists independently of the A series, and is incompatible with the results we have already reached.

For time, as we have seen, involves change, and the only change we can get is from future to present, and from present to past.

The characteristics, therefore, are incompatible. But every event has them all. If M is past, it has been present and future. If it is future, it will be present and past. If it is present, it has been future and will be past. Thus all the three incompatible terms are predicable of each event, which is obviously inconsistent with their being incompatible, and inconsistent with their producing change.

It may seem that this can easily be explained. Indeed it has been impossible to state the difficulty without almost giving the explanation, since our language has verb-forms for the past, present, and future, but no form that is common to all three. It is never true, the answer will run, that M *is* present, past, and future. It *is* present, *will be* past, and *has been* future. Or it *is* past, and *has been* future and present, or again *is* future and *will be* present and past. The characteristics are only incompatible when they are simultaneous, and there is no contradiction to this in the fact that each term has all of them successively.

But this explanation involves a vicious circle. For it assumes the existence of time in order to account for the way in which moments are past, present, and future. Time then must be pre-supposed to account for the A series. But we have already seen that the A series has to be assumed in order to account for time. Accordingly the A series has to be pre-supposed in order to account for the A series. And this is clearly a vicious circle.

What we have done is this—to meet the difficulty that my writing of this article has the characteristics of past, present, and future, we say that it is present, has been future, and will be past. But ' has been ' is only distinguished from ' is ' by being existence in the past and not in the present, and ' will be ' is only distinguished from both by being existence in the future. Thus our statement comes to this—that the event in question is present in the present, future in the past, past in the future. And it is clear that there is a vicious circle if we endeavour to assign the characteristics of present, future, and past by the criterion of the characteristics of present, past, and future.

The difficulty may be put in another way, in which the fallacy will exhibit itself rather as a vicious infinite series than as a vicious circle. If we avoid the incompatibility of the three characteristics by asserting that M is present, has been future, and will be past, we are constructing a second A series, within which the first falls, in the same way in which events fall within the first. It may be doubted whether any intelligible meaning can be given to the assertion that time is in time. But, in any case, the second A series will suffer from the same difficulty as the first, which can only be removed by placing it inside a third A series. The same principle will place the third inside a fourth, and so on without end. You can never get rid of the contradiction, for, by the act of removing it from what is to be explained, you produce it over again in the explanation. And so the explanation is invalid.

Thus a contradiction arises if the A series is asserted of reality when the A series is taken as a series of relations. Could it be taken as a series of qualities, and would this give us a better result ? Are there three qualities—futurity, presentness, and pastness, and are events continually changing the first for the second, and the second for the third ?

It seems to me that there is very little to be said for the view that the changes of the A series are changes of qualities. No doubt my anticipation of an experience M, the experience itself, and the memory of the experience are three states which have different qualities. But it is not the future M, the present M, and the past M, which have these three different qualities. The qualities are possessed by three distinct events—the anticipation of M, the experience M itself, and the memory of M, each of which is in turn future, present, and past. Thus this gives no support to the view that the changes of the A series are changes of qualities.

But we need not go farther into this question. If the characteristics of the A series were qualities, the same difficulty would arise as if they were relations. For, as before, they are not compatible, and, as before, every event has all of them. This can only be explained, as before, by saying that each event has them successively. And thus the same fallacy would have been committed as in the previous case.[1]

We have come then to the conclusion that the application of the A series to reality involves a contradiction, and that consequently the A series cannot be true of reality. And, since time involves the A series, it follows that time cannot be true of reality. Whenever we judge anything to exist in time, we are in error. And whenever we perceive anything as existing in time—which is the only way in which we ever do perceive things—we are perceiving it more or less as it really is not.

We must consider a possible objection. Our ground for rejecting time, it may be said, is that time cannot be explained without assuming time. But may this not prove—not that time is invalid, but rather that time is ultimate? It is impossible to explain, for example, goodness or truth unless by bringing in the term to be explained as part of the explanation, and we therefore reject the explanation as invalid. But we do not therefore reject the notion as erroneous, but accept it as something ultimate, which, while it does not admit of explanation, does not require it.

---

[1] It is very usual to present Time under the metaphor of a spatial movement. But is it to be a movement from past to future, or from future to past? If the A series is taken as one of qualities, it will naturally be taken as a movement from past to future, since the quality of presentness has belonged to the past states and will belong to the future states. If the A series is taken as one of relations, it is possible to take the movement either way, since either of the two related terms can be taken as the one which moves. If the events are taken as moving by a fixed point of presentness, the movement is from future to past, since the future events are those which have not yet passed the point, and the past are those which have. If presentness is taken as a moving point successively related to each of a series of events, the movement is from past to future. Thus we say that events come out of the future, but we say that we ourselves move towards the future. For each man identifies himself especially with his present state, as against his future or his past, since the present is the only one of which he has direct experience. And thus the self, if it is pictured as moving at all, is pictured as moving with the point of presentness along the stream of events from past to future.

But this does not apply here. An idea may be valid of reality though it does not admit of a valid explanation. But it cannot be valid of reality if its application to reality involves a contradiction. Now we began by pointing out that there was such a contradiction in the case of time—that the characteristics of the A series are mutually incompatible and yet all true of every term. Unless this contradiction is removed, the idea of time must be rejected as invalid. It was to remove this contradiction that the explanation was suggested that the characteristics belong to the terms successively. When this explanation failed as being circular, the contradiction remained unremoved, and the idea of time must be rejected, not because it cannot be explained, but because the contradiction cannot be removed.

What has been said already, if valid, is an adequate ground for rejecting time. But we may add another consideration. Time, as we have seen, stands and falls with the A series. Now, even if we ignore the contradiction which we have just discovered in the application of the A series to reality, was there ever any positive reason why we should suppose that the A series *was* valid of reality ?

Why do we believe that events are to be distinguished as past, present, and future ? I conceive that the belief arises from distinctions in our own experience.

At any moment I have certain perceptions, I have also the memory of certain other perceptions, and the anticipation of others again. The direct perception itself is a mental state qualitatively different from the memory or the anticipation of perceptions. On this is based the belief that the perception itself has a certain characteristic when I have it, which is replaced by other characteristics when I have the memory or the anticipation of it—which characteristics are called presentness, pastness, and futurity. Having got the idea of these characteristics we apply them to other events. Everything simultaneous with the direct perception which I have now is called present, and it is even held that there would be a present if no one had a direct perception at all. In the same way acts simultaneous with remembered perceptions

127

or anticipated perceptions are held to be past or future, and this again is extended to events to which none of the perceptions I now remember or anticipate are simultaneous. But the origin of our belief in the whole distinction lies in the distinction between perceptions and anticipations or memories of perceptions.

A direct perception is present when I have it, and so is what is simultaneous with it. In the first place this definition involves a circle, for the words ' when I have it ' can only mean ' when it is present.' But if we left out these words, the definition would be false, for I have many direct presentations which are at different times, and which cannot, therefore, all be present, except successively. This, however, is the fundamental contradiction of the A series, which has been already considered. The point I wish to consider here is different.

The direct perceptions which I now have are those which now fall within my ' specious present.' Of those which are beyond it, I can only have memory or anticipation. Now the ' specious present ' varies in length according to circumstances, and may be different for two people at the same period. The event M may be simultaneous both with X's perception Q and Y's perception R. At a certain moment Q may have ceased to be part of X's specious present. M, therefore, will at that moment be past. But at the same moment R may still be part of Y's specious present. And, therefore, M will be present at the same moment at which it is past.

This is impossible. If, indeed, the A series was something purely subjective, there would be no difficulty. We could say that M was past for X and present for Y, just as we could say that it was pleasant for X and painful for Y. But we are considering attempts to take time as real, as something which belongs to the reality itself, and not only to our beliefs about it, and this can only be so if the A series also applies to the reality itself. And if it does this, then at any moment M must be present or past. It cannot be both.

The present through which events really pass, therefore, cannot be determined as simultaneous with the specious pre-

sent. It must have a duration fixed as an ultimate fact.
This duration cannot be the same as the duration of all specious
presents, since all specious presents have not the same duration.
And thus an event may be past when I am experiencing it as
present, or present when I am experiencing it as past. The
duration of the objective present may be the thousandth part
of a second. Or it may be a century, and the accessions of
George IV and Edward VII may form part of the same present.
What reason can we have to believe in the existence of such
a present, which we certainly do not observe to be a present,
and which has no relation to what we do observe to be a
present ?

If we escape from these difficulties by taking the view,
which has sometimes been held, that the present in the A
series is not a finite duration, but a mere point, separating
future from past, we shall find other difficulties as serious.
For then the objective time in which events are will be something utterly different from the time in which we perceive
them. The time in which we perceive them has a present
of varying finite duration, and, therefore, with the future and
the past, is divided into three durations. The objective time
has only two durations, separated by a present which has
nothing but the name in common with the present of experience, since it is not a duration but a point. What is there
in our experience which gives us the least reason to believe
in such a time as this ?

And so it would seem that the denial of the reality of time
is not so very paradoxical after all. It was called paradoxical
because it seemed to contradict our experience so violently—
to compel us to treat so much as illusion which appears *prima
facie* to give knowledge of reality. But we now see that our
experience of time—centring as it does about the specious
present—would be no less illusory if there were a real time
in which the realities we experience existed. The specious
present of our observations—varying as it does from you to
me—cannot correspond to the present of the events observed.
And consequently the past and future of our observations
could not correspond to the past and future of the events

observed. On either hypothesis—whether we take time as real or as unreal—everything is observed in a specious present, but nothing, not even the observations themselves, can ever *be* in a specious present. And in that case I do not see that we treat experience as much more illusory when we say that nothing is ever in a present at all, than when we say that everything passes through some entirely different present.

Our conclusion, then, is that neither time as a whole, nor the A series and B series, really exist. But this leaves it possible that the C series does really exist. The A series was rejected for its inconsistency. And its rejection involved the rejection of the B series. But we have found no such contradiction in the C series, and its invalidity does not follow from the invalidity of the A series.

It is, therefore, possible that the realities which we perceive as events in a time-series do really form a non-temporal series. It is also possible, so far as we have yet gone, that they do *not* form such a series, and that they are in reality no more a series than they are temporal. But I think—though I have no room to go into the question here—that the former view, according to which they really do form a C series, is the more probable.

Should it be true, it will follow that in our perception of these realities as events in time, there will be some truth as well as some error. Through the deceptive form of time, we shall grasp some of their true relations. If we say that the events M and N are simultaneous, we say that they occupy the same position in the time-series. And there will be some truth in this, for the realities, which we perceive as the events M and N, do really occupy the same position in a series, though it is not a temporal series.

Again, if we assert that the events M, N, O, are all at different times, and are in that order, we assert that they occupy different positions in the time-series, and that the position of N is between the positions of M and O. And it will be true that the realities which we see as these events will be in a series, though not in a temporal series, and that their positions in it will be different, and that the position of the reality which we perceive as the event N will be between the positions of the realities which we perceive as the events M and O.

If this view is adopted, the result will so far resemble those reached by Hegel rather than those of Kant. For Hegel regarded the order of the time-series as a reflexion, though a distorted reflexion, of something in the real nature of the timeless reality, while Kant does not seem to have contemplated the possibility that anything in the nature of the noumenon should correspond to the time order which appears in the phenomenon.

But the question whether such an objective C series does exist, must remain for future discussion.[1] And many other questions press upon us which inevitably arise if the reality of time is denied. If there is such a C series, are positions in it simply ultimate facts, or are they determined by the varying amounts, in the objects which hold those positions, of some quality which is common to all of them ? And, if so, what is that quality, and is it a greater amount of it which determines things to appear as later, and a lesser amount which determines them to appear as earlier, or is the reverse true ? On the solution of these questions it may be that our hopes and fears for the universe depend for their confirmation or rejection.

And, again, is the series of appearances in time a series which is infinite or finite in length ? And how are we to deal with the appearance itself ? If we reduce time and change to appearance, must it not be to an appearance which changes and which is in time, and is not time, then, shown to be real after all ? This is doubtless a serious question, but I hope to show hereafter that it can be answered in a satisfactory way.

[1] [This question is examined in very great detail, and answered affirmatively in The Nature of Existence, II, Bk. VI ; consult especially chaps. xlv–l.—Ed.]

VI

THE RELATION OF TIME AND ETERNITY [1]

1. The true nature of Time, and especially the question how far it is absolutely real, have been much discussed in philosophy. But there is, I think, no ambiguity in speaking of Time. Everyone means by Time the same characteristic of experience—a characteristic present in the experience of each of us.

2. Eternity is a more ambiguous word. It is used in at least three distinct senses : to denote unending time, to denote the timelessness of truths, and to denote the timelessness of existences.

The first sense need not detain us long. It is admitted to be a rather improper use of the word, and is only important on account of its frequency. The great majority of people, for example, who say that they believe that they will live eternally, do not mean that they believe in a timeless life, but that they believe in a life in time which will never end. This is not the only idea in the popular conception of immortality, nor the best, but it is the most common. In this sense, the relation of Eternity to Time is, of course, very simple. Time—finite Time—is simply a part of Eternity.

We pass on to the deeper meanings of Eternity. But first I should wish to say that, although it may be a shallow view of Eternity to see nothing in it but unending Time, yet I cannot regard the question of unending existence in time with the contempt with which it is sometimes treated. If, for example, it were proved that the true nature of man was timelessly eternal, yet I cannot see that the question of his future existence in time would be either unmeaning or un-

---

[1] Address before the Philosophical Union of the University of California, 23rd August 1907.

132

important. It would, on any theory, have as much meaning as the statement of his present existence in time—which may be partially inadequate, but has certainly some meaning. And it may very well have great importance. This, however, is a digression.

3. The second sense in which Eternity is used is to denote that timelessness which is said to be possessed by all general laws, and, indeed, by all truths, particular as well as general. 'The angles of a triangle are equal to two right angles.' 'The flash of a distant cannon is seen before its report is heard.' 'The date of the battle of Waterloo is the 18th of June, 1815.' Of these truths the last two have reference to time, and the third is not a general law, but a particular fact. Yet, it is said, all three truths are timeless. Any man's knowledge of them, indeed, is an event in time. It begins at a certain moment, and has a certain duration. And there may well have been times when none of these truths was known to any person. But the truth, it is said, must be distinguished both from our knowledge of it, which is in time, and the subject-matter referred to, which may be in time. And the truth, it is said, is always timeless.

There is much to be said for this view; but also, I think, something to be said against it. I do not propose to discuss it here. It would take us too far, and is not essential for our purpose. For, if we define Eternity in this manner, the relation of Eternity to Time is very simple. It is simply the relation of a truth to the subject-matter of the truth. About every substance existing in time, and about every event in time, however slight or ephemeral, many propositions—indeed, an infinite number of propositions—will be true. And since, on this view, nothing that exists will be eternal, but only the truths about them, the relation between Eternity and Time will simply be a case of the relation between a truth and the reality of which it is true. What that relation is, constitutes, indeed, a highly interesting question. But the special natures of Eternity and Time will not enter into it.

Nor does the establishment of an Eternity, in this sense, give us any fresh view of the nature of reality, or afford us a glimpse of any greater permanence or stability in the universe than appears on a *prima facie* view of experience. Everything, no doubt, has on this view a certain connexion with Eternity. But everything has exactly the same connexion, and that without any transformation of its nature, but taking it just as it appears. We can look at ourselves *sub quadam specie æternitatis*, for each of us exists, and the truth of his existence is eternal. But then—for an hour or two— a bridge-party exists, and it can be looked at *sub quadam specie æternitatis*, as easily as a human being. And so can the bubbles in a glass of soda-water—I do not mean the substance of the water, but the shape which it assumes for a moment.

And even events have the same timelessness. If I sneezed on last Christmas Day, the truth which expresses that event is, in this meaning of Eternity, as eternal as the truth of love, or of man's existence, or of God's existence, if he exist. No person and no thing are eternal on this view. But about everything, permanent, ephemeral, high and low, there are numberless eternal truths. The conclusion may be correct, but it cannot be called very interesting or significant.

The contemplation of eternal truths, indeed, may be in the highest degree interesting and significant, though whether it is—as Spinoza seems to have held—the highest activity of which spirit is capable may be doubted. But then the contemplation of eternal truths is not itself a truth. It is an activity. And it cannot, therefore, be eternal in the sense which we have so far discussed.

4. We pass to the third meaning of Eternity, which will occupy us for the rest of the paper, in which it is used of the timelessness of existences. Existence is, I think, like Time, too ultimate to admit of definition. But it is not difficult to determine the denotation of the word. In so far as substances, or the qualities and relations of substances, are real at all, they exist. In so far as events are real, they exist. On the other hand, if truths, and the ideas which are the constituent parts of truths, have any independent reality, it is not a reality of existence—though of course our *perceptions* of such truths exist, since they are psychical events. Thus

the Emperor of China exists. His moral character, and the reciprocal influences between him and his subjects exist. So do the events of his daily life. On the other hand, the Law of Excluded Middle, the Law of Gravitation, and other true propositions do not exist, although my knowledge of the Law of Excluded Middle exists as an event in my mind.

Whatever is temporal exists. This seems to be generally admitted, for those thinkers who hold that truths and ideas have a reality which is not existence, admit that such reality would be timeless. Whatever is temporal then, and is real at all, exists. But is the converse true? Is all existence temporal?

All existence which presents itself as part of our ordinary world of experience presents itself as temporal. But there may be reality which does not present itself to us in the ordinary course of things, though search may reveal its presence. And, again, a thing may present itself in a more or less deceptive fashion. And it is frequently maintained that we have reason to believe that some reality which exists, exists timelessly—not merely in the sense that its existence endures through unending time, but in the deeper sense that it is not in time at all.

5. The possibility of timeless existence has been denied. Lotze, for example, makes time an essential characteristic of existence—his terminology is different but it comes to this. But the general opinion of thinkers has been the other way. For most men have believed in the existence of a God, and most of those who have not believed in a God have believed in the existence of some impersonal Absolute. And God or the Absolute has generally been conceived as timeless. This has not been universal. Lotze regards God as existing in time. And among theological writers there have doubtless been some who, when they called God eternal, only meant that he existed through endless time, or that his nature did not change. But as a rule philosophy and theology have held that God exists timelessly.

It seems to me that this opinion—that timeless existence is possible—is correct. To exist and to be in time seem to me two characteristics, each quite distinct from the other. And, while it seems clear that nothing could be in time without existing, I fail to see any corresponding impossibility in something existing without being in time. If so, timeless existence is possible. Whether it is actual—whether we have reason to believe that anything does exist out of time—is a question which I shall not discuss in this paper. My object here is only to discuss the relation of existence in Time to existence in Eternity, should there be any such eternal existence.

6. We, who are endeavouring to estimate the relation, appear to ourselves to exist in time, whether we really do so or not. It is not strange, therefore, that men should have endeavoured to express their relation to the Eternal by terms borrowed from Time, and to say that the Eternal is present, past, or future. We shall consider which of these terms is the most appropriate metaphor, and whether any of them are more than metaphors.

In the first place, we may consider that existence in Time and existence in Eternity are equally real. Then, since the same thing clearly cannot exist both in Time and timelessly —if both predicates are taken in the same sense and as equally real—the only possibility would be that some existent being was in time, and some existent being was out of it. (This is exemplified in the very common theological view, according to which God exists timelessly, but everything else exists in time.) What would the relation be, in such a case, between the temporal and the eternal?

The eternal is often spoken of, under these circumstances, as an ' eternal present.' As a metaphor this has, as we shall see, some appropriateness, but it cannot, I think, be taken as more than a metaphor. ' Present ' is not like ' existence,' a predicate which can be applied in the same sense to the temporal and the timeless. On the contrary, its meaning seems to include a distinct reference to time, and a distinct reference to past and future. The Present has been future and will be past. I do not say this is an adequate definition of the present, but it does seem to be an essential characteristic of the present. If so, the timeless cannot be present. The eternal, the timeless, must be distinguished from what exists unchanged in time. The Pyramids exist in time, but they have existed through thousands of years, through all of which they have been present. And supposing that human beings were really in time, but also immortal, we could say of every man, after he had been born, that he would be endlessly present, since in every moment of future time he would exist. But persistence through time is, as we have seen, quite a different thing from timeless existence.

7. There is one reason which has, I think, led to regarding the eternal as an eternal present, which rests on a confusion. Of anything which exists in time, my judgment ' It is true that X exists now ' is true when X is in the present and not when X is in the future or past. Now supposing that Z exists eternally, my judgment ' It is now true that Z exists ' will be always true. Hence, I believe, it is sometimes supposed that Z is always present. But this is a confusion. For ' It is now true that Z exists,' where the ' now ' refers to the truth of the judgment that Z exists, is by no means the same as ' It is true that Z exists now,' where the ' now ' refers to the existence of Z. A judgment is a psychical event in my mind, and is in time, even if I am judging of the timeless, so that ' now ' is an appropriate word to use about it. But ' now ' cannot be used about the existence of the timeless itself.

8. As a metaphor, however, there is considerable fitness in calling the eternal a present. In the first place, the future and the past are always changing their positions in regard to us. The future is always coming nearer, while yet remaining future. The past is always going farther away, while yet remaining past. The present, however, while it remains present, does not change in this way. It is continually being born out of what was the future. It is continually changing into the past. But as present it does not change in its relation to us.

This affords a certain analogy to the timeless which, of course, is not capable of change. The timeless does not change, and therefore nothing in the timeless can bring it

137

nearer to us or farther from us. And the constancy which this involves has an analogy with the constancy of the present while it remains present.

9. In the second place the present is always regarded as having more reality than the past or future. So much is this the case that we feel no inappropriateness in saying of something which is not existing at present that it does not exist. We should not feel the expression unusual if we said that the Holy Roman Empire does not exist, which is the same expression we should use of More's Utopia. And yet we no more mean to deny the past existence of the Holy Roman Empire than we mean to deny the present existence of the United Kingdom. Now the eternal does not appear with the diminished reality of the past and future. It has all the reality of which its nature admits. And the eternal is generally considered as more real than the temporal, for, when some reality is held to be eternal and some temporal, it is God or the Absolute which is considered eternal, and the created or finite which is considered temporal. It will thus resemble the reality of the present more than the reality of the past or future, and so it will be an appropriate metaphor to regard it as present. This is especially the case when we consider our emotions toward the eternal—a point of great importance since the eternal in this case would be, as we have just said, God or the Absolute. It is clear that the emotions of a man who loved an eternal God would stand much closer to the emotions of a man who loved a being existent in present time than they would to the emotions of a man who loved a being who had ceased to exist, or who had not yet come into existence.

10. In the third place it must be remembered that it is only the present, and not the past or future, which we regard as capable of exercising immediate causal influence. The future is not conceived as being a cause at all—since causality always goes towards what comes later, and never back towards what is earlier. The past is certainly regarded as acting as a cause, but not immediately. The past has produced the present, and so is the remote cause of what the present is

now occupied in producing. But it is not the immediate cause of what is now being produced. This, I think, is the inevitable way of looking at causality in connection with time. If it leads to contradictions—and I do not say that it does not—they are contradictions which spring from the nature of time. They may affect our judgment as to whether time is ultimately real, but we cannot get rid of them while we are looking at things in time.

Now the eternal can be looked on as a cause. I do not wish to inquire whether the view is correct, which is often held, that the eternal can be the sole cause of anything. But there is no doubt that, if anything eternal exists, it can be a part-cause of an effect, so that the result would be different from what it would have been except for that eternal being. And the causation of this eternal being must be regarded as immediate, in the same way as the causation of a being present in time. For this reason, also, then, the present is an appropriate metaphor for the eternal. But it cannot be more than a metaphor. Presentness involves time, and cannot be predicated of the timeless.

11. We must now consider another theory on the subject of timeless existence. This holds that all existence is really timeless, and that the *prima facie* appearance of Time which our experience presents is, in reality, only an appearance, which disguises the nature of the timeless reality. In this case we shall not, as in the previous case, divide all existence into two facts, one eternal and one temporal. All existence will be eternal. And though this will exclude the possibility of any of it being really temporal, yet it will leave the possibility open that some, or even all, of it may appear to us as temporal.

The theory of the unreality of Time is doubtless very difficult to grasp fully. And doubtless it presents very many difficulties. I do not intend, in this paper, to advocate it,[1] or even to develop it at length, but merely to consider, as before, what would be the relation of Time to Eternity, should the theory be true. It cannot be doubted that it is worth while to consider the consequences of this theory. For

---

[1] [Cf. Essay V—*Ed.*]

it is one which is very largely held by philosophers. The exact nature of Eternity in Spinoza's philosophy, and its relation to time is a very difficult problem, especially since it is not improbable that Spinoza himself did not distinguish with sufficient clearness between the timelessness of truths and the timelessness of existence. But the doctrine that all reality is timeless was unquestionably held by Kant—though he would not perhaps have used this expression. It was held by Schopenhauer. It was a fundamental doctrine of Hegel's philosophy, and in this respect Hegelians have followed their master more closely than has been the case with other doctrines. And, at the present day, it is held by the greatest of living philosophers, Mr. Bradley. If we turn from philosophers to theologians we shall find the same doctrine. The view that all reality is timeless is not so general, of course, among theologians, as the view that some reality is timeless. But theology has never in any country or in any age, remained for long together untouched by mysticism. And the unreality of time, although it is not held by all mystics, is one of the most characteristic mystical tenets.

Once more, in the Far East, where philosophy and theology do not admit even of that partial distinction which is possible in the West, we find the doctrine of the unreality of time assumes cardinal importance.

A theory which has attracted so much support, and which continues to attract so much at the present day, must, right or wrong, have much to be said in its favour. Teachers so great, and so different, do not adopt such a doctrine without grave reasons   For my part I am convinced that in spite of the very great difficulties which belong to the theory, it must be accepted as true. But at present I am merely concerned to point out that, whether the theory be true or false, it is no waste of time to consider any consequences that would follow from accepting it.

12. What is the precise description which we must give to Time on this theory ? We cannot call it a mistake, for to perceive things in time does not necessarily involve an erroneous judgment. If a person who perceives things as in time

believes that they really are in time, that would of course be an erroneous judgment. But if the theory is true, a person who believed the theory would not be making any erroneous judgments on the subject. His judgment would be ' I perceive things as in time, and I cannot perceive them any other way, but they are not really in time, but timeless.' In this judgment there would be no error. And thus the perception of things in time must not be called a mistake. It hides, more or less, the true nature of things, but it does not involve making any false judgment about their nature.

And since the perception of things in time does not necessarily involve an error, it follows that, when the error has been there, and is removed, it will not alter the perception of things in time. If I begin by holding the view—which may be wrong, but which is certainly the most obvious view —that things are really in time, and am then convinced by philosophical arguments that they are really timeless, I shall, none the less, continue to perceive the things in time.

Thus we must conceive our perception of things in time to be an illusion, of the same character as those which make us see the sun at sunset larger than at midday, and make us see a straight stick crooked when it enters the water. I do not, after childhood, suppose the stick to be really crooked. But however clearly I may satisfy myself, either by reasoning or by the sense of touch, that the stick has not changed its shape since it was put in the water, I shall continue to get visual sensations from it resembling those which would be given me by a crooked stick in the air. Of this sort is the illusion of time—though it is far more general, and far more difficult to grasp. It hides part of the truth, it suggests a wrong judgment—for the obvious conclusion from our experience, as I said just now, is to hold that things are really in time. But it does not necessarily involve a wrong judgment, and it is not removed by a right judgment.

13. What relation, then, does Time bear to Eternity on such a theory as this ? The answer will, I think, vary. When we see existence under the form of time, the theory tells us, we see it more or less as it really is not. At the same time,

the appearance is not *mere* illusion. We perceive, in spite of this illusive form of time, some of the real nature of the timeless reality. So if we look through a window of red glass we shall see the objects outside correctly as to their form, size, and motion though not correctly as to their colour. The question is, of course, much more complicated here. We cannot get round on the other side of time, as we can on the other side of the glass, and so discover by direct observation what part of our previous experience was due to the form of time. And to reach and justify an idea of what the true timeless nature of existence may be is a very hard task, though I think not an impossible one. We must content ourselves here with the general result that where existence appears to us under the form of time, we see it partly, but not entirely, as it really is.

Thus the way in which, at any moment of time, we regard existence is more or less inadequate. And it seems to me that the relation of Time to Eternity depends on the relative inadequacy of our view of reality at different moments of time.

The decisive question—this is the theory I wish to put before you—is whether there is any law according to which states in time, as we pass from earlier states to later, tend to become more adequate or less adequate representations of the timeless reality.

14. Let us first consider what would happen if there were no such law. In that case there would be no tendency for the future, because it was future, to resemble the timeless reality more or less than the present does. There might be oscillations, even then, in the adequacy with which time represented Eternity. At one moment my view of the universe might distort the truth either more or less than my view of the moment before had distorted it. But such oscillations are like the waves of the sea. At a particular moment the surface at a particular point may be higher than at the moment before. But this does not give us the least reason for concluding that an hour later on it will also be higher than it was at the past moment, or that the average height is rising.

If the adequacy of the time-representations is in this

142

condition, the relation of Time to Eternity will, I think, be expressible in the same way in which we expressed it when Time and Eternity were taken as equally real. That is to say, the most appropriate metaphor for the relation is to consider Eternity as a present, but this is nothing more than a metaphor.

The metaphor is appropriate for the same reasons as it was before. In the first place, the relation of Eternity to Time is constant. In some particular moments of time we may, as I have said, get a less adequate representation of Eternity than at others, but if we take time as a whole it neither approximates to Eternity nor diverges from it. And, for the reasons explained above, there is a certain appropriateness in using presentness as a metaphor for this unchanging relation.

In the second place, the metaphor is appropriate here, as it was before, to express the reality of the eternal. The eternal has not that diminished reality which we attribute to the past and the future. Indeed, its reality is relatively greater here than it was on the other theory. In that theory the Eternal was generally the most real, for it generally included God or the Absolute. But here it is an inevitable result of the theory that the Eternal is not only the most real, but the only true, reality. It is more important than before, therefore, to express it by a metaphor drawn from the greatest reality in time.

In the third place, the Eternal must certainly, on this theory, be regarded as exercising immediate causal influence, or, rather, as having a quality of which causal influence is an imperfect representation. For everything depends on the nature of the eternal, which is the only true reality.

At the same time, to say that the eternal is eternally present remains a metaphor only. It is not a literally correct description. For the present, as we saw, is essentially a time-determination, and the eternal is not in Time.

15. So far, I think, I have not said much that is controversial, and certainly nothing that I should claim as original. But I have now a thesis to put forward which, whether it is original or not, is certainly controversial. I submit that although to

us, who judge from the midst of the time-series, the present-ness of the eternal can never be more than a metaphor, yet, under certain conditions, the assertion that the eternal was past or future might be much more than a metaphor. This statement will doubtless seem highly paradoxical. The eternal is the timeless, and how can the timeless have a position in the time-series ? Still, I believe this position can be defended, and I will now attempt to sketch my defence of it.

16. So far we have considered what would happen if there were no law according to which states in time, as we pass from earlier states to later, tend to become more adequate or less adequate representations of the timeless reality. But what would happen if there were such a law ?

Events in time take place in an order—a fixed and irreversible order. The flash of a distant cannon is perceived before the report. The report is not perceived before the flash. The Battle of Waterloo was fought before the Reform Bill was passed. The Reform Bill was not passed before the Battle of Waterloo was fought. Now what determines this order ?

The mere form of time does not do so. If things happen in time they must happen in an order, and a fixed and irreversible order. So much the nature of time demands. But it gives us no help as to what the order shall be. If the Battle of Waterloo and the passing of the Reform Bill are to take place in time at all, the nature of time requires either that they shall be simultaneous or that the Battle shall precede the Bill, or that the Bill shall precede the Battle. But it gives us no help towards determining which of these three alternatives shall be taken.

What does determine the order of events in time, on the supposition, which we are now discussing, that Time is only an illusory way of regarding a timeless reality ? I believe myself that there is good reason to hold that the order is determined by the adequacy with which the states represent the eternal reality, so that those states come next together which only vary infinitesimally in the degree of their adequacy,

144

and that the whole of the time-series shows a steady process of change of adequacy—I do not say yet in which direction.

I think something can be said towards proving this statement, but it would want far more than a single lecture to say it, and I do not propose even to sketch it now.[1] Nor is it necessary for our present purpose, which is only to consider what relation of Time to Eternity would be under various circumstances. Let us now proceed to consider what that relation would be under these circumstances.

17. Let us suppose, then, that the states of the time-series were such that each state was a more adequate expression of the reality than the state on one side of it, and a less adequate representation of reality than the state on the other side of it, so that they formed a continuous series in respect of the adequacy of their representation. And let us suppose that the most adequate of these representations—which will be, of course, at one end of the series—differs from the reality it represents only by an infinitesimal amount. What is the relation here between Time and Eternity?

This will depend upon the direction in the series in which greater adequacy is to be found. It may be, in the first place, that the later stages of the time-series are more adequate than the earlier stages. In that case the present stage will be more adequate than any of the past, and less adequate than any of the future.

We may go farther than this. If time is unreal, as we have supposed, then the illusion that time exists can no more be in time than anything else can. The time-series, though a series which gives us the illusion of Time, is not itself in time. And the series is really therefore just a series of representations, some more adequate and some less adequate, arranged in the order of their adequacy. This—the series of adequacy—is the only serial element which remains as real, if time is to be condemned as unreal.

When, therefore, we say that a certain stage in the time-series is still in the future, the real truth, if the theory we are considering is correct, is that the stage in question is a

[1] [Cf. footnote to p. 131—*Ed.*]

less inadequate representation of the timeless reality of existence than our present stage.

Now the timeless reality itself contains all its own nature. And therefore it will stand to the least inadequate of the representations of itself as this stands to the next least inadequate, and so on. Since, by our hypothesis, the representations of reality in the time-series approach the reality till the inadequacy finally becomes infinitesimal, the last of the series of time-representations will differ only infinitesimally from the reality itself. And, since time is continuous, the stage before the last will differ from the last in the same way—by being infinitesimally less adequate.

Thus the timeless reality—the Eternal—may itself be considered as the last stage in a series, of which the other stages are those which we perceive as the time-series,—those stages nearest to the timeless reality being those which we perceive as the later stages in time. When, therefore, we are looking at things as in time—as we must look at them—we must conceive the Eternal as the final stage in the time-process. We must conceive it as being in the future, and as being the end of the future. Time runs up to Eternity, and ceases in Eternity.

18. This conclusion will doubtless be rejected by many people without further examination as grossly absurd. How can the timeless have a position at the end of a time-series ? How can Eternity begin when Time ceases ? How can Eternity begin at all ?

The answer to these objections, I think, is as follows : Of course, on this view, Eternity is not really future, and does not really begin. For Time is unreal, and therefore nothing can be future, and nothing can begin. What, then, is the justification of regarding Eternity as future ? It lies, I maintain, in the fact that Eternity is as future as anything can be. It is as truly future as to-morrow or next year. And, therefore, when, taking Time as real, as we must do in everyday life, we are endeavouring to estimate the relation of Time to Eternity, we may legitimately say that Eternity is future. From the point of view of time, the events of to-morrow and next year are future. And if Eternity is as truly future as they are, it is legitimate to say that Eternity is future. It is not absolutely true, but it is as true as any other statement about futurity. And it is much truer than to say that Eternity is present or past.

Let us recapitulate. If time is unreal then the time-series is a series of more or less adequate representations of the timeless reality, and this series itself is not really in time. If what determines the position of the stages in the time-series is the different degrees of adequacy with which they represent the timeless reality, then the series which is not really a series in time, is really a series of degrees of adequacy. If the most adequate of these stages has only infinitesimal inadequacy, then the timeless reality, in its own completeness, forms the last stage of the series. And if the distinction between earlier and later stages is that the later are the more adequate, then—since the future is later than the present—we must place the timeless reality in the future, and at the end of the future.

Thus to say that Eternity is future on this theory is far more accurate than it was, in the two previous cases, to say that Eternity was present. For in those cases Eternity, though it had some analogy to the present, was not as fully present as to-day's sunlight is, which is in the fullest sense present. But in this case Eternity is as really future as to-morrow's sunlight, which is in the fullest sense future. The presentness of Eternity was only a metaphor. Its futurity, in this case, is as true as any futurity.

19. Let us pass to another case. Let us suppose, as before, that the truth of the time-series was a series of representations arranged by their degrees of adequacy, and running on until the extreme term of the series only differed from the timeless reality itself by an infinitesimal amount. But let us suppose that the series runs the other way, so that it is the more adequate members which appear as the earlier stages of the time-series, and the less adequate members which appear as the later stages of the time-series. In this case we should have to regard the timeless reality as the beginning

of the past, instead of as the end of the future. We should have to regard ourselves as having started from it, not as destined to reach it. It is obvious that from a practical point of view the difference between these two cases may be very great—I shall return to the practical importance of the relation later on. It seems to me that there are reasons for supposing that the first of the two cases is the one which really exists, and that Eternity is to be regarded as in the future and not as in the past. But our object here is merely to realize that, if the second case is true, and it is the more adequate members which appear as the earlier, then Eternity must be regarded as in the past.

20. I may mention a third case, though I think it one which is very improbable. Let us suppose that the stages of the series were arranged, not simply in order of adequacy, but on some principle which placed the least adequate in the middle, and made them more adequate as they diverged from this at either end. And let us suppose, as before, that the more adequate representations only differed from the timeless reality infinitesimally. Then it is clear that the timeless reality would stand to the earliest member of the series, as that stood to the next earliest. And it is also clear that the timeless reality would stand to the latest member as this stood to the next latest. And therefore the timeless reality would be a term at each end of the series, which would start from it and would return to it. In that case we should have to consider the Eternal both as the beginning of the past, and the end of the future.

21. Thus we see that, under certain suppositions, the Eternal may be said to be past or future, not only as a metaphor, but with as much truth as anything else can be past or future. But this is not the case about the present. On no supposition could we be justified in saying now that the Eternal was present. If it were present, it would bear the relation to our present position in the time-series that the present does—that is, of course, it would have to be identical with it. And the timeless reality is certainly not identical with a position like our present one, which represents it as in time, and, therefore,

according to our theory, represents it inadequately. On several suppositions, as we have seen above, the most appropriate *metaphor* for the Eternal is that of an eternal present. But on no supposition can it be more than a metaphor.

22. It remains to say, as to the cases in which the Eternal is regarded as being the end of the future or the beginning of the past, that it is possible that the past or the future in question might be infinite in length. I do not see anything which should exclude this supposition, and enable us to assert that the present has been reached in a finite time from the Eternal, or that the Eternal will be reached in a finite time from the present.

In mathematics that which only happens at an infinite distance is said to be the same as that which never happens at all. Thus two parallel straight lines are said to meet at an infinite distance. Since mathematicians adopt this method of expression it has probably some real convenience for mathematics. But, apart from the conventions of that special science, it seems to me that there is a very real difference between a series such that it reaches a result after an infinitely long process, and a series such that it never reaches that result at all.

Even, therefore, if the series of stages which intervene between the present and the timeless reality were such as would appear as an infinitely long time, I should see no impropriety in speaking of the timeless reality as the extreme stage of the series, from which it started, or to which it attains. At the same time, I see no more reason to suppose the length infinite than to suppose it finite.

23. I propose to devote the rest of my paper to a consideration of some aspects of the possibility that it may be right to regard Eternity as the end of the future.

It will be seen that this view has a very strong resemblance to a very common Christian view. The Christian heaven is sometimes looked upon as enduring through unending time. But it is also often looked upon as a timeless state. At the same time, it is generally looked on as in the future. We are not in it now. We have not been in it before birth—

indeed, most Christians deny that we existed at all before the birth of our present bodies. We are separated from it by death—not, indeed, that death alone would place us in it, but that we shall not reach it till we have passed through death. This has not been the universal view of Christianity, but I think it cannot be denied that it has generally been held that heaven was in the future. Heaven may be held to be a state of the mind, not a place or an environment. But still it is a state of the mind which is yet for us in the future. 'Now we see in a mirror, darkly; but then face to face' (1st Epistle to the Corinthians xiii, 12). The beginning may be present here, but not the completion. Moreover, even what is attained of it on earth has to be attained, to be gained where it was not before, and so was once in the future and is still for many men in the future.

This view of the Christian heaven has been severely criticized lately, both from inside and from outside Christianity. It has been said that heaven, if it is perfect, must be timeless, and that it is generally admitted to be timeless, and that therefore it is absurd to place it in the future, and it should rather be regarded as an eternal present.

The critics have a certain subjective justification. They have investigated the relation of Time to Eternity more deeply than the majority of those who hold the view criticized. They have perceived the difficulties of giving Eternity a place at the end of the time-series, while many of those who held that heaven was future had not perceived those difficulties at all. Yet we must hold, I submit, that the view of heaven as now future might, under certain circumstances, be much truer than the view of heaven as now present could be under any circumstances.

Let us recapitulate once more the conditions. The Eternal can be rightly regarded as future if time is unreal, if the series which appears to us as a time-series is a series of representations arranged according to adequacy, if the highest of the series only differs by an infinitesimal amount from the reality represented, and if it is the more adequate representations which appear as latest in the series.

Now many people who hold heaven to be future would hold that it was attained gradually, by advancing stages which got higher till the last led into the timeless perfection without any breach of continuity, and that the higher of these stages came later. Three of the four conditions are thus complied with. The first—that time is unreal—is, of course, less frequent. But if this is combined with the other three—as it often is, and may very well be—then it seems to me that the idea of a timeless heaven as future is quite justifiable, and that the Christians who held this belief, while not seeing so deeply as such critics as Mr. Bradley and Mr. Haldane, had in point of fact grasped the truth, though without seeing very clearly why it was true.

24. The practical importance of the question whether the Eternal can be regarded as future appears to me to be enormous. The supreme question, from the point of view of practical importance, is whether good or evil predominates in the universe, and in what proportion. The practical importance of philosophy consists, not in the guidance it gives us in life—it gives us, I think, very little—but in the chance that it may answer this supreme question in a cheerful manner, that it may provide some solution which shall be a consolation and an encouragement.

In what way can we hope to do this ? It cannot be done by empirical induction. Even granting that we have evidence for coming to a favourable conclusion about the state of people on this planet at the present time—and this is all we can know empirically—it would be far too small a basis for an induction which would give us even the least probability as to the universe as a whole through the whole of time.

The belief in a God who is on the side of the good has been one of the supports on which men have most often tried to base an optimistic solution of this question. But, even if we accept the existence of such a God, it will not by itself afford sufficient ground for what we seek. We are wrecked against the old difficulty—the difficulty which Augustine stated with perfect clearness, and which theists, in all the centuries that have passed, have never avoided. Either God can do everything he likes, and then evil, since it exists, cannot be repugnant to him, and his existence affords no ground for limiting its extent or duration. Or else God cannot do everything he likes, and then we cannot be certain that evil, in spite of God's efforts, may not predominate over good now, and be destined to increase in the future.

Attempts have been made to prove the predominance of good from the intrinsic nature of good and evil. But here, as it seems to me, any argument which proves anything proves too much, for they all tend to prove that there is no evil at all. And such an argument may, I fear, be dismissed as a *reductio ad absurdum*.

25. What other course remains—to those of us who are not so happily constituted as to be able to believe a thing because we want to believe it ? One attempted solution remains—that on which was reared the most magnificent optimism that philosophy has ever seen, the optimism of Hegel. This solution rests on the unreality of Time. Only the Eternal really exists, and the Eternal is perfectly good. All the evil which we suppose to be in existence is part of the Time-element which we wrongly suppose to be in existence. And so there is no evil at all.

This solution, however, in the form which it takes with Hegel, will not give us what we seek. In the first place, it has really no optimistic result. To tell us that evil is unreal does not make what we think to be evil in the least less unpleasant to suffer or in the least less depressing to expect. And even if it had that effect on the people who know the truth, how about the people who do not know it ? The only ground of optimism would be found in a belief that this illusion of evil was limited in quantity or transitory in apparent duration. And the assertion of its unreality would not permit us to limit the extent or the duration of our illusion of its reality.

In the second place, I do not think that the theory can be accepted as true. It is possible that there is no sin in existence —indeed, if time is unreal, it seems inevitable that there should be no sin. It is even possible that there should be no pain—though that is not so simple. But evil is wider than sin or pain. And it seems, to me at any rate, certain that even the illusion that I am sinful or in pain is evil. I may not be really sinful or really in pain, but in some sense the illusion of the sin or pain exists, and that is a real evil. If we doubt it, let us ask whether we should not think the universe better if a given illusion of sin or pain was replaced with an experience of virtue or pleasure. Or let us ask whether we should not blame a creator who needlessly inserted such illusions into the universe he created.

26. But if we abandon the attempt to base an optimistic solution on the unreality of time through the unreality of evil, yet there is another way in which the unreality of time may help us.

It is a certain fact—which may some day be accounted for, but which cannot be denied, whether it is accounted for or not—that good and evil in the future affect us quite differently from good and evil in the past. Let us suppose two men, one of whom had been very happy for a million years, and was just about to become very miserable for another million years, while the other had been very miserable for a million years, and was now about to be very happy for the same period. If we suppose them, in some neutral hour between the two periods, to remember the past and to be certain of the future, it is certain that the second would be in a very much more desirable position than the first, although the total amount of life which each would be contemplating shows exactly the same amount of pleasure and pain.

Past evil, as such, does not sadden us like future evil. We may be saddened by the results which it has left behind in the present, or which may be expected to appear in the future —if those results are themselves evil, which of course is not always the case with the present results of past evils. Or the remembrance of past evil may remind us that the universe is not wholly good, and make us fear for evil in the future. And a particular past evil may give us, not merely this general apprehension, but particular reasons to fear some particular future evil. And, once more, if past evil has been caused by the wickedness of any person, the fact that the evil has passed away will not affect the fact that the responsible person is still wicked, unless indeed he has improved and repented.

27. If, therefore, we arrived at a theory of the universe which was unable to deny the existence of evil, or to assert that over the whole of time good predominated over evil, or that it did so at present, there would still be a chance for optimism. If such a theory were able to assert that, whatever the state of the universe now, it would inevitably improve, and the state of each conscious individual in it would inevitably improve, until they reached a final state of perfect goodness, or at least of very great goodness—surely this would be accepted as a cheerful theory. Surely this would give, as much as any belief can give, consolation and encouragement in the evils of the present. Indeed, it is nearly as favourable a theory as could be framed, for if we went much beyond this in the direction of optimism, we should soon reach the denial of evil, and then, as was said above, our theory would break itself against facts which cannot be denied.

28. But how could such a theory be established? No empirical evidence which we could reach would afford even the slightest presumption in favour of such a vast conclusion. And how can we prove *a priori* that good will predominate over evil more in the future than it has in the past, or than it does in the present? What link can *a priori* reasoning find between the later and the better?

I do not see how it can be done if Time is to be taken as real. But if Time is unreal, I do see a possibility—more I do not venture to say at present—of such a demonstration.[1] I do see a possibility of showing that the timeless reality would be, I do not say unmixedly good, but very good, better than anything which we can now experience or even imagine. I do see a possibility of showing that all that hides this goodness from us—in so far as it is hidden—is the illusion of time. And I do see a possibility of showing that the different representations which appear to us as the time-series are in such an order that those which appear as later are the more adequate,

[1] [Cf. *The Nature of Existence*, II, chaps. lxiv.–lxviii.—*Ed.*]

and the last only infinitesimally differs from the timeless reality. In that case we must look on the Eternal as the end of Time ; and on Time as essentially the process by which we reach to the Eternal and its perfection.

The reality of the Eternal can only have comfort for us, then, if we conceive it as future, since it is to the future that optimism must look. Nor do I see how we can regard the future optimistically unless we regard it as the progressive manifestation of the Eternal. Whether this can be done, will be for the future to pronounce—the possibilities of which I have spoken may prove to be demonstrations or to be the merest fallacies. Only I do see a chance of a happy solution in the relation of Time to Eternity, and, as philosophy stands at present, I see it nowhere else.

VII

THE MEANING OF CAUSALITY

In this lecture [1] I propose to discuss what is meant, and what should be meant, by the word Causality. The question whether Causality, defined as we shall find reason to define it, does occur in the universe, will not be discussed. Personally I do believe that various existent realities in the universe are connected with one another by the relation of Causality, but the arguments which lead me to this conclusion would require more than a single lecture in which to explain them. [2]

We must begin by considering what characteristics have, at different times and by different people, been considered as essential to causality. There are, I think, seven such characteristics, of which the first two are universally admitted to be essential to causality, while the other five are not.

In the first place, it would, I think, be universally admitted that causality is a relation of Determination. If A is the cause of B, then the existence of A determines the existence of B. [3] And it determines it in some way which does not hold between all things in the universe, so that it is possible for A to be the cause of B, and not the cause of C. We must, that is, give causality such a meaning that it is possible to say that the beheading of Charles I was the cause of his death, but that it was not the cause of the death of Julius Cæsar.

What sort of determination is this? It is a determination of Implication. The cause implies the effect. What then do we mean by implication? I am using implication in what

[1] Henry Sidgwick Memorial Lecture for 1914, delivered at Newnham College, Cambridge.

[2] [These are developed in *The Nature of Existence*, I, Bk. IV, particularly in ch. xxv.—*Ed.*]

[3] It is not so universally admitted that the existence of the effect determines the existence of the cause. This will be discussed later.

I believe to be the usual sense. I should say that implication is a relation between propositions, and that P implies Q when, if I know P to be true, I am justified by that alone in asserting that Q is true, and if I know Q to be false, I am justified by that alone in asserting P to be false. That is, the beheading of Charles I implies his death, because, if I knew that he had been beheaded, I should be justified by that alone in asserting that he was dead, and, if I had known that he was not dead, I should have been justified by that alone in asserting that he had not been beheaded.

Strictly speaking, as we have seen, implication is a relation between propositions, or truths, and not between events. But it is convenient to extend our use of it, so as to say that, if one proposition implies another, then the event asserted in the first implies the event asserted in the second. It is in this sense that we say that the cause implies the effect.

It must not be supposed that implication is a subjective or psychological relation only. For we have not said that one event implies another because our knowledge of one causes us to assert the other, but because our knowledge of one *justifies* us in asserting the other. And this justification must be due to a relation between the events themselves, and not merely to a relation between our thoughts of them.

In the second place, the relation of causality is always held to be a relation between realities which exist. We should not say that the definitions and axioms of Euclid were the cause that two of the sides of a triangle were longer than the third side, although this is implied in the definitions and axioms. For neither the definitions and axioms nor the proposition about the sides *exist*. But if an existent figure— some particular drawing or some particular piece of paper— was a triangle, we should, I think, naturally say that *its* triangularity caused two of its sides to be longer than the third. Again, we should not say that the law of the tides was partly caused by the law of gravitation, but we should say that the height of the sea at a particular time and place had the attraction of the moon as part of its cause.

Again, the beheading of an English king in the eighteenth

century implies the death of that king. But we should not say that it caused it, because, in point of fact, no English king was beheaded in the eighteenth century, and so the relation of implication is not between terms which exist. All that we should say would be that, if a king of England had been beheaded in the eighteenth century, it would have caused his death—that is, to assert that, if the terms had been existent, the relation of causality would have held between them.

These two characteristics of causality are, I think, admitted by everyone to be essential to that relation. But we now come to others, which are asserted by some thinkers to be essential to causality, while others deny this.

The first of these—the third in our general list—is that a certain activity is exerted by one term of the relation or the other, the name of cause being appropriated to the term which exerts the activity, and that of effect to the term on which it is exerted. Causation, it is said, is more than uniform conjunction. Even if the presence of A is invariably followed by the presence of B, this is not, it is maintained, sufficient to give causation, unless there is also present this activity. If it is asked exactly what is meant by such an activity, the usual answer is that each of us can observe it by introspection whenever an act of his own volition is the cause of the event which is willed in the volition.

The fourth point—which, as we shall see later, is very closely connected with the third—is that the cause determines the effect in some way in which the effect does not determine the cause. It is often held, for example, that our choice between resisting a temptation and yielding to it would be undetermined, if it were not caused, even if it were itself the inevitable cause of certain effects.

Fifthly, it is sometimes held that when the relation of causality holds between A and B, it involves that one of those terms is explained by its holding that relation to the other. When such an explanatory quality is attributed to causation, it is often held that the cause explains the effect, while the effect does not explain the cause. But sometimes the explanation is held to be reciprocal.

THE MEANING OF CAUSALITY

Those existent realities which are considered to be causes and effects are generally, though not always, events in time. This brings us to the sixth point. It is asserted that the cause cannot be subsequent to the effect. So much is very generally agreed, but there does not seem any general agreement that the cause must be prior to the effect. It is sometimes held that it can be simultaneous with it in time. Also it is held that a timeless existent reality can be the cause of events in time. For example, it is often held by theists that the creator who caused all temporal things is himself timeless. Nor would it be unusual, I think, to say that the Nicene Creed regarded the First and Second Persons of the Trinity as the causes of the Third, in spite of the fact that all three, and the Procession which relates them, are regarded as timeless.

In these cases, when the cause is not prior to the effect, it would only be distinguishable from it by a discovery that one of the terms, and not the other, was the one which exerted an activity, or determined the other term, or explained the other term.

We pass to the seventh and last point. Here a word of preliminary explanation is wanted. When we look at what exists, we find that there are Qualities and Relations, and that there are things which have qualities, and which stand in relations. We may call qualities and relations by the general name of Characteristics. Characteristics have themselves other characteristics ; but, besides this, we find that there are other things, which have characteristics, but which are not themselves characteristics. It will be convenient to call all of these Substances. It should be noted that if we define substance in this way—which I think, besides being the most convenient definition, is also the most usual—it will include more than is usually realized. For an event is something which has characteristics, and is not itself a characteristic. And thus not only can we so call by the name of substance such things as England, myself, and a pebble, but also such things as the battle of Waterloo or a flash of lightning.[1]

Now a causal relation is always between substances. It is

<hr>

[1] [Cf. editorial footnote, p. 85.—*Ed.*]

generally, though not always, between events, but it is always between substances. But—and here we come to the seventh characteristic—although it is itself between substances, it always rests on a relation between characteristics. The typical form of a causal proposition is that, whenever a substance occurs with the characteristic X, it causes a substance with the characteristic Y. We may say that the beheading of Charles I caused his death, where we are speaking of particular substances. Or we might say that the most interesting event which has taken place in Whitehall caused the event from which the reign of Charles II is measured. But we can only do this because ' the beheading of Charles I ' and ' the most interesting event which has taken place in Whitehall ' are descriptions of an event which is the beheading of a human being, and ' the death of Charles I ' and ' the event from which the reign of Charles II is measured ' are descriptions of another event which is the death of the same human being, and because there is a causal law that the beheading of a human being always causes the death of that human being.

Of these seven characteristics, which have been asserted to be essential to causality, which shall we include in our definition ? I think we should include the first two only, and should say that causation is a relation of implication between existent realities—or, to put it more precisely, between existent substances.

My reason for leaving out the seventh characteristic from the definition is that, as I shall endeavour to show in a few minutes, it is implied in the two first. It is therefore true of all cases of causality, defined as I have defined it, but, since it follows from what is already in the definition, it is superfluous to add it.[1]

With regard to the other four the case is different. I propose to leave them out for a different reason. I believe

---

[1] [In *The Nature of Existence*, I, section 208, McTaggart does, however, add this ' seventh characteristic ' to the two already mentioned, thus holding ' there are three things which would be universally admitted to be necessary ' to causality, and that all three are ' beyond dispute.'—*Ed.*]

that by rejecting them we shall have a definition which is both more convenient, and, on the whole, more in accordance with ordinary usage. For, by the definition, I propose all that we assert, if we assert the validity of causality, is that the facts of the existent world are so connected with one another that it is possible, at any rate in certain cases, to infer one of them from another, and so form a basis for practical life and the validity of the empirical sciences. Now I believe that this is what people in general mean by causality, and that where these conditions are fulfilled, it would be in accordance with usage and convenience to say that there was causality. If that is the case, we ought not to put the other four characteristics under the definition of causality, even if they were true of all cases of causality.

There is also another reason why it is convenient to leave these other four characteristics out of the definition of causality. It is, I think, convenient, if possible, to reserve the term causality for some relation that actually does occur between all or most existent substances. Now, as I shall try to show, there is reason to judge that these four characteristics do *not* belong to any relation which holds among all or most existent substances.

If, on the other hand, we define causality, as I have proposed, as a relation of implication between existent substances, there is no reason whatever to believe that such a relation does not occur throughout the universe. That, of course, does not involve that there is any reason to believe that it *does* occur. I believe, as I said at the beginning of the lecture, that it can be proved to occur, but that is a point which we cannot consider to-day. But it remains the fact that it cannot be proved not to occur, and that almost everyone does believe that it occurs—everyone in fact who is not so thorough-going a sceptic as Hume. And, even if the relation does not occur, it is certain that the illusion that it does occur is one of which we cannot get rid. No one realized more completely than Hume himself that, whether one event did imply another or not, we should always believe it, except when engaged in philosophic thought, and should act on our belief—that we should take food when we wished to appease our hunger, and not cut off our neighbours' heads unless we were prepared to cause their death. It seems therefore more convenient all round to define causality as a relation of implication between existent substances.

I must now proceed to justify the statements which I have made—that the seventh characteristic is implied in our proposed definition, and that the remaining four characteristics do not belong to any relation which holds between existent substances.

Let us first consider the seventh characteristic—that a causal relation, while itself a relation between substances, is based on a relation between characteristics of those substances. This, I submit, is involved in the fact that the relation of causality is a relation of implication. For all implication of one substance by another must rest on an implication of characteristics of the first by characteristics of the second.

This will be seen when we consider that implication must fall under one of two heads. Either it is evident *a priori* that the one term cannot occur without the other term in a certain relation to it—as when the triangularity of a particular figure determines the equality of its angles to two right angles. Or it is simply an ultimate fact that they are always found in a certain relation—as when a certain action in my brain causes the sensation of redness in my mind. Now it is clear that *a priori* implication of one substance by another can only happen as a consequence of *a priori* implication of characteristics, since it is only characteristics—qualities and relations—whose nature can be known *a priori*.

As for the second sort of implication, it depends on the terms always being found together, and has therefore no meaning unless they occur more than once. Now characteristics can occur more than once, for they are universal, and can occur in more than one particular case. But substances are themselves particular, and can only occur once. Therefore all implication must be based on the implication of characteristics. We can, indeed, say that one event implies another—for example, that the beheading of Charles I implies the death of Charles I, where the two terms of the implication are both particular events. But this is only because the first event has the characteristic of being the beheading of a human being, and the second event has the characteristic of being the death of the same being, and because the occurrence of an event having the characteristic of being such a beheading involves the occurrence of an event having the characteristic of being such a death.

It has not always been realized in the past that a causal relation must, in the last resort, rest on a relation of characteristics. And many of the difficulties in which writers on causation have involved themselves are, I think, due to their failure to see this, and, consequently, their failure to realize that any causal relation between particulars rests on a relation between universals—since all characteristics are universals. The reason of this failure has often, I think, been the belief that causality had the third characteristic which we enumerated —that there was an activity exerted by a cause or an effect. For, if this had been the case, it might have been maintained that the particular substance which was the cause did intrinsically determine the particular substance which was the effect, by means of this activity, and so implied it directly, and not by the intervention of characteristics. But, as we shall see, this conception of the activity exercised by the cause or the effect must be rejected.

We come now to the four characteristics which, as I have said, there seem to be good reasons for rejecting, as not being characteristics of any relation which does hold between existing realities.

The first of these is the third in our general list, which was spoken of just now—namely that the cause exerts an activity or an effect. No reason, so far as I know, can be given why we should believe that such an activity exists. If we ask for a proof of its existence we are usually referred to the evidence of introspection. When I will to move my arm, and my arm is thereupon moved, I am directly aware, it is said, of an activity which I, the willing subject, am exerting.

Even if there were such an activity in such cases, it would give us no reason to believe that there was any such activity when the cause was not a volition, nor any indication of what the cause would, in that case, be like. And therefore some of the more consistent supporters of this view are driven to maintain that nothing but a volition is ever a cause—all events which are not the effects of human volitions being the direct effects of divine volitions, and having no other causes. As to this we may remark that it would be a very strained and inconvenient use of the word ' cause,' to say that the *only* cause of the death of Charles I was a divine volition, and that the beheading had no effect at all.

But I do not believe that there is any such activity to be perceived even when our volitions are causes. In my own case I can perceive no such activity. And I *can* perceive something else which could be mistaken for such an activity. I am conscious of willing. And then, after an interval of more or less duration, I am conscious that the result which I willed—the movement of my arm, for example—has taken place. In some cases, also, I am conscious of a feeling of tension or strain within myself. But this is all. Now this feeling of tension or strain is not an activity exercised by me on my arm. It is itself an effect of some cause or causes, and it is a psychical state, and falls wholly within the mind. But I venture to think that this feeling of tension is mistaken for an activity exercised by me on the arm. On these grounds I reject the view that we are directly aware of such an activity when our volitions are causes. And no other reasons have ever been given why we should believe such an activity to exist.

The fourth characteristic was that the cause determines the effect in some way in which the effect does not determine the cause. And it is for this reason that it is supposed that there must be a first cause in any chain of causation, while there need not be a last effect—that an unending series of causes of causes is impossible, while an unending series of effects of effects is quite possible. But, in truth, we do not find this characteristic in any relation of implication which holds between existing substances.

One reason why it has been thought that there is this non-reciprocal determination is, once more, the belief that the cause exerts an activity on the effect. If this were so, it is supposed, the term which determines the activity would determine the other term in a way which was not reciprocated. But this is of course invalid, if, as has been maintained above, there is no such exertion of activity.

Of course—and this may have contributed to the mistake—there really is a non-reciprocal determination between characteristics. Beheading determines death, but death does not determine beheading, since there are many other ways in which death can arise. But this will not justify us in saying that the cause has a non-reciprocal determination of the effect. Very often the determining characteristic belongs to the term which would be called effect, and not to the one which would be called cause. In the case given above, beheading and death, it belongs to the term which would be called cause—the event of beheading. But, to take another case, we should certainly say that drinking alcohol was the cause of getting drunk, and not that getting drunk is the cause of drinking alcohol. And here the characteristic of what would be called the effect determines the characteristic of what would be called the cause, and not *vice versa*. For I cannot get drunk without drinking alcohol, but I can drink alcohol without getting drunk. It is therefore the characteristic of getting drunk which determines the characteristic of drinking alcohol, and not *vice versa*.

The fact is that it is impossible to say that either event determines the other non-reciprocally, because each event can be described by close and precise characteristics, or by vague and wide ones. And in proportion as it is described by vague and wide ones, they are likely to be such that they are determined without determining. We have seen that drinking alcohol is determined by getting drunk, and does not determine it. But any event which is a drinking of alcohol is also the drinking of a definite amount M under conditions N. And if we take *this* more definite characteristic we find that the drinking now determines the drunkenness and not *vice versa*.

For it would be impossible to drink that amount under these circumstances without getting drunk, while it would be possible to get drunk without drinking that amount under these circumstances—a much less amount, for example, might be sufficient for a man with a different constitution.

Thus, of two events causally connected, we cannot say that the one which would generally be called the cause determines the other more than it is determined by the other. Nor can we say that whichever of the two does determine the other ought to be called the cause. Firstly, this would, as we have seen, involve that the one which was later in time should in many cases be called the cause, and the earlier the effect—which would be so contrary to usage as to be very inconvenient. Secondly, because the same event would often have to be called cause if you described it in one way, and effect if you described it in the other. An event, for example, which was described simply as drinking alcohol, would be called the effect of the subsequent drunkenness; but if it were more precisely described as the drinking of an amount M under conditions N, it would be called the cause of that drunkenness. This also would be extremely inconvenient. For all those reasons we must give up the fourth characteristic.

The fifth characteristic was that the discovery of a causal relation between two events explained those events, or, at any rate, explained the event taken as the effect. Now, if explanation here merely means that the events are taken as an instance of a general rule, then of course causality does give an explanation. If I ask why event B occurs, and am told that it was the death of a human body, that the beheading of the same body had immediately preceded it, and that there is a general law that the beheading of a human body is immediately followed by its death, then, in this sense, the event will be explained. But it will not be explained in any other sense, except that of being brought under the law. And, of course, in this sense, the law itself has not been explained. It, in its turn, may be explained by being shown to be a case of some more general law, but we must at last reach a causal law which is ultimate, and cannot be explained further.

But it is more than this which is meant when the characteristic we are considering is asserted. It is supposed that a causal law does not only say that every occurrence of X implies the occurrence of Z, but that in some way it shows us *why* every occurrence of X implies the occurrence of Z, and, that, as a consequence of this, a particular case of Z is explained by its causal relations in some deeper and more thorough manner than by being shown to be an example of a general rule.

Now it is very important to realize that every ultimate causal law—every causal law which is not a case of a more general law—asserts an ultimate connection of two things— that is, a connection of which we know that it does exist, but do not know why it exists.

This view is one which many people have been very unwilling to accept. They have been very anxious that causal laws should offer some explanation of that relation of characteristics which they assert, and their anxiety has led them in many cases to an entirely distorted view of the nature of causal laws.

In the first place, it has led to the belief that cause and effect are identical. If the cause is the same thing as the effect, it is thought that the relation between them—or rather the relation it has to itself—will be so obvious that it will be self-explanatory. But then any relation of a thing to itself cannot be a relation of causality. If, whenever we say that A is the cause of B, A is identical with B, what we mean is that B is its own cause, and the only cause it can have. And it is clear that this is not what is really meant by causation, and that it explains nothing, since it merely connects a thing with itself and gets us no farther than we were before.

This seems so obvious that it seems strange that anyone should deny it. And yet many great philosophers *have* denied it. The explanation is, I think, that what they are thinking of is that a cause and effect often have a common element. The egg is part of the cause of the chicken, and some of the content of the egg is some of the content of the chicken. Sugar and fruit are part of the cause of jam (not the whole cause, for there is also the person who makes it) and the same matter which was the sugar and fruit is the matter which is the jam. And we may perhaps say that the energy which was in the cause is also in the effect. But there are cases where there is no such common element. An east wind may be the cause of a bad temper. And the ambition of Napoleon may be the cause of bullet-holes in the walls of Hougoumont. And in neither of these cases is there any common element that I can see, except those which are also common to things not causally connected.

But even when there is a common element this does not make the cause and the effect identical. Sugar and fruit may have a common element with jam, but they are not the same thing as jam, or we could not distinguish jam from them, which we can do. And when we say that sugar and fruit (*and* the jam-maker) cause jam, what they cause are just the elements in the jam which are not identical with any elements in the sugar and fruit. The elements which are the same are not caused, but persist. We do not say that in making jam we cause its weight or its impenetrability.

Cause and effect, then, are not identical. And we must go farther. That any cause A has an effect B is never a self-evident proposition, in the way that it is self-evident that two straight lines cannot enclose a space. And, still further, it is never a proposition that can be proved by *a priori* considerations, in the way in which we can prove that the angles of a triangle are equal to two right angles. All ultimate causal laws are empirical truths. We know that they are so because, in point of fact, we find them to be so.

We have good reason to believe that, if a man's head is cut off, he dies. But our reason is purely empirical. We believe it either because it has been observed that, in none of the many cases in which a man has been beheaded, he fails to die, or else because it can be deduced from some wider law which itself rests on experience. Apart from experience we should have no reason to suppose that cutting off a man's head would kill him than to believe that cutting his hair would kill him. Apart from experience, we have no more reason to suppose that cutting off my head would kill me than we have to suppose it would kill the executioner, or blow up the Taj Mahal, or destroy a mountain in the moon. We have good reason to believe that it will do the first, and not any of the other three. But our reasons are all empirical. All ultimate causal laws, in other words, are what is sometimes called ' brute facts.' But the name is misleading, since it rather suggests that there is some defect or imperfection about these facts, or about our knowledge of them, whereas the truth is that such facts not only have no reasons, but do not require any reasons.

There is one case in which it might seem particularly hard to admit that causal relations are here brute facts, and that is the case when a volition to do something—say to move one's arm—causes the movement. Surely, it might be said, even if it is not possible to be certain, apart from experience, that such volitions have such results, it could be seen, apart from experience, that it is likely to have such a result, and the probability, though not the certainty, is more than a brute fact ? But this is mistaken. Except for empirical experience, it is just as probable that my volition to move my arm should move my leg, or Mount Everest, as that it should move my arm. This may be made more obvious if we reflect that the *immediate* effect of my volition to move my arm is to produce various changes in my brain, nerves, and muscles, which I am not willing, and of which, perhaps, I know nothing whatever, and that, if for any reason this effect, which is not willed, fails, the effect which is willed fails with it.

The fifth characteristic, then, must be rejected. No relation of causality gives any explanation, except in the sense that it gives a general rule of which the particular case is an example. How about the sixth characteristic ? This was that the cause could not be subsequent to the effect.

To answer this question, we must consider, in the first place, that we have not as yet found any criterion by which to distinguish the cause from the effect in a causal relation. The definition of causality which we have adopted was that it was a relation of implication between existing substances.

The only difference between the two substances concerned which this relation involves is that one of them implies the other, while the second does not (except in cases of reciprocal causation) imply the first. But, as we saw when we were discussing the fourth characteristic, it would be impracticable to call the determinant substance the cause, and the other the effect. And thus our definition of causality gives us no criterion for distinguishing one term as cause and the other as effect. The third, fourth, and fifth characteristics would have given us such a criterion, but we have found it necessary to reject them.

Accordingly, if we are to distinguish one term as cause and the other as effect it will have to be exclusively by means of a criterion based on the sixth characteristic. The earlier of the two terms connected by a causal relation will be called the cause, and the later the effect. But there will be considerable difficulties about such a use of words. If the distinction between cause and effect depends solely on temporal order, then there could be no causal relation between strictly simultaneous events. And, again, there could be no causal relation between two substances, one or both of which is out of time.[1] A timeless God, for example, could not be the cause of the world, and between such a God and the world there could be no causal relation at all. Whether there is a God, and, if so, whether he is timeless, is another question ; but there is, I think, no doubt that a use of the word ' cause ' would be very inconvenient if it prevented us from saying that such a God, if he existed, could be a cause.

Moreover, although it has been very generally held in the past that the earlier of the two terms should be called the cause, it has by no means been very general to hold that priority by itself is sufficient to make the earlier term the cause. It is generally, I think, believed that the earlier term is the cause because it is the earlier term which exerts an activity,

---

[1] [In *The Nature of Existence*, I, p. 225, McTaggart appends the footnote : ' We might, however, reasonably call one term the cause if it *appeared* as being in time, and as being prior to the other, though in reality both terms were timeless.'—*Ed.*]

or which determines the other, or which explains the other. And now that we have had to reject this view, it does not seem that we should be in very much harmony with ordinary usage, if we called the earlier term the cause, merely because it was earlier.

The course that I think most convenient therefore is to speak of causal relations as existing between two terms, but not to speak of one of those terms as cause, and of the other as effect. Of course, I am speaking here of philosophical usage. In ordinary life one should doubtless continue to say that a particular drinking of alcohol is the cause of a particular state of drunkenness. But philosophically we should say only that the drinking and the drunkenness stood in a causal relation to one another, since they were existent substances which stood in a relation of implication. What the implication, or rather the implications, may be, depends on the various characteristics of each. We saw above that, if the drinking is described only as a drinking of alcohol, it is determined by the other, described as a state of drunkenness, and does not determine it, but that this is reversed if it is described as a drinking of an amount M under conditions N.

Of course it might be objected that, after all we have given up, we ought not to speak of causal relations at all. If we have given up all idea of activity, and of explanation, and of the non-reciprocal determination of the later term by the earlier, and if we have given up the designation of one of the terms as cause, and of the other as effect, ought we not to give up causality altogether? This view is taken by Mr. Russell, who, in his paper before the Aristotelian Society on the Notion of Cause, says that the idea of causality ' is a relic of a bygone age, surviving . . . only because it is erroneously supposed to do no harm.' [1]

There is, no doubt, something to be said for this view, but, as I said previously, I think the balance is the other way. It is admitted that, for example, the occurrence of an event which is the beheading of a human being implies the occur-

[1] [*Proceedings of the Aristotelian Society*, 1912–13 ; reprinted in *Mysticism and Logic* : London, 1921 ; pp. 180–208.—*Ed.*]

rence of an event which is the death of the same human being. And I think that in this we have the essence of causality, and that we ought therefore to say that there is a causal relation between the beheading of Charles I and the death of Charles I. Still this is, after all, a matter of definition. The results which we have reached which are more than matters of definition are that we ought to reject the conceptions of a cause which exerts activity, of a cause which explains its effects, and of a cause which non-reciprocally determines its effect, together with the further result that these rejections do not involve the rejection of the implication of one event (or other substance) by another.

We have then defined causality. The further question arises of the universal validity of causality. The question of whether causation *is* universally valid, or, indeed, valid at all, is beyond the scope of this lecture. All that I shall try to do is to state precisely what its universal validity would mean.

For causality to hold universally it would be necessary that each characteristic of any substance, in each case in which it occurred, should be implied by some other characteristic which had occurred. It would be necessary, then, that the following statement should be true. Let G be any characteristic which occurs, that is to say, which is found in any existing substance. Then, in each case in which G occurs, a characteristic, $H\alpha$, can be found, which occurs in a relation, $L\alpha$ to that occurrence of G, and which is such that, in each case in which $H\alpha$ occurs, it will stand in the relation $L\alpha$ to some occurrence of G.

Thus G might be the death of a human body. The $H\alpha$ that we might find in connection with a particular case of G might be the beheading of a human body. The relation $L\alpha$ would then be that they were characteristics of the same body, and that the death immediately followed the beheading. And it is the case that whenever the beheading of a human body occurs the death of a human body is found in that relation to it.

I do not say that this is the form which causal laws invariably take. They do take it in some cases, but in others

THE MEANING OF CAUSALITY

(especially, though not exclusively, in the sciences of inorganic matter) the laws of most importance take a quantitative form. For example, a change in the temperature of water determines a change in the space it occupies, and the amount of the one change is connected with the amount of the other according to some definite formula. But, although such a law as this does not take the form of the proposition given above, yet many propositions of this form must be true, if the law is to be true. If the changes of temperature and size are connected in this way, then, whenever the change takes place from some particular temperature to another, there must be a change from some particular size to another. And then these two changes will be the G and the Hα, of which one is always found in a certain relation to the other. Such a law as that which correlates temperature and size will imply many such propositions as these, and cannot be true unless these propositions are true. And thus our statement above will have to be true in any field—whether the universe or a part of the universe—in which causality is universal, even though many of the causal laws are not expressed in this form.

The universality of causality is what is meant when we speak of the Uniformity of Nature, and we may therefore give the name of the Law of the Uniformity of Nature to our proposition which asserts that a causal law can always be found by which any particular occurrence of G is determined.

It will be noticed that our statement of the Law of the Uniformity of Nature does not assert reciprocal determination. The Hα which can be found for any occurrence of G is to be such that every occurrence of Hα stands in the relation Lα to an occurrence of G, but it has not been said that every occurrence of G will have an occurrence of Hα standing in the relation of Lα to it. It may well be that different occurrences of G may be related respectively to occurrences of Hα, Hβ, and Hγ, by the relations Lα, Lβ, and Lγ, and therefore, while every occurrence of Hα stands in a relation Lα to a G, not every G has an occurrence of Hα standing in the relation Lα to it. Thus, in our previous example, the beheading of a body is always followed by its death, but the

173

death of a body is not always preceded by its beheading. The death may be determined by hanging or poisoning.

Of course, if G does not reciprocally determine Hα, it will be necessary, if the law of the uniformity of nature should be true, that Hα, whenever it occurs should be determined by some other characteristic. Since, for example, the death of a body does not imply the previous beheading of that body, there must, if the law of the uniformity of nature be true, be some other characteristic, the occurrence of which on any occasion implies the beheading of a body. This need not be a characteristic of the body itself. The law may be that whenever a certain characteristic occurs in something in a relation to a body that body will be beheaded.

Why does the law of the uniformity of nature lead to this apparently one-sided result—that for every occurrence of G we can find an Hα which determines G, while there is no guarantee that any Hα can be found which G will always determine ? The answer is that G stands in the law for any characteristic which occurs in the universe, whether that characteristic is a description so minute that it applies only to one case in the universe, and is so closely defined and so narrow in its application as ' the death of a King of England,' or is as broadly defined and as wide in its application as ' event,' ' substance,' ' thing.' Hα, Hβ, etc., on the contrary, are not *any* characteristics, but only such as fulfil the required conditions with reference to G. They can therefore be chosen so as to be as closely defined and as narrow in their application as is necessary to ensure that there shall be no occurrence of Hα, or of Hβ, which does not determine an occurrence of G.

The law of the uniformity of nature, then, does not imply the reciprocal determination of characteristics. How must a law be stated which would assert that reciprocal determination ?

It is clear, in the first place, that any law which asserted that, whenever there was determination, there was reciprocal determination, would be false. We know that drunkenness determines the drinking of alcohol, and we know that the drinking of alcohol does not determine drunkenness, since there have been cases in which men have drunk alcohol without getting drunk. Here, then, is at least one case of causal determination which is not reciprocal. Again, if an existent thing is red, that fact determines that the same thing shall be coloured. But the fact that an existent thing is coloured does not determine that it should be red.

If, then, universal reciprocal determination is taken to mean that every determination of one characteristic by another is reciprocal, it is clear that reciprocal determination does not hold universally. And when it has been said that all causal determination is reciprocal, something else, less far-reaching than this, has, I think, been meant. It has been meant, not that every determination of a characteristic is reciprocal, but that every characteristic has at least one determination which is reciprocal. The determination of death by beheading, it would be admitted, is not reciprocal, but, it would be asserted that all deaths by beheading have some particular characteristic which is found in no other sort of death, and that this particular sort of death and beheading are in reciprocal determination. Again, it would be asserted that there was some characteristic which occurred whenever the characteristic of death occurred, and only then, so that it stands in reciprocal determination with death.

If such reciprocal determination were universal, the law asserting it might be expressed as follows : Let G be any characteristic which occurs. Then, in each case in which G occurs, a characteristic H can be found, which occurs in a relation L to that occurrence of G, and which is such that in each case in which H occurs it will stand in the relation L to an occurrence of G, and that in each case in which G occurs, an occurrence of H will stand in the relation L to it.

It is impossible to prove empirically that this law does not hold universally. There may be many cases in which we do not see it to hold. There may be many characteristics, even among them for which we can find determinants, for which we cannot find any case of reciprocal determination with another characteristic. Yet for each of them there *may* be a determinant, unknown to us, where the determination is reciprocal. But, on the other hand, it would seem that it must be impossible to prove the law of reciprocal causal determination from the law of the uniformity of nature, even if the latter were itself established. For it is obvious that there is no contradiction in a determination which is not reciprocal, since, as we have seen, many determinations—such as the determination of death by beheading—are not reciprocal.

There is one more question about laws of causation which we may profitably consider. It has sometimes been asserted that complete knowledge of any substance would imply complete knowledge of any other substance, so that, if it were possible for us to know all that was true about any other substance, it would be ideally possible, with a sufficiently powerful intellect, to infer from this all that is true about every other substance in the universe, and the universe itself. This is apparently what Tennyson means when he says that if he could know completely what the flower was that he plucked from the crannied wall, he would know what God and man were. It is often said that this implication of the nature of each substance with that of every other must happen if the law of the uniformity of nature were universally valid, and could not happen unless it were universally valid.

This seems to me to be mistaken. In one sense this implication of the nature of each substance with that of every other is true, and it is true quite independently of the law of the uniformity of nature. In another sense it could be false even if the law of the uniformity of nature—and the law of universal reciprocal determination—were true.

The sense in which it is true, independent of the uniformity of nature, is as follows. Every substance in the universe is related to every other substance in the universe. Complete knowledge of all that was true about any substance A would include knowledge of all its relations to all other substances. This will include complete knowledge of all those other substances. For, if A has the relation L to B, then every fresh fact, C, about B is also a fresh fact about A, since it tells us that A has the relation L to something of which C is true. My relation to Julius Cæsar is not a very close one, but there *is* a relation, and therefore complete knowledge of me will include complete knowledge of Cæsar, since without complete knowledge of Cæsar it will not be known exactly what it is to which I stand in this relation. So a complete description of A—including all facts true of A—would include complete descriptions of all other substances. It would scarcely be correct to say that complete knowledge of B could be *deduced* from complete knowledge of A, but it would be true that, if we had complete knowledge of A we should have complete knowledge of B, and of every other substance.

But this inclusion of knowledge of all other substances in knowledge of A is not what is meant by the theory we are discussing. That theory asserts that from a knowledge of A which does not include knowledge of B, complete knowledge of B might be inferred by anyone who had sufficient knowledge of the laws by which one substance causally determines another, and sufficient power of reasoning to carry out the arguments required. And there seems no reason to suppose that this would necessarily be true, even if universal reciprocal causal determination were true.

That causal determination should be universal means that every occurrence of a characteristic in the universe is implied by the occurrence of some other characteristic in the universe. Now there is nothing in this to prevent it from being the case that there should be two substances, A and B, such that there is no characteristic of B the occurrence of which is implied, directly or indirectly, by the occurrence of any characteristic in A. (It is, of course, as we have just said, impossible that there should be any two substances in the universe which are not related in some way, but it does not follow from this that any two substances must be related by a relation of implication, since there are many other sorts of relation.)

And, even if it should be the case that every substance in the universe were connected with every other substance by relations of implication, the theory we are considering would not be proved. For it might still be the case that, though some characteristics of B were implied by characteristics of A, there were other characteristics of B which were not implied, either directly or indirectly, by any characteristic of A. And, in this case, no knowledge of A will enable us to infer all the characteristics of B.

We have thus attempted to decide what should be meant by the word causality, and what would be meant by the universal validity of causal determination. The question whether causal determination *is* valid is beyond the scope of this lecture. Yet it may be pointed out that, if it is to be shown to be valid, it can only be in one way. To attempt to prove it empirically is hopeless, for all empirical proof must rest on induction, and induction itself rests on the uniformity of nature, so that any such argument would move in a vicious circle. And it is clear that the universal validity of causal determination is not *self-evident a priori*. In the mere assertion that it is not valid, taken by itself, there is nothing self-contradictory nor absurd. Only one alternative remains—that it should be capable of proof by a chain of reasoning resting on premises known *a priori*. It is further to be noticed that it does not follow that causal determination cannot be proved or be valid at all, unless it is proved to be valid universally. It might conceivably be proved to be true with respect to characteristics of certain classes, if it could not be proved about all.

VIII

PROPOSITIONS APPLICABLE TO THEMSELVES

1. Mr. L. Wittgenstein in his *Tractatus Logico-Philosophicus* (p. 57) remarks, what has often, of course, been said before, that no proposition can ' say anything about itself' (' etwas ueber sich selbst aussagen '). There is a sense in which, I think, this is clearly true. But the statement is rather ambiguous, and requires further specification.

2. The proposition ' Charles I was crowned ' is clearly about Charles I. It is only a definite proposition if it contains an exclusive description of the man—one which is true of nothing but him. But how about ' all kings of England are mortal ' ? This cannot be said to be about Charles I. It can have a definite meaning for a person who knew no exclusive description of Charles I, or even for one who supposed that all kings of England were named Henry. Yet whatever is said of all kings of England is true of Charles I. I cannot tell from Mr. Wittgenstein's words whether he would say that this was or was not a proposition about Charles I. The terminology I propose to adopt is that the first proposition is *about* Charles I, while the second is not *about* him, but *applies* to him.

3. It is clear that no proposition can, in this sense, be about itself. Let us take an example. ' The proposition which I am now asserting is known to God.' (It is better to say ' known to God ' than ' true ' or ' false,' since the last two predicates have special relations to propositions which might raise a suspicion that they were not fair representatives of all other predicates.) Let us call this A. Now it is clear that this assertion depends for its meaning on the meaning of the proposition which I assert, and which is known to God.

179

But to the question ' what proposition am I asserting,' the only answer is ' it is the proposition " the proposition which I am now asserting is known to God." ' And this raises the same question, which can only receive the same answer, and so on to infinity. And this infinite will be vicious. No link in the chain can have any meaning until the chain is finished. And it never is finished. The original statement, then, is neither true nor false, and is not a proposition.

4. A proposition, then, cannot be about itself. But can it apply to itself ? How about ' all propositions asserted by me are known to God ' ? But ' all ' here is ambiguous. In the proposition ' all Cambridge Colleges in 1922 had at least twenty members,' the assertion really is, as it professes to be, about each Cambridge College in 1922. And it depends on the truth of seventeen separate propositions, such as ' Peter-house in 1922 had at least twenty members.' Any one of these seventeen could be true without the proposition about ' all Cambridge Colleges ' being true, but it cannot be true unless all the seventeen are true.

But then this proposition is not deducible from the nature of a Cambridge College in 1922. Something which had only ten members could have been such a College—only nothing was. But take the proposition ' all Cambridge Colleges in 1922 have privileges under the Law of Mortmain.' This is quite different. It is not dependent on propositions about each of the existent Colleges, nor even on the existence of any of them. If every Cambridge College had been abolished in 1921, and no more founded, it would still be true, unless the Law of Mortmain had been altered, that ' all Cambridge Colleges in 1922 have privileges under the Law of Mortmain.' And the explanation is that the proposition is incorrectly expressed. It is not an assertion about Cambridge Colleges in 1922, but about the *characteristics* ' being a Cambridge College in 1922,' and ' having privileges under the Law of Mortmain.' And it asserts that the possession of the first characteristic implies the possession of the second.

5. Now if the sentence ' All propositions asserted by me are known to God ' is taken in the first of these senses (let us

call this B), then it, like A, has no meaning. For it is an assertion dependent on each of the propositions asserted by me, and its meaning depends on the meanings of each of them. But B itself, if it is a proposition at all, is a proposition asserted by me. Its meaning, therefore, will depend, *inter alia*, on its meaning. And when we ask what is the meaning of B on this second occurrence the answer will be that it, again, depends on the meaning of B. And this infinite series will be vicious, since the meaning of B could only be determined on the completion of the series, which never is completed. B, therefore, has no meaning, and is not a proposition.

6. But the case is very different if the words ' all propositions asserted by me are known to God ' are taken in the second sense mentioned in Section 4. (Let us call this C.) For C is not an assertion about a proposition, or about a number of propositions. It is an assertion that the possession of the characteristic ' being a proposition asserted by me ' implies the possession of the characteristic ' being known to God.' And this is a proposition about characteristics, not about one or more propositions. It is not, therefore, a proposition about itself, or about a number of propositions of which it itself is one. The determination of its meaning does not depend on the previous determination of its meaning. And therefore it can, and does, have a meaning. And it is a proposition.

But, of course, it applies to itself, since it is a proposition asserted by me. And so, from the fact that I assert the proposition C, can be deduced the further proposition, D, ' the proposition C is known to God.' But this creates no difficulty, for neither proposition is about itself. C is about the implication of characteristics, and D is about C.

7. We may remark, in parenthesis, that, not only can a proposition apply to itself, but it can apply, in some cases, to itself alone. If the possession of the characteristic ' being a proposition asserted by me ' implies the possession of the characteristic ' being known to God,' then it is clear that the possession of the characteristic ' being the last proposition asserted by me before my next death ' implies the possession of the characteristic ' being known to God.' Now only one

thing can possess the characteristic of being the last proposition asserted by me before my next death. And if I should assert this implication, and die before I asserted anything else, then the proposition would apply to itself, and to nothing else but itself. But it would not be about itself in the manner in which I have taken that phrase, and it would not be liable to the difficulties, mentioned in Section 3, which prevent A from being a proposition.

8. To return from this digression. It has often been pointed out that the complete scepticism which says that all propositions are false is self-contradictory, because it is itself a proposition, and therefore its truth would prove its falsity. To this I have heard the objection that a proposition cannot be about itself, and that therefore such a scepticism is not self-contradictory, but impossible.

Now, no doubt, if the words ' all propositions are false ' were taken in sense B, they would be unmeaning, for the reasons given in Section 5. But not even an absolute sceptic would have so much confidence in his own omniscience as to suppose that he had examined all propositions, and found each of them individually to be false, as each Cambridge College was found to have at least twenty members. If the words are ever used, they will be used in sense C—that the possession of the characteristic of being a proposition implies the possession of the characteristic of being false. Now this, for the reasons mentioned in Section 6, has a meaning, and is a proposition. But it is a self-contradictory proposition. For it applies to itself, and so the proposition, C, implies the further proposition, D, that C is false. Thus the truth of C implies its falsity.

In the same way the words ' all propositions which are believed are false ' have a meaning, and are the statement of a proposition. Here the proposition is not strictly speaking *self*-contradictory, but its truth, together with the truth of the assertion that the sceptic believes it, implies its falsity.

IX

INTRODUCTION TO THE STUDY OF PHILOSOPHY

I. Introduction [1]

1. Metaphysic is not a subject which can be made easy for everyone. But for those who have some power of thought, and training in thought, it is possible to give a comparatively brief account of its nature, methods, problems, and utility : not of its results, for none are universally accepted.

2. Its definition may be—provisionally—taken to be, The systematic study of the ultimate nature of Reality. Philosophy is a rather wider term, for it includes Ethics—the systematic study of the ultimate nature of the Good. Its systematic nature separates it from such study of reality as is found in poetry. Theology deals with metaphysical problems, but not always in a metaphysical way.

3. Science also consists in the systematic study of Reality.

---

[1] [To those at Cambridge who were not studying philosophy, McTaggart became widely known through a course of introductory lectures he used to deliver at Trinity on Friday evenings every year from 1899 to 1914, and after the War until his death. The Syllabus of that course, from which the present paper is reprinted, was prefaced by this note : ' These lectures are chiefly intended for those students who, though not engaged in the systematic study of Philosophy, may desire to learn something of the objects, methods, and present problems of Metaphysic. No previous knowledge of the subject will be assumed, nor will any course of reading be required in connection with the lectures. The treatment adopted will not be historical, but will deal mainly with the present position of metaphysical inquiries.'—That these lectures were brilliantly successful in the ways that are the most important philosophically is commonly agreed and known. This Syllabus conveys simply, concisely, and yet comprehensively what is very characteristic of McTaggart's attitude to his subject. It seemed fitting therefore, in spite of the unavoidably ' staccato ' manner of its paragraphs, to include it in this volume.—*Ed.*]

Now Metaphysic is not the aggregate of the sciences, nor merely their common principles. In the first place, Metaphysic considers certain subjects not dealt with at all by science—as God, immortality, the highest good, etc.

4. And then science is not interested in the ultimate nature of reality in the subjects it deals with, but only in what is—comparatively—on the surface. Thus science assumes as ultimate, without inquiry, certain premises.

5. Metaphysic has also to start with certain assumptions—for all reasoning requires premises. But it does not make them uncritically, as Science does.

6. And—at any rate according to some systems—Metaphysic criticizes the validity of the conceptions of Science, and with respect to some of them, while admitting that they have their uses for practical purposes, denies that they are exactly true, or that they would be adequate for the study of the ultimate nature of Reality.

7. What is the practical utility of Metaphysic? Does it give us guidance? I do not think that a man's views on questions of practice are much affected by his views on metaphysical problems. This is fortunate, for there is so little agreement about Metaphysic that, if it were otherwise, our moral life would become chaotic.

8. The utility of Metaphysic is to be found rather in the comfort it can give us—which is still more directly practical. When we look round the world we find much misery due partly to the action of matter on spirit, partly to the actions of one spirit on another, and partly to the internal defects of spirits.

9. Some people are not troubled by the general question of how much evil there may be in the universe, but are only interested in the amount which they can directly observe, or anticipate in the immediate future. For such persons there is no practical utility in Metaphysic.

10. But people who have no interest in the more general question are rare, since, for example, all theological interest is incompatible with such a position. And interest of this sort is likely to increase as the immediate evils of our present life are mitigated by the advance of society.

11. Now the most natural attitude, as we shall see, upon these questions is Dualism, i.e., that Mind and Matter are equally real, and each exists in its own right. And Dualism would tend to confirm those fears as to the general state of the universe which had been excited by ordinary observation.

12. And if we think rather more deeply, the most natural tendency is towards Materialism, which is still more depressing.

13. But if we go farther, we may succeed in arriving at a belief in Idealism, and that gives us a much more cheerful view of the universe.

14. Some people, of course, succeed in arriving at Idealist views, without the aid of Metaphysic, by the help of some form of religion claiming to be revealed. But the number of those who are unable to do this is increasing.

15. The practical need for Metaphysic is thus growing. Of course we have no right to believe a particular metaphysical theory because we could not be happy unless it is true. But if our only chance of believing it to be true is to study Metaphysic, then its connection with our happiness gives us ample practical justification for the study.[1]

16. Metaphysic and Science advance in quite different

[1] [In *Some Dogmas of Religion*, p. 295, McTaggart observes : ' The study of metaphysics will perhaps never be very common, but it may be more common in the future than it is at present. The world's leisure is increasing, and much of it may be devoted to study. And if study at present is rarely study of metaphysics, that is largely because metaphysics seems unpractical. If, however, people find that they cannot have religion without it, then it will become of all studies the most practical. Its results, indeed, may not be more practically useful than those of some other subjects. For some results of study are, in our present civilization, essential to life, and life is a condition precedent of religion. But elsewhere we can enjoy the results without investigating them ourselves. I can eat bread, although I have never learnt to plough or bake. I can be cured of an illness, though I have never learnt medicine. But if— and this is the case at present—I have no right to rely on any metaphysical result which I have not myself investigated, then the study of metaphysics will be for many people the most momentous of all studies. And this may produce important results. For, after all, one great reason why so few people have reached metaphysical conclusions for themselves is to be found in the fact that so few people have tried to reach them.' See also, *ibid.*, chaps. i, ii, and Conclusion. —*Ed.*]

ways. Science, by small and frequent additions to a body of generally admitted truths. Metaphysic, by the substitution of one complete system for another. And in Metaphysic there is no decisive consensus of opinion on any point of importance.

17. The reason of this difference is to be found partly in the greater difficulty of the subject, and partly in its closer connection with our practical interests. But it is chiefly due to the fact that metaphysical problems are much more closely connected with one another than scientific problems.

18. The continual succession of opposed systems in philosophy may be regarded dogmatically—from the point of view of one of the systems, or sceptically — as a ground for distrusting all of them.

19. Or we may consider that each of them has some truth in it, though not the whole truth. In this case we shall be able to view the multiplicity of systems not merely as so many errors (with the possible exception of one) but as approximations towards the truth, which we may find reason to believe are becoming gradually closer.

20. We shall classify the views we shall consider according to their attitude to the relation of Matter and Mind. This will give us three forms, Dualism, Materialism, and Idealism. But before discussing these, we must inquire whether we can know anything at all, and so consider Scepticism.

II. Scepticism and Agnosticism

1. Scepticism—other than mere general caution—is either absolute, which denies the possibility of all knowledge about philosophy or anything else, or else Agnosticism, which, breadly speaking, admits the knowledge of science and everyday life, but denies the possibility of philosophical knowledge.

2. Causes which tend to make us generally cautious about all our knowledge, and which especially tend to prevent us from being too dogmatic in philosophy.

3. There is far less dogmatic certainty about philosophy at

present than in earlier times. This is largely due to the greater attention paid to the history of philosophy. But caution and reserve as to the results we have reached do not paralyse inquiry. Absolute Scepticism—which tells us that we never *can* know anything—would, of course, paralyse all inquiry.

4. How are we to find any ground from which to attack Scepticism? For, as the sceptic denies everything, it would seem that we could have no common ground with him. But the Sceptic does not deny the truth of his own position.

5. Thus we may say to him—' Either you are certain that nothing can be known—and then this is a proposition which you think can be known [1]—or you are not certain that nothing can be known—and then you have given up Absolute Scepticism.'

6. Nor can he escape by saying only, ' Perhaps nothing can be known.' For if he does assert this, then he asserts that this possibility can be known, and if he does not assert it, it cannot help him.

7. If the Sceptic will not admit these arguments, then, indeed, we cannot argue with him. But these arguments would be denied by so few people—if by any—that we have strengthened our position by resting it on them, till it is practically impregnable.

8. It does not follow from what has been said that we should be entitled to dispose of Scepticism by saying that we had an immediate certainty of its falsehood. There are ultimate propositions which neither require nor admit of proof, but the falsity of Scepticism cannot be one of them.

9. Nor are we justified in disposing of Scepticism by asserting that its defenders cannot believe what they say. For there is no reason to suppose they do not, nor would the fact, if true, be relevant. Nor would it be relevant to say—what,

[1] [It has been objected that this reply (designed to show that the assertion of absolute scepticism is self-contradictory) assumes that a proposition can be about itself, and that this assumption is false. McTaggart allowed the objection, and treats of it in Essay VIII.— *Ed.*]

no doubt, is to a certain degree true—that they do not act as if they did believe it.

10. We now proceed to Agnosticism—which admits that we know what is presented to our senses, and can reason on it to a certain extent, but denies that we can know the reality behind the presentations. These presentations are called Phenomena. The reality is called Noumena, or Things-in-themselves.

11. The name is sometimes, but incorrectly, applied to an absence of certainty on metaphysical subjects, or to an assertion that nothing *has been* discovered about them, without raising the question whether such discoveries are impossible.

12. Agnosticism, in the strict sense, generally rests itself on the subjective element in all knowledge, which is asserted to render that knowledge untrustworthy so far as the representation of Absolute Reality goes, though it may have some practical value.

13. But the supposition that there is an irremovable subjective element of such a nature as to vitiate our knowledge of Absolute Reality is not justifiable.

14. And, again, if the Agnostic says there is nothing behind the Phenomena, his Agnosticism vanishes. For then there is nothing beside the Phenomena, and, in knowing them, we know all the Reality that there is.

15. And if he says there is something behind the Phenomena, then he knows something about it—namely its existence—which is inconsistent with Agnosticism. And, again, his theory will require that he knows some relation which exists between the Phenomena and the Noumena. Also he must know that its nature is such that it never can be known to us.

16. All this is a good deal of knowledge about that which cannot be known to us. And not only is this inconsistent with Agnosticism, but no reason could be given why we could never know any more of that of which we admittedly know so much.

17. The Agnostic is quite right when he says that we can only start with what is given us in experience. His error lies in supposing that we cannot go beyond it.

18. On the general question of how far we are entitled to trust the power of the mind to find out truth, it leads equally to contradictions to distrust it altogether, or to trust it completely. All we can say is, that the mind is capable of making mistakes, and is also capable of correcting them.

III. DUALISM, ABSOLUTE AND RELATIVE

1. The view of Dualism—the independence of Mind and Matter—is practically the same as that taken by Common Sense before beginning Metaphysical thought. In Absolute Dualism, they are taken as neither dependent on one another, nor on anything else. In Relative Dualism, Matter and Finite Spirit are taken as independent of one another, but dependent on a third reality, usually conceived as a creative Infinite Spirit.

2. *Absolute* Dualism, however, is scarcely a position natural to Common Sense. The tendency of the latter is to regard Mind and Matter as externally connected—as in Relative Dualism.

3. The strength of Absolute Dualism lies in the fact that the world we see so strongly suggests that something analogous to our reason has considerable, but not complete, power in it. This does not go well with Materialism or Idealism, but would be quite compatible with Absolute Dualism.

4. But we cannot deny (except by passing into Scepticism or Materialism) that Mind and Matter act causally on one another. And this makes some kind of unity between them. Now it may well be doubted if such a unity could exist, unless Mind and Matter had to some degree a common nature. And if they had, Absolute Dualism would be false.

5. Again, have we any conception of what Matter would be, independently of its observation by Mind? Our idea of Matter has certain components received by means of our five senses. It also contains other elements, such as Substance, Causality, and the like, which are not given by the senses, but added by the work of the Mind.

6. The Secondary Qualities are admitted not to exist in Matter taken by itself. But then that Matter has a nature which we have never experienced, and cannot even imagine—one which consists of Primary Qualities without Secondary Qualities.

7. Again, take Extension, the most fundamental of the Primary Qualities. Can we form any idea of it apart from an observing Mind ? It cannot be Extension as seen, nor yet as touched, for these differ from each other with the same object, and each of them also varies according to the circumstances under which we see or touch.

8. Nor can it be any common quality of visual and tactual Extension, for no such quality can be observed.

9. All we are entitled to infer from the facts is that there is some reality outside us which is a part-cause of our sensations. But we have no right to suppose that it in any way resembles them. Therefore the Primary Qualities can no more be ascribed to Matter in itself than the Secondary could be.

10. As for such Categories as Substance and Causality, we do not get them through sensations, and they can therefore only be the work of the mind.

11. But what reason have we to accept them as valid ? None, except that, without them, we could not make a coherent theory of things. But, if Matter in itself exists quite independently of our minds, what right have we to say that its nature must be such as would admit a theory of it which would be coherent to our minds ? If we keep Absolute Dualism, we have no right to predicate of Matter categories due to the working of our minds.

12. Thus, if we separate Matter from an observing mind, no part of the conception is left, and the assertion of its existence is meaningless. Now mind is not in the same position. For, even if it could only exist *in company with* Matter, it certainly exists for itself, and not merely *for* Matter. Whereas the whole nature of Matter has been resolved into its relation to Mind.

13. We now pass on to Relative Dualism. This is very close to the position of the natural man before he studies

Metaphysic. But it loses the advantage that Absolute Dualism had of being specially able to explain such an apparently heterogeneous universe as this. For it refers all things to a single mind, and so the *prima facie* partial irrationality of the universe is as much a difficulty for it as for Idealism.

14. With Relative Dualism the difficulty which, in the case of Absolute Dualism, arises as to interaction does not take place, since the theory admits some common nature belonging to both Mind and Matter.

15. But still, if Matter and finite Mind are to be on an equality, it will be necessary that Matter should have some existence in itself, independent of its existence for Mind. And then the same difficulties will occur, as to Primary and Secondary Qualities, which occurred in the case of Dualism.

16. It is no doubt reasonable to hold that my sensations are not exclusively caused by myself. But this does not justify a belief in a self-existent Matter, for the cause in question might be another self, either divine or human.

17. Berkeley's explanation would account for the existence and the regularity of the sensations as well as a Dualistic theory, while avoiding the difficulties of such a theory.

18. Nor is it legitimate to appeal to our ' instinctive ' belief in Matter, nor to demand that people who disbelieve in it shall consent to thrust their hands into the flame of a candle.

IV. MATERIALISM AND PRESENTATIONISM

1. Materialism holds that Matter is the only reality in the universe, and that all activities commonly ascribed to Mind are really activities of Matter.

2. Materialism has the recommendation of being a Monism, and therefore a more perfect explanation of the universe than a Dualism can be.

3. And, starting from the natural position of Dualism, it seems more natural to reduce the universe to Matter than to Mind. In the first place the number of laws relating to

Matter which we know is much greater than the number of laws relating to Mind.

4. And Matter forms one great whole, persisting through many ages. Mind appears in the form of separate individuals, isolated from each other by Matter, and each ceasing, so far as our observation goes, after a very few years.

5. Also the changes which we can observe Mind to make in Matter are comparatively insignificant, while a very slight change in Matter will either destroy Mind, or, at least, remove it from the only circumstances in which we can observe its existence. All these characteristics make Matter appear much more powerful and important than Mind.

6. Also Idealism was weakened by being supposed to be bound up with certain theological doctrines which became discredited. All these things account for the great strength of Materialism some years ago.

7. There has been a reaction against this, but the extent of the reaction has been exaggerated. It still remains the belief to which most people tend on first leaving an unreflecting position. And many remain there. Science is a large element in our lives now, and if we try to make Science serve as Metaphysic, we get Materialism.

8. Nor is it to be wished—even by Idealists—that Materialism should become too weak. For Idealism is seldom really vigorous except in those who have had a serious struggle with Materialism.

9. Materialism cannot be disproved by the *prima facie* difference between thought and motion. For there is a great *prima facie* difference, e.g., between heat and motion. Nor can such imperfect order and symmetry as we are able to observe in the universe be said to be incompatible with Materialism.

10. It would be very difficult to disprove Materialism, if we once accepted the reality of Matter, as a Thing-in-itself. But, as we saw when considering Dualism, such a reality of Matter is untenable (III. §§ 5–12). And this conclusion is even more obviously fatal to Materialism than it was to Dualism.

11. And, again, if Materialism is true, all our thoughts are produced by purely material antecedents. These are quite blind, and are just as likely to produce falsehood as truth. We have thus no reason for believing any of our conclusions—including the truth of Materialism, which is therefore a self-contradictory hypothesis.

12. We now come to Presentationism, which rejects the existence alike of Matter and of Selves, and which makes the ultimate reality to be units of mental occurrences, combined either by pure chance, or by laws analogous to those of mechanics.

13. It may seem curious to rank a theory which denies Matter with Materialism. But what is important is not the name which is given to Reality, but the sort of action which is held to express its real nature.

14. Now Presentationism denies that the ultimate nature of Reality is adequately expressed by any of the characteristics which *prima facie* appear in Mind. And it asserts that the ultimate nature of Reality causes it to act in ways which are adequately expressed by the laws *prima facie* evident in Matter. It thus makes the nature of Reality resemble Matter more closely than Mind, and so is properly ranked by the side of Materialism.

15. It is generally approached through Materialism, and is more difficult to reach than Materialism, though not so difficult as Idealism. It escapes, of course, the objection to Materialism which rests on the impossibility of conceiving Matter as a Thing-in-itself.

16. But the other argument against Materialism (cp. § 11 above) applies equally to Presentationism. As this is the only argument against Presentationism it should be carefully considered.

17. Presentationism is incompatible with the truth of general propositions—and therefore with itself, since it can only be expressed by a general proposition.

18. And closer analysis shows that it is incompatible even with particular propositions, since these (*a*) involve the union of two terms, (*b*) involve the use of general ideas.

19. Thus the theory breaks down because it leads to complete scepticism, invalidating both general and particular propositions. And complete scepticism is, as we have seen before, self-contradictory.

20. The theory is more often called Sensationalism or Phenomenalism. But neither of these names is completely satisfactory.

V. DOGMATIC IDEALISM

1. This may be defined as an attempt to prove the truth of Idealism otherwise than by a direct inquiry into the nature of Reality. The two most usual forms are (a) it is true, because it is believed; (b) it is true, because such disastrous consequences would follow if it were not true.

2. And the first of these falls into three subdivisions :
(i) It is true, because I cannot help believing it to be true.
(ii) It is true, because everyone does believe it to be true.
(iii) It is true, because most people believe it to be true.

3. It is generally of some particular doctrine, rather than of a whole system of Idealism, that such assertions are made.

4. (i) If anyone has a belief in the truth of a doctrine for which he cannot give any reasons, and which cannot be shaken, it is no doubt useless to argue with him. But, he, again, has no right to argue with anyone else. This, however, is often ignored.

5. That X should have an inevitable belief in a proposition involves that he must believe it. But that X must believe it, is no reason why Z should believe it, and, by the hypothesis, X has no other reason for his belief to give to Z. The fact of X's irresistible conviction is only interesting to other people if they are interested in his biography, or in psychological statistics.

6. Again, many opinions which appear to be immediate, are really based on arguments. And some opinions which are not based on arguments can yet be refuted by them—as in certain cases of prejudice.

7. Nor can positions of this sort derive strength from the undoubted fact that every argument must begin with some premises which must be assumed as true.

8. (ii) This argument, in its strict sense, is either false or useless. For if everyone does believe a certain conclusion what is the good of proving what no one doubts?

9. If we say that the belief is one which all people believe unless they have become sophisticated, the word sophistication begs the question. And why should we believe that our original convictions are more likely to be true than later ones? Especially as many of our original convictions are admitted by everyone to be erroneous.

10. (iii) The argument from the opinion of the majority is of but little value, when it is considered how many people are affected by irrelevant considerations. And if experts are to be distrusted in philosophy, on account of their want of unanimity, it scarcely warrants a trust in those who are not experts.

11. We now come to the second variety of Dogmatic Idealism, that which concludes the truth of a proposition from the unsatisfactory results which would follow from its falsity. Here again there are two subdivisions, according as the unsatisfactory results would affect, (a) happiness, or (b) virtue.

12. (a) The first asserts that the world would be an intolerable place unless some form of Idealism or Relative Dualism were true. The assertion must be admitted to have considerable weight. The world as we see it has much that is unsatisfactory.

13. Materialism would give us no reason to suppose that the universe as a whole was better than what we see. And, in particular, it can give us no hope that either we ourselves or the human race will escape annihilation.

14. Absolute Dualism would give us no more cheerful prospect. It leaves, indeed, a chance of Immortality, but of an Immortality exposed to so many evils that most people would think it worse than none.

15. But then what ground have we to assert that the universe is not intolerable? Perhaps it *is* intolerable. If we were

already Idealists, we might possibly be sure it was not so, but it would beg the question to use a belief obtained in this way to prove Idealism.

16. (b) It is argued, to begin with, that no theory but Idealism would be compatible with the existence of virtue, while the existence of virtue cannot be denied. This is not strictly an argument from consequences. It is invalid, for there is no reason why virtue should not arise in a universe whose fundamental nature was indifferent to virtue.

17. Then it is argued that no theory but Idealism would ensure the eventual triumph of virtue, and then it would be absurd to be virtuous. But, if this were so, how can we be certain that it is not absurd to be virtuous ? And why should it be absurd to be virtuous because virtue cannot be completely triumphant ?

18. It is argued also, that, if virtue were not assured of complete success, people would not, in point of fact, be virtuous. This could only prove, at the most, the necessity of people believing in the success of virtue. It could not prove the reality of the success.

19. But there is not the least reason to suppose that people would be less virtuous because they did not believe in a complete triumph of virtue hereafter.

20. To argue that a thing cannot be real because it is very bad is to subvert the foundations of morality. For it follows that, if it were real, it could not be very bad. And then moral judgments have ceased to be supreme in their own sphere.

VI. THE CRITICAL POSITION

1. What method is adequate to the direct proof of Idealism ? The deductive methods recognized by Formal Logic are insufficient, for they cannot give us new knowledge, but only make explicit what is already known.

2. Nor would Induction be adequate, for all Induction rests on the law of the Uniformity of Nature. It is one of the most important tasks of philosophy to consider if this law is true,

and it would not be justified, therefore, in starting by assuming its truth.

3. Moreover, almost every proposition which we wish to examine in Metaphysic is of such enormous extent as compared with the range of our direct experience, that any induction about it, having only that direct experience as its basis, will be quite worthless.

4. Let us try inquiring what conditions are necessary in order that we may have experience at all. Such a method does not involve, as Induction does, the assumption of the Uniformity of Nature.

5. And we can legitimately make our conclusions universal. For they will apply to all experience. Now, in the first place, anything outside actual or possible experience is at any rate of no practical interest to us.

6. And, more than this, something outside the range of possible experience has no meaning for us, even as a possibility. For we can form no idea of it, and it would have no common basis with anything we know.

7. Possibilities with nothing positive about them are valueless. If we say that something of which we know nothing may be possible, because we do not know anything which makes it impossible, this is an empty and idle ' possibility.'

8. And, again, this method will not be sterile like pure deduction. For it is based on observation, though on the observation of *a priori* element only in experience.

9. This method was first explicitly developed by Kant. But he did not realize its full force. And many philosophers before Kant used arguments which were essentially critical.

10. We may illustrate the position by the metaphor of a man looking through a window of red glass, who knows that everything he sees will be seen by him as red, and so is able to make a universal judgment on the matter without waiting for the actual experience.

11. But the metaphor is deceptive. For the things have a real colour of their own, which the glass does not permit us to see. And we should know them more truly if the glass were broken.

12. There is a tendency to interpret the critical theory this way, but it is quite erroneous. The conditions which it discovers are essential to any experience, not to a particular kind of experience. And if they were removed, instead of knowing more truly, we should know nothing at all.

13. This inquiry into the conditions of reality is *not* a psychological inquiry, though it is sometimes supposed to be one. Psychology deals with the *fact* of knowledge, which is *part* of Reality. Our present inquiry deals with the *contents* of knowledge, which is the *whole* of Reality.

14. And Psychology is on the same comparatively uncritical level as the other sciences, while our present inquiry is on the level of philosophy.

15. It is to be noted that when this method tells us that the principle A is involved in the truth of B, it does not mean that everyone who believes B must be aware of A, but there is a contradiction in affirming B to be true and at the same time denying the truth of A.

16. A critical argument is always *ad hominem*. For it starts from the validity of some experience, and would be of no value against a sceptic who denied that validity. Hence critical arguments are of very different degrees of value.

17. We cannot say in a general way what can be proved by this method. But, merely as an example, I will sketch a proof of causality, substantially identical with Kant's proof of it, which was directed especially against Hume.

18. Hume denied the validity of the idea of Causation. But he did not deny the validity of the idea of Objective Succession, i.e. that ideas may be known by our thoughts to have occurred in an order different from the order of our thoughts about them. And he could not have denied this, consistently with the rest of his system.

19. Kant's argument is that there is nothing in our experience which can suggest an Objective Succession of events which is distinct from, and may be contrary to, the Subjective Succession of apprehension.

20. Unless therefore we are certain *à priori* that the events have a fixed and definite order among themselves, we could

have no reason to believe in such an order. And such an order could only be determined by Causation. Either, then, we must reject Objective Succession, or we must admit Causation to be valid *a priori*.

VII. THE DIALECTIC POSITION

1. The Critical position was, as we have seen, *ad hominem*. It does not possess any special starting point, and the arguments which form a Critical system do not form a single train of reasoning.

2. The Dialectic position, on the other hand, which is a modification of the Critical, is one according to which the entire system forms a single chain of argument proceeding from one definite starting point.

3. This position is very closely associated with Hegel. Indeed, we may say that there has as yet been no dialectic system which has not been very distinctly Hegelian.

4. Hegel has been dead more than seventy years, and his philosophy is not so much accepted as formerly. But this is partly due to the general diminution of interest in philosophy—at any rate in some countries. The philosophy of the present day is very largely Hegelian.[1]

5. The dialectic begins by determining a starting point which must be accepted as valid by everybody, and not merely by a particular opponent. It finds this in the assertion Something Is, or in other words, in the validity of the Category of Being. We may define a category as a general idea which is of an *a priori* nature, and which is accepted as having fundamental importance in the structure of the universe.

6. The system forms, as has been said, a single chain of argument from this beginning. The method of the advance may be provisionally described as the alternate production and removal of contradictions.[2]

[1] [This is hardly true of philosophy in 1934, or of philosophy since the War.—*Ed.*]

[2] [No clearer or more penetrating exposition and defence of this Method is to be found than that in McTaggart's *Studies in Hegelian*

7. Taking the first step in Hegel's dialectic as an example, we find that the idea of Pure Being, with which we start, turns out to be identical with the idea of Nothing. It must be remembered that it is only the idea of *Pure* Being, not of *Determinate* Being, of which this is said.

8. But the ideas of Pure Being and Nothing are incompatible with one another. And thus we have a contradiction. Hegel removes this by asserting (after an intermediate stage) that the truth lies in the validity of the category of Determinate Being, in which Pure Being and Nothing are reconciled.

9. The new term thus reached develops a fresh contradiction, and a similar process occurs, and is repeated till we reach a final category which develops no contradiction, and is called the Absolute Idea.

10. The movement in each case is from a Thesis to an Antithesis, which is the contrary (and not the contradictory) of the Thesis. From the Thesis and Antithesis the movement proceeds to the Synthesis which reconciles them.

11. A marked peculiarity of the dialectic process is that as it advances it demonstrates the premises from which it started to be only partially true, and to be partly false. It follows from this that the Absolute Idea is the only category in the dialectic which is absolutely valid, though the other categories have all a certain degree of validity.

12. The main object of the dialectic is to arrive at the complete truth of the Absolute Idea, but it also gives us information about the comparative truth of the lower categories, for the later they come in the process, the greater will be their relative truth.

13. The dialectic process has been often said to violate the law of contradiction. But it is very far from doing this. On the contrary, its advance depends entirely on the certainty that a contradiction is a mark of error. Otherwise there would be no reason for going on to the Synthesis.

Dialectic; cf.especially ch. i, 'The General Nature of the Dialectic.' In his *Commentary on Hegel's Logic*, he examines in detail the validity of Hegel's transitions throughout the dialectical passage from Pure Being to the Absolute Idea.—*Ed.*]

14. The process is one of negation and complement. The Antithesis is not merely contrary to the Thesis, but it is the element which, with the Thesis, is found in the Synthesis.

15. Now of these two factors it is that of completion which is essential. In the process of development the idea negates itself, but it only does so because it is driven to complete itself, and the only road to completion is through negation.

16. The idea of the Synthesis is difficult to grasp. It is best done by seeing what ideas Hegel does treat as synthesizing certain contradictions. We do not synthesize two ideas by applying them to different fields, nor by splitting the difference between them.

17. As an example of this let us take the possible ways in which two such ideas as Liberty and Order can be treated.

18. The evidence for the validity of a Synthesis is always in some degree negative, as depending on the impossibility of any other category being discovered which would equally remove the contradiction.

19. Let us now consider what are the most general results that Hegel gets out of his dialectic. We may say that they are two—the balance of Unity and Differentiation, and Freedom.

20. The universe is clearly a differentiated unity. What Hegel does is to prove that unity and differentiation are so intimately connected that anything can only be a close unity in proportion as its parts are clearly differentiated, and *vice versa*.

21. And he also proves that the nature of the whole must be in each part in such a way as to render each part self-determined, and therefore free.

VIII. THE RESULTS OF IDEALISM

1. It does not follow, from the validity of the Critical or the Dialectic methods, that we could prove Idealism by their means. The result might be of a different nature. We have not time to examine in detail in this course what could

be proved by either method ; but shall here consider what
varieties of Idealism are possible.

2. Idealism holds that Spirit is the sole absolute Reality.
But with reference to Personality, Spirit may be regarded as
being essentially personal, or as not being so. The latter
view can be subdivided, according as it is held (a) that Spirit
is adequately expressed in a personal form, but can also be
adequately expressed otherwise, (b) that personality is not an
adequate expression for Spirit.

3. Of these (a) rests mainly on the large amount of the
universe which is *prima facie* not personal, and would be
refuted, if at all, by some theory which would explain this
fact in a way compatible with all Spirit being personal.

4. (b) is mainly supported by an attempted demonstration
that the finite is, as such, contradictory, and that therefore
the finite self is not an adequate expression of Spirit. This
view may be doubted.

5. The difficulty about both these views is to understand
what the nature of Spirit could be, if it was not personal, since
all the Spirit which we know directly, or which we empirically
infer, is personal.

6. Should all Spirit be personal, it would not follow that
it must all be one person or else not all be one unity. It
might quite well be a perfect unity, which was not itself a
person, but of which all the parts were persons.[1]

7. On the theory that all Reality consists of persons, how
can we account for the part of our experience which is *prima
facie* not personal ? There are two methods. (a) Berkeley's
solution, which we may call the Consistent Dream theory, by
which all matter is resolved into sensations in the mind of
some person—sensations without any outside reference at all.

8. This does not destroy the reality of knowledge. For by
this theory our waking experience still differs from dreams

---

[1] [This is McTaggart's own position in ' The Further Determination of the Absolute ' (X), p. 214 ff. ; and a modification of it (viz.
that all the ' primary parts ' of the universe are selves), he regards
as established by the argumentation of *The Nature of Existence* :
cf. section 433.—*Ed.*]

in just those characteristics that determine real knowledge—coherency, continuity, and community.

9. The other explanation [1] (b) is to ascribe the appearance of impersonal reality, which I experience, to some reality, not myself, which is personal. The appearance of impersonality is referred either to a defect in my observation, or to an imperfection in the selves observed, or to both.

10. The mechanical nature of the actions of this reality might be accounted for either by the imperfect development of the selves, or by the supposition that we only see the resultant of the actions of a great number of selves.

11. Each theory has its weaknesses. The second theory (b) has the advantage of accounting more simply for the sub-human life which we perceive round us.

12. We pass to the relation of Idealism to our desires and aspirations. They are so closely bound up with our personality, that those forms of Idealism which admit of impersonal Spirit are almost—though not quite—as unfavourable to them as Materialism or Absolute Dualism would be.

13. With those forms of Idealism which make Spirit essentially personal, there is no longer a presumption against the harmony of the universe with our desires. But that harmony is by no means proved.

14. It would be impossible to prove it in this course. I can only indicate a way in which it might be possible, by means of the ideas of unity and differentiation.

15. The question of the satisfaction of our natures depends partly on the relation of the self to the environment, and partly on whether the nature of the self is such that any environment could satisfy it.

16. A mere causal unity between the self and its environment would not help us to a harmony between the self and its environment. But it would be different if we found reason to believe that they were included in a unity whose nature was just to be manifested in each of its differentiations, while

---

[1] [This is the alternative McTaggart himself eventually adopted. How such ' appearance of impersonality ' is possible, he discusses fully in *The Nature of Existence*, II, Bk. VI.—*Ed.*]

the nature of each of the differentiations was just to manifest the whole nature of the unity.

17. Such a unity as this is sometimes called an organic unity. But such a name is misleading, for an organism has more in its nature than its manifestation in its parts, and the parts have a nature besides their connection in the organism.

18. The unity of which we speak might be called a Community of Selves, if we guarded against atomistic implications. For the importance of the unity and of the differentiations would have to be exactly balanced, if the unity is to be such as can help us.

19. And such a unity as this might also remove the doubt whether the nature of the self is such as could be satisfied by any possible environment. But at this point the subject must be left for treatment elsewhere than in this course.

20. But if such results as I have sketched here could be proved, should we not have proved too much by proving that we could experience no disharmony, while we notoriously do experience some disharmony? This leads us on to the final division of these lectures—the problem of good and evil.

IX. The Problem of Good and Evil

1. We have now to consider whether any *a priori* conclusion can be arrived at as to the relative importance of Good and Evil, and whether in the long run, or over the whole universe, one is completely or very greatly preponderant.

2. The universe could *result* in producing only, or mostly, good, without having a *purpose* to do so. But, if it had the purpose, it must have the result, for nothing could thwart the purpose of the whole universe. Let us consider the question of purpose first. This need not necessarily be a conscious purpose.

3. The view that the purpose of the universe is only to produce the good is confronted with the fact that evil does exist. This has been met, at times, by the assertion, that evil, whether sin or pain, has no reality.

4. But if this were so, everything which was not good would be sinful, and everything which was not happy would be painful. The example of a stone is sufficient to refute this. There are senses in which evil is the negation of good, but it is impossible to take it as a bare negation.

5. Then there is the argument which says that although evil exists when we look at a part of the universe by itself, yet when we look at the whole, it is not nearly counterbalanced, but vanishes away.

6. But then evil does exist for all the finite persons we know, and it seems futile to say that it does not exist at all. If it does not exist for omniscient beings, if any exist, that does not prevent its existing for us.

7. If it be said that every finite being may become omniscient, it must be admitted that some of them are not omniscient at present. Thus the argument no longer denies the evil of the universe at the present time ; and the attempt to reconcile present evil with future or eternal good is another question which we must consider later.

8. Another argument says that if we looked at the whole course of the world in time, the events, which when taken separately were evil, would be seen to be completely good. This is a stronger argument than the last because it is not so clear that each moment in a person's life has worth in itself as it is that each person has worth in himself.

9. But the world, according to this theory, is only good when we see the whole of it at once. And we do not do so now. If it is said that we shall do so in the future, this would not make the world completely good. For the past, though less important to us, is as much part of the world as the future, and the past would be admitted to be bad.

10. Or shall we say that true perfection is to be found, not in a temporal future, but in some timeless state, in which all its successive temporal states should be timelessly summed up, and which is the true reality, all the isolation of these elements into successive steps in time being unreal.

11. This is too subtle a point to discuss here. But even if substantiated, the theory would not do what was wanted.

For if we are not conscious of this state, the evil remains for us.

12. And what right have we to suppose that we shall ever be conscious of this state, even if some suicide of time could be imagined ? For if the imperfect time process is incompatible with the timeless perfection, we must be wrong in believing in the timeless perfection, since the time process certainly exists. But if the time process is compatible with the perfection now, why not always ? And if always, *we* shall never get rid of evil, since the time process will be left.

13. This is the fundamental difficulty of all theories which attempt to prove Reality to be completely good. If the evil is really evil, its existence proves that Reality cannot be wholly good. If it is not really evil, the goodness of Reality affords us no ground for hoping that we shall get rid of it, while it remains just as unpleasant for us.

14. Efforts are continually made to deduce the vanishing of evil in the future from the fact that Reality is in its ultimate nature completely good, but they are all invalidated by this difficulty.

15. Can we, we must now inquire, account for evil by accepting it as real, and explaining it as an indispensable condition for the realization of some good purpose ?

16. It is sometimes asserted that we can see for ourselves that good could not exist except as opposed to existent evil, and that therefore evil is an indispensable condition of good. But when we inquire into the grounds for this view it does not seem correct.

17. A more general application is to ascribe the universe to a cause—for example, a personal God—which is wholly directed towards good, and then to account for the evil by asserting that the cause worked under such limitations that it could not have produced the good unless it also produced the evil.

18. The theory has this in its support—that the conception of a will which did not work under limitations would be meaningless. For the laws of logic would not apply to it. And, again, could it create something which it could not destroy?

19. (The use of means always implies that the power which uses them is limited. For means are not employed for their own sake, but because the agent cannot accomplish his end without them.)

20. The facts would be equally consistent with the theory that the cause was working for evil, and that it was the good which resulted from the limitations of its power. And, in any case, the purpose of the whole universe could not be good. If the purpose of the cause was good, the purpose of the limitations on its power could not be.

21. And if the universe is produced by a cause directed towards good, then the whole of the universe has not a good purpose. For those evils in the universe which are due to the limitations of the power of the cause, are clearly not due to any good purpose.

22. And this theory, while it would involve that good could never be completely destroyed in the universe, would put no limit to the possible excess of evil over good. However bad the universe was, it might still be the best that the good cause could produce under the limitations to which it was subject.

23. All this is on the assumption that we are not able to know anything else about the limitations on the power of the good cause except that they do limit it, and do produce evil.

24. There have been attempts to maintain an omnipotent good cause, in spite of the existence of evil, by trusting to the feebleness of our intellects. But this is suicidal, for exactly the same argument might be used to suppose any other conclusion on the same subject.

25. And any attempt to determine empirically that good is more than evil, or is gaining on evil, is illegitimate because of the small proportion which the facts observed must bear to the conclusion.

26. Abandoning the attempt to prove that the universe has a purpose directed to good as such, can anything be made of the attempt to prove that it had some other purpose which secured a preponderance, though not an unmixed state, of

good ? This, at any rate, if proved, would prove neither too much nor too little.

27. Have we any reason to suppose that evil has an essentially subordinate position in Reality, i.e., on the Idealist hypotheses, in Spirit ?

28. With sin this does seem to be the case. For a complete state of sin—unlike a complete state of virtue—is impossible. And again all action, good or bad, is for something conceived, rightly or wrongly, as being in some aspect good.

29. It is more difficult to prove the subordinate character of pain. But it is to be noticed that all pain comes from want of harmony, and that if the want of harmony became too great, the pain would cease. Thus pain has an intrinsic limit. This consideration, however, is perhaps hardly strong enough for our purpose.

30. Coming to a more general point—suppose that the conception of the One and the Many, which we have seen was held by Hegel, was the adequate interpretation of Reality.

31. In that case harmony would be clearly preponderant over disharmony. For the nature of each individual would just be to manifest the whole. And the nature of the whole is just that it should be manifested, not only in that individual, but in all of them. Consequently the nature of each individual requires, for its own realization of its nature, that the others should also realize their nature. For if not, then the whole cannot realize its nature, and then the part originally spoken of cannot realize its nature either.

32. But doesn't this go too far and prove that there can be *no* disharmony, and so *no* pain ? For then we should be back in the same difficulties as previously. What we want is a theory which will allow disharmony, and so pain, a place in Reality, but will ensure that it shall be a subsidiary place.

33. I cannot go farther into the question here, but will only say that I believe the solution might possibly be found in regarding the harmony as eternal, and the disharmony as caused by the manifestation of the eternal in time.[1]

34. At any rate, this would be consistent with a view which

[1] [Cf. *The Nature of Existence*, II, ch. lxvi.—*Ed.*]

has other grounds to support it—that the determination of the relation of time to eternity is at present the most pressing and important question in philosophy.

35. This theory, unlike the one which we discussed previously (cp. 10 above), does not seek to prove that there is no evil, but only that the evil is subordinate. It therefore does not involve the same difficulties.

36. It may be objected that such a theory, while giving us a hopeful view of the universe, could not enable us to regard the cause of the universe as a being deserving veneration. For the theory involves that evil is not inconsistent with the purpose of the universe, and a being with whose purpose evil is not inconsistent is a morally evil being.

37. But this difficulty is avoided if (a) we are able to regard the universe as the work of a conscious being acting under limitations. For then *his* purpose might be completely good, although that of the whole universe (which includes his limitations) was not so.

38. Or (b) the universe might be regarded as not caused by a conscious being at all, in which case the question of moral nature would not arise.

X

THE FURTHER DETERMINATION OF THE ABSOLUTE [1]

'To love unsatisfied the world is mystery, a mystery which love satisfied seems to comprehend.'
—F. H. BRADLEY, *Appearance and Reality*, p. xv.

The progress of an idealistic philosophy may, from some points of view, be divided into three stages. The problem of the first is to prove that reality is not exclusively matter. The problem of the second is to prove that reality is ex-

[1] [This essay is McTaggart's earliest published writing in philosophy, with the exception of a juvenile contribution on John Stuart Mill to the *Cliftonian*. It was 'printed for private circulation only' in 1893, two years after his election to a Fellowship at Trinity. 'I felt almost ashamed to write it at all,' he says in a letter, 'it was like turning one's heart inside out.' But the paper had been shown to 'one or two people who are rather authorities (Caird of Glasgow and Bradley of Oxford) and they have been very kind and encouraging about it,' and 'several people have cared enough for it to make me glad I wrote it' (Cf. G. Lowes Dickinson, *J. McT. E. McTaggart*: Cambridge, 1931, p. 37).
It is in this essay, Lowes Dickinson thinks, that McTaggart 'expresses more perfectly perhaps, and more freshly than anywhere else, the essence of his philosophical belief.' It may also be taken as the most faithful general expression of his final position, and McTaggart remained convinced of its substantial correctness throughout his life. About half the material of this essay was incorporated, with little modification, in his *Studies in Hegelian Cosmology* (1901), and the essential conclusions reappeared, though differently supported, in the second volume of *The Nature of Existence*, posthumously published in 1927.
In the original pamphlet, the text is prefaced by the following note : ' It would be difficult for anyone to be more conscious than I am of the extreme crudeness of this paper, and of its absolute inadequacy to its subject. My excuse must be that I knew the conclusions at which it arrived were held by scholars whose right to pronounce on such points was different indeed from my own. It seemed that, if my arguments could not justify my conclusions, my

THE FURTHER DETERMINATION OF THE ABSOLUTE

clusively spirit. The problem of the third is to determine what is the fundamental nature of spirit.

The importance of the second of these stages is very great. The universe stands transfigured before our eyes. We have gained a solution of our difficulties—still abstract, indeed, but all-extensive. Because the fundamental nature of ourselves and of the universe is the same, we are enabled to say that the universe and ourselves are implicitly in harmony—a harmony which must some day become explicit. The world can present no problem which we cannot some day solve ; it is therefore rational. And our nature can make no demand, can set no aim before itself which will not be seen some day to be realized in the world, which is therefore righteous. The harmony in question holds good, no doubt, not of the irrational and unrighteous self of the present, but of the rational and righteous self of the future. But we know that whatever turns out to be the fundamental fact of our nature will have complete realization and satisfaction, and this fundamental fact of our nature is not only superior to all other aspects of us, but is the only reality, of which they are merely phases and misconceptions. And we know, therefore, that not a thought, not a desire, can affect us, however apparently false and trivial, which will not be found to be realized in its truth by the ultimate reality of things. All that we know, all that we want, must be found in that reality, and will not be found the less, because much more than we can at present perceive or desire will be found there too.

conclusions might excuse my arguments. And I hoped that an attempt to explain my position to a few of my teachers and fellow-students might produce criticisms or refutations which should be profitable either in improving or preventing any further work on my part. I fear that, in my uncertainty as to whether I meant to write for people who were interested in my reasoning or people who sympathized with my conclusions, I have failed in both attempts, and that I have been at once too technical and too personal. It is not easy, in the borderlands of metaphysics, to avoid both these errors at once, and I can only hope that between the two something may be found which someone may care to read. If anyone thinks I have been talking about things which should not be spoken, or at any rate be written about, it may interest him to know that I am very much inclined to agree with him.'—Ed.]

But this result, though comprehensive, is still abstract, and is therefore defective even from a theoretical point of view. It does not enable us to see the ultimate nature of the universe, and to perceive that it is rational and righteous. We only know in an abstract way that it *must* be rational and righteous, because it fulfils the formal condition of rationality and righteousness—harmony between the nature of the universal and the nature of the individual. Such a skeleton is clearly by no means complete knowledge. And it is therefore, to some extent, incorrect and inadequate knowledge; for it is knowledge of an abstraction only, while the truth, as always, is concrete. The content of the universe has not been produced by, or in accordance with, a self-subsistent law. It is the individual content of the universe which is concrete and self-subsistent, and the law is an abstraction of one side of it, with which we cannot be contented. From a theoretical point of view, then, the assertion of the supremacy of spirit is comparatively empty unless we can determine the fundamental nature of spirit.

The practical importance of this determination is not less. As a guide to life, the knowledge of the absolutely desirable end is, no doubt, not without drawbacks. Christ's remark ' Be ye perfect, even as your father in heaven is perfect ' reveals a fundamentally wrong principle. A certain degree of virtue, as of knowledge and happiness, is appropriate and possible for every stage of the process of spirit. By the aid of reflection we may perceive the existence of a stage much higher than that in which we are. But the knowledge that we shall some day reach it is not equivalent to the power of reaching it at once. We are entitled to as much perfection as we are fit for, and it is useless to demand more. An attempt to live up to the Summum Bonum, without regard to present circumstances, will be not only useless, but, in all probability, actually injurious. The true course of our development at present is mostly by thesis and antithesis, and an attempt to become virtuous as the crow flies will only lead us into some *cul de sac* from which we shall have to retrace our steps.

Nevertheless, the knowledge of the goal to which we are

going may occasionally, if used with discretion, be a help in directing our course. It will be something if we can find out what parts of our experience are valid *per se*, and can be pursued for their own sake, and what are merely subsidiary. For however long it may take us to reach the Absolute, it is sometimes curiously near us in isolated episodes of life, and our attitude towards certain phases of consciousness, if not our positive actions, may be materially affected by the consideration of the greater or less adequacy with which those phases embody reality.

In close connection with the attitude which we take up towards any experience is the emotional significance which it bears for us. And the success of a more complete determination of the nature of spirit would not be unimportant with regard to its effect on our happiness. The position from which we start has indeed already attained to what may be called the religious standpoint. It assures us of an ultimate solution which shall only differ from our present highest ideals and aspirations by far surpassing them. From a negative point of view, this is complete, and it is far from unsatis-factory as a positive theory. But it is clear that, if so much knowledge is consoling and inspiriting, more knowledge would be better. It is good to know that reality is better than our expectations. It would be still better to be able at once to expect the full good that is coming. If the truth is so good, our hopes must become more desirable in proportion as they become more defined.

And, if we descend to more particular considerations, we shall find that in other ways more complete knowledge might conduce to our greater happiness. For there are parts of our lives which, even as we live them, seem incomplete and merely transitory, as having no value unless they lead on to something better. And there are parts of our lives which seem so funda-mental, so absolutely desirable in themselves, that we could not anticipate without pain their absorption into some higher perfection, as yet unknown to us, and demand that they shall undergo no further change, except an increase in purity and intensity. Now we might be able to show of the first of these groups of experiences that they are, in fact, mere passing phases, with meaning only in so far as they lead up to and are absorbed in something higher. And we might even be able to show of the second that they are actually fundamental, lacking so far in breadth and depth, but in their explicit nature already revealing the explicit reality. If we can do this, and can justify the vague longings for change on the one hand, and for permanence on the other, which have so much effect on our lives, the gain to happiness which will result will not be inconsiderable.

Let us now endeavour to consider what data we have for our inquiry. Hegel (*Encyclopædia*, Section 236) defines the Absolute Idea, which is the content of Spirit, as ' der Begriff der Idee, dem die Idee als solche der Gegenstand, dem das Objekt sie ist.' If we translate this into terms more applicable to our present purpose, we shall find, I think, that it means that Spirit is ultimately made up of various finite individuals, each of which finds his character and individuality by relating himself to the rest, and by perceiving that they are of the same nature as himself. In this way the Idea in each individual has as its object the Idea in other individuals.

To justify this conception of the nature of Spirit would be a task beyond the limits of this paper. Indeed it could only be done by going over the whole course of Hegel's Logic. But it may not be impossible to indicate briefly some reasons why it should recommend itself to us.

In the first place it is quite clear that Spirit cannot be an undifferentiated unity. It must have some character, or it would be reduced to the state of mere Being, which is the same as Nothing. And character implies relations. Now ultimate reality cannot, of course, have any relations with things external to itself, since no such things exist. Ultimate reality must, therefore, be taken as a whole which is differentiated into an organism of parts, which by their relations to one another constitute its character.

And these parts again must, each for itself, partake of the essential nature of Spirit. For although Spirit is only realized in them in so far as they are united, it is nevertheless realized in each part, and not merely in the union. That the Idea has itself as a ' Gegenstand ' and an ' Objekt ' indicates that the Idea is manifested in numerically distinguishable centres. Besides this, we have seen that reality must be regarded as differentiated, and if the Idea is not present in each differentiated part, then the relative independence of the parts must be considered as something alien to the Idea. And if anything did remain alien to it, the Idea could not yet be called Absolute. Each part of Spirit must therefore itself be spirit, and expresses (at present, of course, only implicitly) its full nature. And Spirit is thus made up of spirits—to use a common expression—each a part of the whole, but each at the same time a perfect individual, because it expresses the whole nature of Spirit. In other words the Absolute realizes itself in a community of individuals like ourselves—in what has been termed the Civitas Dei.

We may arrive at this conclusion from another point of view, if we consider that the course of development is always from a whole which has no differentiated parts, and therefore no real unity, to one which is a real unity of differentiated parts. Here again, for a detailed proof, a reference to Hegel would be necessary, but the fact is one which can be easily observed. The lowest abstractions in Nature are Space and Time, the parts of which are, in themselves, absolutely indistinguishable, and have not the slightest independent existence. And unity is as much lacking to Space and Time as individuality. Any part of either can be separated from any whole of which it may be a part without the slightest alteration in its nature. We find here at once infinite divisibility, and an entire absence of objective divisions. Advancing to the subject matter of physics we find that parts have now slightly differentiated themselves from one another, and, at the same time that the wholes have gained some slight degree of unity. In chemistry both the individuality of the parts and the coherence of the wholes have again increased. And in any case which falls under the category of organic life we find that the parts lose all meaning on being separated from the whole, just because they are so highly differentiated into a scheme which finds its unity in that whole. When we arrive at the Absolute, the unity has become perfect, and so must the differentiation. That which is most completely differentiated is the individual, and we again reach the conclusion that the Absolute must consist of individuals bound together by a unity closer than any which we know at present, who are, for that very reason, more completely individuals than we can at present imagine.

Or once more. It is certain that finite spirits exist at present. If they ceased to exist as such in the Absolute, they must either have gone out altogether, or be merged in something else. The first alternative is scarcely possible, since Spirit is the fundamental reality of the universe, for it is difficult to see what cause could be contained in the universe which would be adequate to the destruction of even a part of absolute reality. The only destruction we know is that of forms and combinations, and we have no reason to believe— I doubt if we can even conceive—that the content of a form is ever destroyed. Moreover, if spirit could cease to be, its existence would be in time. It is, however, a consequence of an idealism based on the Dialectic, that time is not an adequate expression of ultimate reality, and if spirit is ultimate reality it cannot be conceived as merely in time.

The suggestion, on the other hand, that finite spirits may possibly be merged in the infinite without actual destruction, involves a fallacy. It implies that in Spirit, as in the material world, there is a substance or matter which is indifferent to the form it takes, and which can go from one form to another.

Without tracking this error to its roots it must suffice us to observe here that such a view inevitably involves the application of the conception of quantity to Spirit. The Absolute must be considered as in some way affected by the absorption of the finite spirits into itself. If it were not there could be no valid distinction between absorption and the absolute destruction already considered. And, *ex hypothesi*, it is not affected by their form, for the form is supposed to disappear. Either the form is conceived as destroyed altogether, or as

216

passing into the higher form characteristic of the Absolute. In either case the form of the Absolute is left unaffected. We can only conceive it then as affected by the magnitude of the finite spirits which it absorbs. But to speak of an individual as containing a certain quantity of Spirit, as a bottle does of whisky, is a glaring misapplication of a quite inadequate category. We are thus forced to the conclusion that finite spirits can no more be merged than they can be annihilated, that, since they unquestionably exist at present, they must be taken as existing in the Absolute.

I have endeavoured to summarily recapitulate the grounds which make it probable that the Absolute is composed of individuals closely connected with one another, although all actual proof must depend on a detailed study of the Dialectic. We must now inquire in what manner those individuals will be able to express, at once and completely, their own individuality and the unity of the Absolute.

Human consciousness presents three aspects. On the one hand we have knowledge. Here we endeavour to effect our unity with that which is outside us, by constructing in our own minds a faithful representation of the outside reality. On the other hand, in volition we postulate something as demanded by our own nature, and endeavour to produce a harmony between ourselves and our environment by discovering or producing an agreement between our demands and the facts. Besides these, there is feeling. In so far as we perceive ourselves to be out of harmony with our surroundings, we feel pain ; in so far as we feel ourselves in harmony with them, we feel pleasure. Feeling accompanies every mental state. Even if pleasure and pain be exactly balanced, there is an equilibrium, but not an absence of feeling.

We may observe that knowledge and volition are correlative methods of endeavouring to obtain that unity between individuals which is the perfection of spirit, while feeling is not so much a struggle towards the goal as the result of the process, so far as it has gone. Through knowledge and volition we gain harmony, and, according as we have gained it more or less completely, our feeling is pleasurable or painful.

The absence of any independent movement of feeling renders it unnecessary, for the present, to consider it separately.

I shall first inquire what general aspect would be presented by spirit, if we suppose knowledge and volition to have become as perfect as possible. It will then be necessary to ask whether knowledge and volition are permanent and ultimate forms of the activity of spirit. I shall endeavour to show that they are not, that they both postulate, to redeem them from paradox and impossibility, an ideal which they can never reach, and that their real truth and meaning is found only when they imply and lead on to a state of the mind in which they themselves, together with feeling, are swallowed up and transcended in a more concrete unity. I believe that this unity will be found to be essentially the same as that mental state which, in the answer to our first question, we shall find to be the practically interesting aspect of knowledge and volition in their highest perfection as such. This state will thus have been shown to be, not only the result which the process of the universe tends to produce as its final outcome, but also to be the only truth and reality of spirit, of which all other spiritual activities are only distortions and abstractions, and into which they are all absorbed. It will not only be the highest truth, but the only truth. We shall have found in it the complete determination of Spirit, and therefore of reality.

Let us turn to the first of these questions, and consider what would be the result in our attitude towards the universe, when both knowledge and volition had reached perfection. To answer this we must first determine in rather more detail what would be the nature of perfect knowledge and volition.

In the first place we must eliminate knowledge as the occupation of the student. The activity and the pleasure which lie in the search after knowledge can form no part of the Absolute. For all such activity implies that some knowledge has not yet been gained, and that the ideal, therefore, has not yet been reached. The ideal must be one, not of learning, but of knowing.

And the knowledge itself must be enormously changed in

its nature. At present much of our knowledge directly relates to matter; all of it is conditioned and mediated by matter. But if the only absolute reality is Spirit, then, when knowledge is perfect, we must see nothing but Spirit everywhere. We must have seen through matter till it disappears. How far this could be done merely by greater knowledge on our parts, and how far it would be necessary for the objects themselves, which we at present conceive as matter, to first develop explicitly qualities now merely implicit, is another question; but it is clear that it would have to be done, one way or another, before knowledge could be said to be perfect.

Nor is this all. Not only must all matter, but all contingency, be eliminated. At present we conceive of various spirits— and even of Spirit in general—as having qualities for which we can no more find a rational explanation than we can for the primary qualities of matter, or for its original distribution in space. But this must disappear in perfected knowledge. For knowledge demands an explanation of everything, and if, at the last, we have to base our explanation on something left unexplained, we leave our system incomplete and defective.

Since knowledge essentially consists of argument from data, it would seem that such perfection could never be attained, since each argument which explained anything must rest upon an unexplained foundation, and so on *ad infinitum*. And it is true that we can never reach a point where the question ' Why ? ' can no longer be asked. But we can reach a point where it becomes unmeaning, and at this point knowledge reaches the highest perfection of which, as knowledge, it is susceptible.

The ideal which we should then have reached would be one in which we realized the entire universe as an assembly of spirits, and recognized that the qualities and characteristics which gave to each of these spirits its individuality, did not lie in any contingent or non-rational peculiarity in the individual himself, but were simply determined by his relations to all other individuals. These relations between individuals, again, we should not conceive as contingent or accidental, so that the persons connected formed a mere miscellaneous crowd. We should rather conceive them as united by a pattern or design, resembling that of a picture or of a living organism, so that every part of it was determined by every other part, in such a manner that from any one all the others could, with sufficient insight, be deduced, and that no change could be made in any without affecting all. This complete interdependence is only approximately realized in the unity which is found in æsthetic or organic wholes, but in the Absolute the realization would be perfect. As the whole nature of every spirit would consist exclusively in the expression of the relations of the Absolute, while those relations would form an organic whole, in which each part, and the whole itself, would be determined by each part, it follows that any fact in the universe could be deduced from any other fact, or from the nature of the universe as a whole.

If knowledge reached this point, the only question which could remain unanswered would be the question, ' Why is the universe as a whole what it is, and not something else ? ' And this question could not be answered. We must not, however, conclude from this the existence of any want of rationality in the universe, for the truth is that the question ought never to have been asked. For it is the application of a category, which has only meaning within the universe, to the universe as a whole. Of any part we are entitled and bound to ask ' why,' for, by the very fact that it is a part, it cannot be self-subsistent, and must depend on other things. But when we come to an all-embracing totality, then, with the possibility of finding a cause, there disappears also the necessity of finding one. Self-subsistence is not in itself a contradictory or impossible idea. It *is* contradictory if applied to anything in the universe, for whatever is in the universe must be in connection with other things. But this can of course be no reason for suspecting a fallacy when we find ourselves obliged to apply the idea to that which has nothing outside it with which it could stand in connection.

To put the matter in another light, we must consider that the necessity of finding causes and reasons for phenomena depends on the necessity of showing why they have assumed the particular form which actually exists. The inquiry is thus due to the possibility of things happening otherwise than they did, which possibility, to gain certain knowledge, must be excluded by assigning definite causes for one event rather than the others. Now we can imagine the possibility of any one thing in the universe being different from what it actually is. But there is no meaning in the supposition that the whole universe could be different from what it is. On this subject we may refer to Mr. F. H. Bradley, who has demonstrated (*Logic*, Book I, ch. vii) that a possibility is meaningless unless it has some element in common with what actually exists. If, however, the actual universe was shown to be a completely interdependent organism, then nothing could be different from it in part without being entirely different from it, for the existence of one feature of such an organism would involve all the rest. And the possibility that the universe might have been entirely different from what it now is, would leave no feature common to it with actual existence, and would be therefore unmeaning. If the possibility of variation is unmeaning, there can be no need to assign a determining cause.

We can thus reject any fear that the necessity which exists for all knowledge to rest at last on the immediate shows any imperfection which might prove a permanent bar to the development of Spirit. For we have seen that the impulse which causes us even here to demand fresh mediation is unjustified and even meaningless. But we shall have to consider in the second part of this essay whether the possibility of even making the unjustified demand does not indicate that for complete harmony we must go on to something which embraces and transcends knowledge.

Let us now pass on to the ideal of volition. We can in the first place exclude, as incompatible with such an ideal, all volition which leads to action. For action involves that you have not something which you want, or that you will be deprived of it if you do not fight for it, and both these ideas are fatal to the fundamental and complete harmony between desire and environment which is necessary to the perfect development of Spirit.

Nor can virtue have a place in our ideal, even in the form of aspiration, whatever Mr. Green may say to the contrary. Like all other vices, however dear, it will have to be left outside the door of heaven. For virtue implies a choice, and choice implies either uncertainty or conflict. In the completed ideal neither of these could exist. We should desire our truest and deepest well-being with absolute necessity, since there would be nothing to deceive and tempt us away. And we should find the whole universe conspiring with us to help us onward. Under these circumstances there would be no more virtue in obeying the law, for example, of courage, than in obeying the law of gravitation. The use of the word law in both cases would no longer be misleading, for all difference between precepts and truths would have ceased, when the righteous was *ipso facto* the real.

The ideal of volition is rather the experience of perfect harmony between ourselves and our environment which excludes alike action and choice. This involves, in the first place, that we should have come to a clear idea as to what the fundamental demands and aspirations of our nature are. Till we have done this we cannot expect harmony. All other desires will be in themselves inharmonious, for, driven on by the inevitable dialectic, they will show themselves imperfect, transitory, or defective, when experienced for a sufficiently long time, or in a sufficiently intense degree. And, besides this, the very fact that the universe is fundamentally of the nature of Spirit, and therefore *must* be in harmony with us when we have fully realized our own natures, proves that it *cannot* be in the long run in harmony with us so long as our natures remain imperfect. For such a harmony with the imperfect would be an imperfection, out of which it would be forced by its own dialectic.

And this harmony must extend through the entire universe. If everything (or rather everybody) in the universe is not in harmony with us our ends cannot be completely realized. For the whole universe is connected together, and every part of it must have an effect, however infinitesimal, upon every other part. Our demands must be reconciled with and realized by every other individual.

And again we cannot completely attain our own ends unless everyone else has attained his own also. For, as was mentioned in the last paragraph, we cannot attain our own ends except by becoming in perfect harmony with the entire universe. And this we can only do in so far as both we and it have become completely rational. It follows that for the attainment of our ends it would be necessary for the entire universe to have explicitly developed the rationality which is its fundamental nature. And by this self-development every other individual, as well as ourselves, would have attained to the perfection of volition. Moreover, looking at the matter from a less formal point of view, we may observe that some degree of sympathy seems inherent to our nature, so that our pleasure in some one else's pain, though often intense, is never quite unmixed. And on this ground also our complete satisfaction must involve that of all other people.

We have now determined, as well as we can, the nature of perfected knowledge and volition, as far as the formal conditions of perfection will allow us to go. What is the concrete and material content of such a life as this ? What does it come to ? I believe it means one thing, and one thing only—love. When I have explained that I do not mean benevolence, even in its most impassioned form, not even the feeling of St. Francis, I shall have cut off the one probable explanation of my meaning. When I add that I do not mean the love of Truth, or Virtue, or Beauty, or any other word that can be found in the dictionary, I shall have made confusion worse confounded. When I continue by saying that I mean passionate, all-absorbing, all-consuming love, I shall have become scandalous. And when I wind up by saying that I do not mean sexual desire, I shall be condemned as hopelessly morbid—the sin against the Holy Ghost of Ascalon.

For let us consider. We should find ourselves in a world composed of nothing but individuals like ourselves. With these individuals we should have been brought into the closest of all relations, we should see them, each of them, to be rational and righteous. And we should know that in and through these individuals our own highest aims and ends were realized. What else does it come to ? To know another person thoroughly, to know that he conforms to one's highest standards, to feel that through him the end of one's own life is realized—is this anything but love ?

Such a result would come all the same, I think, if one only looked at the matter from the point of view of satisfied knowledge, leaving volition out of account. If all reality is such as would appear entirely reasonable to us if we knew it completely, if it is all of the nature of spirit, so that we, who are also of that nature, should always find harmony in it, then to completely know a person and to be known by him must, as I conceive, end in this way. No doubt knowledge does not always have that result in every-day life. But that is incomplete knowledge, under lower categories and subject to unremoved contingencies, which, from its incompleteness, must leave the mind unsatisfied. Perfect knowledge would be different. ' Tout comprendre, c'est tout pardonner '—even the world knows that. Philosophy might go a step farther. How much more if besides the satisfaction attendant on mere knowledge, we had realized that it was through the people round us that the longings and desires of our whole nature were being fulfilled.

This would, as it seems to me, be the only meaning and significance of perfected Spirit. Knowledge and volition would still remain, but their importance would consist exclusively in their producing this result. For it is only in respect of the element of feeling in it that any state can be deemed to have intrinsic value. This is of course not the same thing as saying that we always act for our own greatest happiness, or even that our own greatest happiness is our only rational end. We do not deny the possibility of disinterested care for the welfare of others. We only assert that the welfare of any person depends upon the feeling which is an element of his consciousness. Nor do we necessarily assert that a quantitative maximum of pleasure is the Summum Bonum. It is possible that there may be qualitative differences of pleasure, which might make a comparatively unhappy state more truly desirable than one of far greater happiness. But this does not interfere with the fact that it is only with regard to its element of feeling that any state can be held to be intrinsically desirable.

Now, perfected knowledge and volition, taken in connection with the consequent feeling, not only produce personal love, but, as it seems to me, produce nothing else. There are, it is true, many other ways in which knowledge and volition produce pleasure. There are the pleasures of learning, and of the contemplation of scientific truth ; there are the pleasures of action, of virtue, and of gratified desire. But these all depend on the imperfect stages of development in which knowledge and volition are occupied with comparatively abstract generalities. Now all general laws are abstractions from, and therefore distortions of, the concrete reality, which is the abstract realized in the particular. When we fail to see the abstract in the particular, then, no doubt, the abstract has a value of its own—is as high or higher than the mere particular. But when we see the real individual, in whom the abstract and particular are joined, we lose all interest in the abstract as such. Why should we put up with an inadequate falsehood, when we can get the adequate truth ? And feeling towards an individual, fully known as such, has only the one form.

It may be objected that I am making the whole thing too cut and dried. What right have we to talk of love coming as a necessary consequence of anything ? Is not it the most unreasoning thing in life, choosing for itself, often in direct opposition to what would seem the most natural plan ? I should explain the contradiction as follows—an explanation which I am scarcely prepared to defend, but only to suggest. Nothing but perfection could really deserve love. Hence, when it comes in this imperfect world, it only comes in cases in which the affection is able to disregard the other as he now is—that is, as he really is not—and to care for him as he really is—that is, as he will be. Of course this is only the philosopher's explanation of the matter. To the un-philosophic subject of the explanation it simply takes the form of a wild conviction that the other person, with all his faults, is somehow *in himself* infinitely good—at any rate, infinitely good for his friend. The circumstances which determine in what cases this strange dash into reality can be made are not known to us. And so love is unreasonable. But only because reason is not yet worthy of it. It cannot reveal—though in philosophy it may predict—the truth which can alone justify love. When reason is perfected, love will consent to be reasonable.

Fantastic as all this may seem, the second part of my essay, on which I must now enter, will, I fear, seem much worse. I have endeavoured to prove that all perfect life would lead up to and culminate in love. I want now to go farther, and to assert that as life became perfect all other elements would actually die away—that knowledge and volition would disap-pear, swallowed up in a higher reality, and that love would reveal itself, not only as the highest, but as the only thing in the universe.

If we look close enough, we shall find, I think, that both knowledge and volition postulate a perfection to which they can never attain ; that consequently if we take them as ulti-mate realities we shall be plunged into contradictions, and that the only way to account for their existence at all is to view them as mere sides or aspects of a higher reality which realizes the perfection they postulate. This perfection lies in the production of a complete harmony between the subject and the object, by the combination of perfect unity between them with perfect discrimination of the one from the other. And this, as I shall endeavour to prove, is impossible without transcending the limits of these two correlative activities.

In the first place, is it possible that the duality which makes them two activities, rather than one, can be maintained in the Absolute ? For if it cannot be maintained, then know-ledge and volition would both be merged in a single form of spirit. We have seen that the object of both is the same—to produce the harmony described in Hegel's definition of the Absolute Idea. What is it that separates them from one another, and is the separation one which can be considered as ultimate ?

The most obvious suggestion is that volition leads directly to action, which knowledge does not, except indirectly by affecting volition. If however we look more closely we shall find that this is not a sufficient distinction. We may perhaps leave out of account the fact that a desire, however strong, for something which we know is perfectly impossible, or something which no action can affect, does not provoke us to action at all. No action tends to be produced by a desire that two and two may make five, or by a desire that the wind may blow from the west. But even in cases where the process of development is taking place, and the harmony between desire and reality is being gradually brought about, it is by no means always the case that it is brought about by action. There are two other alternatives. It may be brought about by a discovery in the field of knowledge, which reveals a harmony which had previously escaped observation. Discovery is itself, certainly, an action. But it is not the act of discovery which here produces the harmony, but the truth which it reveals, and the truth is not an action. We have not gained the harmony because we have changed the environment, but because we have understood it. And the act of discovery is the result of our desire to understand, not of our desire for the result discovered.

The other possible means of reconciliation is by the desire changing itself into conformity with the environment, either through an intellectual conviction that the previous desire was mistaken, or by that process of dialectic development inherent in finite desires.

Let us suppose, for example, that a desire that vindictive justice should exhibit itself in the constitution of the universe finds itself in conflict with the fact, known by empirical observation, that the wicked often prosper. Some degree of harmony between desires and facts may be attained in this case by means of action as affecting the political and social environment. But this alone could never realize the demand. We have however two other possible methods of reconciliation. Philosophy or theology may assure us that there is a future life, and that in it our desires will be fulfilled. Or we may, either by argument or by a gradual development of our notions of the desirable, so change our views as no longer to require that the universe should exhibit vindictive justice. In either case we should have attained to harmony without action following as a consequence of our volition.

Or, secondly, it may be suggested that the distinction lies in the activity or passivity of the mind. In knowledge, it might be said, our object is to create a picture in our minds, answering to the reality which exists outside them, and based on data received from external sources. Since the test of the mental picture is its conformity to the external reality, the mind must be passive. On the other hand, in volition the mind supplies an ideal by means of which we measure outside reality. If the reality does not correspond to our desires, we condemn it as unsatisfactory, and, if the thwarted desires belong to our moral nature, we condemn it as wrong. Here, it might be urged, the mind is in a position of activity.

There is unquestionably some truth in this view. The greater weight is no doubt laid, in knowledge on the external object, in volition on the consciousness of the agent. But we must seek a more accurate expression of it. For the mind is not passive in knowledge, nor purely active in volition. In considering the last argument we saw that the harmony may be produced, wholly or in part, by the alteration of the desires till they coincide with the facts. In so far as this is the case, the mind is in a passive position, and is altered by external facts, whether the result comes from arguments drawn from the existence of those facts, or by reaction from the contact with them in actual life.

We may go farther, and say, not only that this may happen in some cases, but that it must happen in all cases to some extent. For otherwise in the action of mind on the environment we should have left no place for any reaction, and by doing so should deny the reality of that member of the relation

which we condemn to passivity. But if the as yet unharmon-
ized environment was unreal, when compared with the as yet
unembodied ideal, the process will cease to exist. If the
environment, as such, has no existence our demands cannot
be said to be realized in it. If it has real existence, it must
react on our demands.

And again it cannot be said that the mind is purely passive
in knowledge. The data which it receives from outside are
subsumed under categories which belong to the nature of
the mind itself, and the completed knowledge is very different
from the data with which it began. Indeed if we attempt to
consider the data before any reaction of the mind has altered
them we find that they cannot enter into consciousness—
that is, they do not exist. If conceptions without perceptions
are empty, it is no less true that perceptions without conceptions are blind.

Let us make one more effort to find a ground of distinction.
I believe that we may succeed with the following—in knowledge we accept the facts as valid and condemn our ideas if
they do not agree with the facts ; in volition we accept our
ideas as valid, and condemn the facts if they do not agree
with our ideas.

Suppose a case of imperfect harmony. That which, as far
as we can see at the time, is the fundamental nature of our
desires, disagrees with what, as far as we can see at the time,
is the true state of the facts. What is to be done ? The
first thing is, of course, to recognize that something must be
wrong somewhere, since, in the case supposed, there would
be a want of the ideal harmony both in knowledge and volition.
But, when we have realized this, what can we do ? Since
the two sides, the internal and external, are not in harmony,
we cannot accept both as valid. To accept neither as valid
would be impossible—because self contradictory—scepticism
and quietism. We must accept one and reject the other.
Now in knowledge we accept the facts as valid, and condemn
our ideas, in so far as they differ from them, as mistaken.
In volition, on the other hand, we accept the ideas as valid,
and condemn the facts in so far as we differ from them, as

wrong. If it should appear to us that a rational and righteous universe would involve personal immortality, while there were reasons to disbelieve that personal immortality existed, then we should have to take up a double position. On the one hand we should be bound to admit that our longing for immortality would not be gratified, however much we wanted it. On the other hand we should be bound to assert that the universe was wrong in not granting our desires, however certain it was that they would not be granted.

Two words of explanation seem necessary here. In the first place, what has been said assumes that every effort has been made to produce the harmony. We have no right to condemn the universe as evil on account of an unfulfilled desire till we have inquired carefully if it is a mere caprice, or really so fundamental a part of our nature that its realization is essential to permanent harmony. And we are not bound to condemn our ideas as untrue because the facts seem against them at first sight. Secondly, when I have spoken of internal and external, or ideas and facts, I have meant to indicate the opposition of subject and object. An internal phenomenon, whether an idea or a feeling, when taken as an object to be observed by the active subject, counts as an external fact.

I am far from wishing to assert—in fact it is incompatible with the idealist position with which this paper started—that there is in reality any possible want of harmony. That some harmony must exist is evident. Without it we could not have any knowledge at all, and so could never become conscious of any possible want of harmony. And the possible want of *complete* harmony from the point of view of volition involves the existence of *some* harmony between our needs and the facts. For without it we could never demand that the facts should realize our desires—nor indeed could we exist at all. There must be some harmony then, and it is the aim of the critical philosophy—culminating in the Dialectic —to prove that the existence of any harmony involves its existence in full completeness. But, however that may be, some philosophers reject this endeavour, and even those who admit it, must acknowledge that in an infinite number of particular cases they are quite unable to see *where* the harmony is, although on philosophic grounds they may be certain that it must exist somehow. And, finally, even in some cases where we may intellectually perceive the harmony our nature may not be so under the control of our reason, as to enable us to feel the harmony, if it happens to conflict with our passions. In all these cases it will be necessary to act in the face of a want of harmony, and in all these cases we must give the facts the supremacy in the sphere of knowledge and the ideals the supremacy in the sphere of volition upon pain of spiritual high treason.

It has become rather a commonplace lately, since science, for its sins, received the somewhat severe punishment of popularity, that one of our most imperative duties is intellectual humility, to admit the truth to be true, however unpleasant or unrighteous it may appear to us. But, correlative to this duty there is another no less imperative—that of ethical self-assertion. If no amount of ' ought ' can produce the slightest ' is,' it is no less true that no amount of ' is ' can produce ' ought.' It is of the very essence of human will, and of that effort to find the fundamentally desirable which we call morality, that it claims the right to judge the whole universe. This is the categorical imperative of the idealists, and we find it again in Mill's preference of hell to the flattering of an unjust deity. Nor is it only in the interests of virtue as such that the will is categorical. Pleasure, unless absolutely wrong, is no more to be treated lightly than virtue. If all the gods of all the universes, from Oannes of the Chaldeans to the Unknowable of Mr. Herbert Spencer united to give me one second's unnecessary toothache, I should not only be entitled, but bound, to judge and to condemn them. We have no more right to be servile than to be arrogant. And while our desires must serve in the kingdom of the true, they rule in the kingdom of the good.

We must note in passing that we are quite entitled to argue that a thing is because it ought to be, or ought to be because it is, when we have once satisfied ourselves that the harmony does exist, and that the universe is essentially rational and righteous. To those who believe in a benevolent God, for example, it is perfectly competent to argue that we must be immortal because the absence of immortality would make life a ghastly farce, or that toothache must be good because God sends it. It is only when, or in as far as, the harmony has not yet been established, that such an argument is an unhallowed assignment unto God of the things which are Cæsar's, and unto Cæsar of the things which are God's, to the embarrassment of both parties.

If, then, we have succeeded in finding the distinction between knowledge and volition, we must conclude that it is one which can have no place in the Absolute. For we have seen that the distinction turns upon which side of the opposition shall give way, when there is opposition, and not harmony, between the subject and the object. In the Absolute there can be no opposition, for there can be no want of harmony, as the Absolute is, by its definition, the harmony made perfect. And not only can there be no want of harmony, but there can be no possibility that the harmony should ever become wanting. Everything must have a cause, and if it were possible that the harmony which exists at a given time should subsequently be broken, a cause must coexist with the harmony capable of destroying it. When the harmony is universal, the cause would have to exist within it. Now when we speak of things which are only harmonious with regard to certain relations, or to a certain degree, we can speak of a harmony which carries within it the seeds of its own dissolution. Such is the life of an organism, which necessarily leads to death, or the system of a sun and planets, which collapses as it loses its energy. But when we come to consider a harmony which pervades objects in all their relations, and which is absolutely perfect, anything which could produce a disturbance in it, would be itself a disturbance, and is excluded by the hypothesis. This will be seen more clearly if we remember that the harmony is one of conscious spirit. The consciousness must be all-embracing, and therefore the cause of the possible future disturbance must be recognized as such. And the possibility of such a disturbance must produce at once some degree of doubt, fear, or anxiety, which would itself and at once be fatal to harmony.

It follows that, since not even the possibility of disturbance can enter into the Absolute, the distinction between knowledge and volition, depending as it does entirely on the course pursued when such a disturbance exists, becomes, not only irrelevant, but absolutely unmeaning. And in that case the life of Spirit, when the Absolute has been attained, will consist in the harmony which is the essence of both knowledge and volition, but will have lost all those characteristics which differentiate them from one another, and give them their specific character.

Before passing on to further arguments, we must consider some objections which may be raised to what has been already said. The most obvious, perhaps, is that no trace of the asserted union of knowledge and volition is to be found in our experience. We often find, in some particular matter, a harmony which is, at any rate, so far complete that no want of it is visible, in which our desires and our environment show no perceptible discordance. And yet knowledge and volition, though in agreement, do not show the least sign of losing their distinctness. On the one hand we assert that a given content is real, and on the other hand that it is desirable. But the difference of meaning between the predicates ' true ' and ' good ' is as great as ever.

But no harmony to which we can attain in the middle of a life otherwise inharmonious can ever be perfect, even over a limited extent. For as we saw above (pp. 222–3) the universal reciprocity which must exist between all things in the same universe would prevent anything from becoming perfect, until everything had done so. And a harmony between two imperfections could never be complete, since the imperfect remains subject to the dialectic, and is therefore transitory. Even supposing, however, that such a limited harmony could be perfect, it could never exclude the possibility of disturbance. The possibility was excluded in the case of a universal harmony, because the ground of disturbance could not exist within the harmony, and there was nowhere

233

else for it to exist. But here such a ground might always be found outside. And while there is any meaning in even the possibility of a discrepancy between our demands and reality, there is no reason to expect the separation of knowledge and volition to cease.

To our assertion that knowledge and volition, as they become perfect, are merged in a unity which is neither of them, it may be objected that we have already said that this unity will contain all that part of both activities which constitutes their real meaning—what Hegel calls their ' truth.' All that would be found in perfect knowledge and volition is to be found there, and nothing is left out except the negative element, which, in so far as it *is* found, marks the imperfection of the subject matter. Ought we not rather to say, therefore, that in the Absolute we find both knowledge and volition, instead of saying that we find neither. It is no doubt true that all the ' truth ' of both sides will be found in the resulting unity, and that nothing but a negative element is left out. But then it is just this negative element which distinguishes knowledge and volition from one another, and so makes them what they are in ordinary life, where they are unquestionably distinguished from one another. The ' truth ' of the two may be found in the unity. But the point of our argument has been that, as separate things, they are imperfect, and therefore it is that element in their present condition which is not their ' truth,' which separates them, and makes them the activities we know. To say that they are both contained in a unity is really equivalent to saying that neither of them is there. For all that makes their duality, is their opposition to one another, and before they could be brought into such a unity, their opposition, and therefore their duality, must have vanished.

Again, it may be said that the Absolute, as the end of the dialectic process, and as summing up in itself all the meaning of that process, must contain not only the positive element which is found in knowledge and volition, but also that quality, whatever it was, which caused them in the lower stages of the process to appear as independent and opposed activities.

If we admit that this demand is one which may fairly be made on the synthesis of a process, we may answer the objection by pointing out that, if the meaning of the past imperfection is to be found in the synthesis, it must be a meaning which explains it away. For in no other form could the explanation of the opposition be found in the unity. And if the meaning is one of this sort, then it still remains true that knowledge and volition, as such, can have no place in the Absolute.

Our attention has so far been directed to an attempt to prove, by means of a comparison between the nature of the Absolute itself and the nature of knowledge and volition, that the process of the dialectic must have passed beyond knowledge and volition before it can reach the Absolute. It is also, I think, possible to arrive at this conclusion without carrying our inquiries beyond the characteristics of the two separate forms. For these bear in themselves the mark of their finitude and transitoriness, since they postulate, throughout their activities, a goal which they can never reach. We started this inquiry on the basis of an idealistic philosophy, and we are therefore entitled to assert that every postulate which Spirit makes must be realized, either in itself, or by the attainment of a higher end in which it is transcended. If knowledge and volition, then, cannot realize their own ideal, we are bound to hold that the dialectic process will not stop with them, but will carry us forward to some higher stage where the realization will be found. Or—to directly apply to this special case the grounds on which idealism bases its conviction of the general rationality of the universe—we may put the case this way. If it be found that each act of knowledge and volition postulates the ideal, we shall have to choose between admitting the validity of the ideal, and denying the validity of all knowledge and volition. The latter is impossible, because self-contradictory. The very statement or thought which explicitly made the assertion would implicitly deny it—deny it as to volition, because to make an assertion is to act, and deny it as to knowledge because we should assert the validity of a proposition. If an ideal is implied in all

235

knowledge and volition, therefore, we have no alternative but to admit its validity, and to account nothing ultimate which leaves it unrealized.

This ideal is (cp. p. 226) the combination of complete unity between the subject and object with complete differentiation between them. Leaving volition for the present, let us consider, first, whether knowledge does postulate this, and then whether it can realize it.

Knowledge is a state of the subject's mind which gives information as to the nature of the object. This implies a unity between the two. Of the elements of knowledge some are given as data from outside by the object, and that these should be able to pass into the mind of the subject indicates a connection between them. On the other hand, some elements of knowledge—the categories—are supplied by the mind itself, and that we should be able to predicate of the object that which is supplied us by the nature of the subject clearly implies a community of nature between them. And the differentiation is no less necessary than the unity. From the point of view of knowledge, the primary importance of differentiation may be said to lie in the necessity that the object should get its due, though the individuality of the subject is as essential. If the fact that the knowledge is ours, involves the unity of the subject and object, the fact that the knowledge is of something outside us involves their differentiation. To destroy the reality or significance of the external object of knowledge, is to destroy the reality or significance of knowledge, to which the assertion that it is true of something outside itself is essential. No one is likely to deny the existence of the subject in knowledge, and so, if the unity is pressed to the exclusion of the differentiation, it is the object that must suffer. But as the object vanishes, knowledge changes into dreams or fancies, and these, however interesting as objects of knowledge, are absolutely different from knowledge itself.

All knowledge thus requires the combination of unity and differentiation. Complete knowledge will require the combination of complete unity with complete differentiation.

But, more than this, all knowledge, however imperfect and fragmentary, implies the completeness of both elements, and has only truth and validity, in so far as it is justified in demanding this postulate. In all knowledge we combine and arrange the data by means of some category. As was mentioned in the last paragraph, we have no direct evidence whatever of the applicability of these categories to anything outside us, for they are not given in the data which we receive from outside. They cannot be communicated by the senses which are our only avenues of approach to the object. We cannot smell Casuality, nor taste Teleology, nor see Organic Unity. And yet we apply these categories drawn from the nature of our own minds to the outside reality. In so far as we do so, we assume a unity of nature between the mind which is the subject of knowledge, and the external reality which is its object. Now the Dialectic shows that to assert any one category of reality is to assert all. And therefore any single act of knowledge involves the predication of all the categories as part of the nature of the object, as we already know them to be of the subject. This again is an assertion of the entire unity between the two, so that my knowledge of a single truth about an object involves the assertion that it is possible for me to know it through and through. But we have seen that if the unity overpowers the differentiation knowledge ceases. If therefore complete unity is implied, there must be also implied complete differentiation.

Knowledge postulates, then, this combination of antithetical qualities. Is it possible that the postulate can ever be realized in knowledge itself?

The action of knowledge consists in ascribing predicates to the objects of knowledge. (In logic, that to which the predicates are ascribed is termed the subject. But since I have been using the word subject, in its epistemological sense, to denote the knowing consciousness, I shall continue to speak of the subject of the propositions which that consciousness contains as the object as distinguished from its qualities, or specifically as the *logical* subject). All our knowledge of the object we owe to the predicates which we ascribe to it. But our object is not a mere assembly of predicates. There is also the unity in which they cohere, which may be called epistemologically the abstract object, and logically the abstract subject.

Here—as in most other places in the universe—we are met by a paradox. The withdrawal of the abstract object leaves nothing but a collection of predicates, and a collection of predicates, taken by itself, is a mere unreality. Predicates cannot exist without a central unity in which they can cohere. But when we inquire what is this central unity which gives reality to the object, we find that its unreality is as certain as the unreality of the predicates, and perhaps even more obvious. For if we attempt to make a single statement about this abstract object—even to say that it exists—we find ourselves merely adding to the number of predicates, and not attaining our purpose—to know what the substratum was in which all the predicates inhere, which is not assisted by knowing that another predicate inheres in it.

Thus the abstract object is an unreality, and yet, if it is withdrawn the residue of the concrete object becomes an unreality too. Such a position is not uncommon in metaphysics. All reality is concrete. All concrete ideas can be split up into abstract elements. If we split up the concrete idea which corresponds to some real thing into its constituent abstractions, we shall have a group of ideas which in their unity correspond to a reality, but when separated are self-contradictory and unreal.

The position of the abstract object reminds us of a similar abstraction which has received more attention in metaphysics—the abstract subject. This has been called by Kant the synthetic unity of apperception, and is sometimes spoken of less technically, though not without ambiguity, as personality or self-consciousness. While on the one hand mental phenomena could not be a part of spiritual life, or indeed be conceived as existing at all, unless they cohered in, or referred to, a central unity, by virtue of their connection with which they all form part of one self-conscious life—on the other hand, this central unity, considered apart from the phenomena which find their centre in it, is a mere blank, a form without content, of which nothing can be said. This analogy between the abstract object and the abstract subject is very suggestive, especially when we remember that in an idealist philosophy all reality is Spirit, and that consequently its central unity is both an abstract subject and an abstract object. We shall have to return to this point later on.

This abstract object is described by Mr. F. H. Bradley, in an article entitled ' Reality and Thought ' (*Mind*, xiii, p. 370), from which I first got the idea of this paper. He speaks of it as the This of the object, in opposition to the What, which consists of the predicates we have found to be applicable to it. While knowledge remains imperfect, the This has in it the possibility of an indefinite number of other qualities, besides the definite number which have been ascertained and embodied in predicates. When knowledge becomes perfect—as perfect as it is capable of becoming—this possibility would disappear, as it seems to me, although Mr. Bradley does not mention this point. In perfect knowledge all qualities of the object would be known, and the coherence of our knowledge as a systematic whole would be the warrant for the completeness of the enumeration. But even here the abstract This would still remain, and prove itself irreducible to anything else. To attempt to know it is like attempting to jump on the shadow of one's own head. For all propositions are the assertion of a partial unity between the subject and the predicate. The This on the other hand is just what distinguishes the subject from the predicate.

It is the existence of the This which renders it impossible to regard knowledge as a self-subsistent whole, and makes it necessary to consider it merely as an approach to something else. In the This we have something which is at once within and without knowledge, which it dares not neglect and cannot deal with.

For when we say that the This cannot be known, we do not mean, of course, that we cannot know of its existence. We know of its existence, because we can perceive, by analysis, that it is an essential element of the concrete object. But

239

the very definition which this analysis gives us shows that we can know nothing more about the This—that there is, indeed, nothing more to know. To know merely that something exists is to present a problem to knowledge which it must seek to answer. To know that a thing exists is to know it as immediate and contingent. Knowledge demands that such a thing should be mediated and rationalized. This, as we have seen, cannot be done. The impossibility is no reproach to the rationality of the universe, for reality is no more mere mediation than it is mere immediacy, and the immediacy of the This combines with the mediation of the What to make up the concrete whole of the Spirit. But it *is* a reproach to the adequacy of knowledge as an activity of Spirit that it should persist in demanding what cannot and ought not to be obtained. Without immediacy, without the central unity of the object, the mediation and the predicates which make up knowledge would vanish as unmeaning. Yet knowledge, is compelled by its own nature to attempt this suicidal exploit, and to feel itself baffled and thwarted when it cannot succeed. Surely an activity with such a contradiction inherent in it can never be a complete exponent of the Absolute.

In the first place the existence of the This is incompatible with the attainment of the ideal of unity in knowledge. For here we have an element, whose existence in reality we are forced to admit, but which is characterized by the presence of that which is essentially alien to the nature of the knowing consciousness in its activity. In so far as reality contains a This it cannot be brought into complete unison with the knowing mind, which, as an object, has of course its aspect of immediacy like any other object, but which, as the knowing subject, finds all unresolvable immediacy to be fundamentally opposed to its work of rationalization. The real cannot be completely pictured in the mind, and the unity of knowledge is therefore defective.

And this brings with it a defective differentiation. For while the This cannot be brought into the unity of knowledge, it is unquestionably a part of reality. And so the failure of knowledge to bring it into unity with itself involves that the part of the object which *is* brought into unity with the subject is only an abstraction from the full object. The individuality of the object thus fails to be represented, and so its full differentiation from the subject fails to be represented also. The result is that we know objects, so to speak, from outside, whereas, to know them in their full truth, we ought to know them from inside. That every object [1] has a real centre of its own appears from the dialectic. For we have seen that the conclusion from that is that all reality consists of spirits, which are individuals. And, apart from this, the fact that the object is more or less independent as against us—and without some such independence knowledge would be impossible, as has been already pointed out—renders it certain that every object has an individual unity to some extent. Now knowledge fails to give this unity its right. The unity of the object is found in its This, and its This is to knowledge something alien. It sees it to be the centre of the object in a sense, but only a dead, mathematical centre, not a living and unifying centre, such as we know that the synthetic unity of apperception is to our own lives, which we have the advantage of seeing from inside. The centre of the object appears to us as a mere *caput mortuum*, produced by abstracting all possible predicates, not a real centre, such as the centre of gravity in a body, much less a vivifying centre, such as the animal life in an organism. And while we thus view the object from our standpoint, and not its own, knowledge can never represent the object so faithfully as to attain its own ideal.

And here we see the reason why knowledge can never represent quite adequately the harmony of the universe.

---

[1] In saying ' every object,' I do not necessarily mean every chair, or even every amoeba. Behind all appearance there is reality. This reality we believe, on the authority of the Dialectic, to be divided into individuals. It is these centres of reality which I here call objects. But as to *how many* centres of reality there may be behind a given mass of phenomena we do not know. Of course each self-conscious spirit is one object and no more. It is with regard to the reality behind what is called inorganic matter that the difficulty arises.

We saw above (p. 220) that when knowledge should have reached the greatest perfection of which it is capable there would still remain one question unanswered, Why is the whole universe what it is, and not something else? The possibility of asking this question depends, as it seems to me, on the existence of the This, which knowledge is unable to bring into unity with the knowing subject. The This is essential to the reality of the object, and it is that part of the object to which it owes its independence of the subject. And the question naturally arises, Why should not this core of objectivity have been clothed with other qualities than those which it has, and with which the subject finds itself in harmony?

The question arises because the existence of the harmony is dependent on the This. The This alone gives reality to the object. If it vanished, the harmony would not change into a disharmony, but disappear altogether. And the This, as we have seen, must always be for knowledge a something alien and irrational, because it must always be an unresolved immediate. Now a harmony which depends on something alien and irrational must always appear contingent and defective. Why is there a This at all? Why is it just those qualities which give a harmony for us that the favour of the This has raised to reality? To answer these questions would be to mediate the This, and that would destroy it.

It may be urged, as against this argument, that we do not stand in such a position of opposition and alienation towards the objective This. For we ourselves are objects of knowledge as well as knowing subjects, and our own abstract personality, which is the centre of our knowledge, is also the This of an object. Now the interconnection of the qualities of all different objects, which would be perfect in perfect knowledge, would enable us to show why all reality existed, and why it is what it is, if we could only show it of a single fragment of reality. The difficulty lies in reaching the abstract realness of the real at all by means of knowledge. And if, by means of our own existence as objects, we were able to establish a single connection with the objective world, in which the immediate would not mean the alien, no other connection would be required. The last remaining opposition of the object to the subject would disappear.

The objection, however, does not hold. For the self as the object of knowledge is as much opposed to the self as the subject as any other object could be. We learn its qualities by arguments from data given by the ' internal sense ' as we learn the qualities of other objects by arguments from data given by the external senses. We are immediately certain of the first, but we are no less immediately certain of the second. And the central unity of our own nature is no more an object of direct knowledge than the central unities of other objects, and for the same reasons. We become aware of its existence by analysing what is implied in having ourselves as objects, and we become aware of the central unities of other things by analysing what is implied in having them for objects. The one is no more immediate than the other. Of course our own selves are not really alien to us, although we know them immediately. But then the existence of knowledge implies, as we have seen, that other reality is not really alien to us, although we know it immediately. It is knowledge which fails to represent the immediate except as alien.

We have thus traced the origin of the abstract possibility of disharmony in the universe. We saw in the first part of this essay that it was unmeaning, since it would be impossible for any reality to be destroyed or altered, unless the same happened to all reality, and the possibility of this, which has no common ground with actuality, is an unmeaning phrase. And we have now seen another reason why the possibility is unmeaning. For we have traced it to the persistence of thought, in considering its essential condition as its essential enemy. The existence of such a miscalled possibility, therefore, tells nothing against the rationality of the universe. But it does tell against the adequacy of knowledge as an expression of the universe. By finding a flaw in perfection, where no flaw exists, it pronounces its own condemnation.

If the possibility is unmeaning, knowledge is imperfect in being compelled to regard it as a possibility.

It seems at first sight absurd to talk of knowledge as inadequate. If it was so, how could we know it ? What right have we to condemn it as imperfect when the judge is *ipso facto* the same person as the culprit ? This is, of course, so far true, that if knowledge could not show us its own ideal, we could never know that it did not realize it. But there is a great difference between indicating an ideal and realizing it. It is possible—and I have endeavoured to show that it is the fact—that knowledge can do the one, and not the other. When we ask about the abstract conditions of reality, it is able to demonstrate that harmony must exist, and that immediacy is compatible with it, and essential to it. But when it is asked to show in detail *how* the harmony exists, which it has shown *must* exist, it is unable to do so. There is here no contradiction in our estimate of reason, but there *is* a contradiction in reason, which prevents us from regarding it as ultimate, and which forces us to look for some higher stage, where the contradiction may disappear.

Let us now turn to volition, and consider, in the first place, whether it also implies the combination of complete unity with complete differentiation, and, in the second place, whether it also is unable to realize the ideal which it sets before itself.

That volition implies unity is tolerably obvious. Its demand is that an ideal which it finds in the mind should be realized in the objects round it—that is, that the mind and the object should be brought into unity. And with the unity must come the differentiation. The primary interest of volition may be said to be in the differentiation of the subject, while in knowledge it lies rather in the differentiation of the object. The desirable would cease to be such, if we so completely identified ourselves with the pursuit, that, in attaining our end, we did not distinguish ourselves from it. That we find satisfaction in a thing proves our unity with it, but that it is we who find satisfaction proves our differentiation. Otherwise we should not so much find satisfaction, as lose ourselves.

But that the subject should be completely differentiated involves that the object should be so too. For the two developments are inseparable. The logical necessity of this can be shown by the dialectic, and empirical examples of it are furnished by psychology, for example, in the observation of the minds of children. As the consciousness of an individual subject to be satisfied disappears, satisfaction gradually becomes, first the passivity of satiated instinct, then the still lower stability which arises when an unconscious thing is in harmony with its environment, and finally even harmony disappears in a blank unity equivalent to nonentity. And in each of these stages the individuality of the object falls out of the unity in proportion to the disappearance of the subject. Besides this, the fact that all volition can be expressed in the form of a demand carries its satisfaction, of necessity, beyond the consciousness which demands it, and so far as it is not perceived to be embodied in some real object, it is not perceived at all.

Thus, in so far as the satisfaction of volition is attained, it involves complete unity and complete differentiation. And, going farther than this, we may say that any satisfaction, however incomplete, implicitly asserts the complete unity and differentiation of the subject which experiences it and the object which affords it. For the existence of any satisfaction shows a unity which is equivalent to the assertion of some community of nature between the two. Now the dialectic shows us that, if we are able to assert of any subject-matter any category of the logic, we are entitled to proceed to the Absolute Idea ; and we are thus able to assert of both subject and object that they are manifestations of that idea, and—therefore—perfectly in accord, and perfectly distinct.

How far can volition carry out the ideal which it thus places before itself ? In considering this question, we find that we must distinguish, in the object of satisfaction, the same two elements which we have already observed in the object of knowledge. The satisfaction which an object affords to us is due to certain qualities which harmonize with the ideals of our volition. But an object is not an assembly of qualities. Besides them we must have the central unity, which gives uniqueness and reality to the object, which is not a quality, but which determines that the qualities exist—the difference, in short, between the hundred thalers which will pay your debts—to use Kant's immortal example—and the exactly similar hundred thalers which only amuse your imagination.

We are confronted, then, in volition, by the same distinction in the object between the This and the What which is apparent in the object of knowledge. And with it recurs the same difficulty. We can no more experience satisfaction, without the This, than we can have knowledge. Yet it is as impossible to find satisfaction in the This, as it is to know it. For the This has no qualities in which we can find the demands of our nature realized. It may be objected that it is a This, that it is real, and so are we, and that this is a community in which satisfaction might be found. But, as Mr. Bradley has shown in his *Logic* (p. 69), this can never be true as a symbol, and we find no community between things in the fact that each of them has a This in it. That to us as real beings there should be opposed in the This an immediate reality is a ground rather of discord than of harmony. The only quality which the immediately real can be said to have is self-assertion, and a common desire for self-assertion is not a ground for concord. The reality of the object would, taken by itself, be in such harmony with our own reality, as was produced between the Emperor and the King of France on the occasion when they wanted precisely the same thing—namely the city of Milan.

The existence of the This in the object will thus be fatal, in the first place, to the unity of satisfaction. For in the This we find an element of the object which will not allow itself to be regarded as a means to our end. In any case, as an independent reality, it offers a negative resistance to our consideration of the universe from our own point of view. And the results of the dialectic make this into a positive challenge, when we learn that all reality must be individual like ourselves, and must, like ourselves, have an end of its own.

The assertion that perfect satisfaction requires us to consider everything else as a means to our own end may arouse some opposition. Is there not such a thing as unselfish action, as self-sacrifice ? And in that highest content of satisfaction which we call moral good, is it not laid down by high authority that the fundamental law is to treat other individuals as ends and not as means ?

It is undoubtedly true that our satisfaction need not be selfish. But it must, I maintain, be self-regarding, and self-centred. This implies no moral blame, and no denial of disinterested action, unless we assume, contrary to the corollaries of Idealism, that the nature of Spirit is essentially selfish. But it does imply, I think, that the existence of objects independent of ourselves, while necessary to satisfaction, is incompatible with its purity.

Many of our desires are not for our own pleasure—such as the desire to win a game, or to eat when we are hungry. But these are still desires for our own good. If the result did not appear to us one which would be desirable for us, we should not desire it. Put in this way, indeed, the fact that volition and its satisfaction are self-centred appears almost a truism. And it is possible that a sense of duty or a feeling of sympathy may determine us to unselfish action— to action painful to ourselves, and which, apart from those feelings, we could not regard as our good. But such action implies that we do regard virtue, or the happiness of others, as our highest good. Even if we take Mill's extreme case of going to hell, we must conceive that the following of virtue as long as possible, even if the result was eternal misery and degradation, presented itself to him as his highest good. Self-sacrifice, strictly speaking, is impossible, and unmoral. We can sacrifice the lower parts of our nature. But if we were not actuated by some part of our nature, the action would cease to be ours. It would fall into the same class as the actions of lunacy, of hypnotism, of unconscious habit. The will is ours, and the motive which determines will must be a motive which has power for us. In other words, our volition is always directed towards our own good, and has always ourselves for its end.

And this is not interfered with by the possibility and the obligation, which unquestionably exist, of regarding other individuals as ends. We may do this with the most absolute sincerity. But if we are asked why we do it, we do not find it an ultimate necessity. We can, and do, insert another term. We may perhaps ascribe our conduct to a sense of sympathy with others. In this case the reference to self is obvious. Or, taking a more objective position, we may say that we do it because it is right. Now the obligation of virtue is admitted by all schools to be purely internal. This is upheld alike by those who imagine it to be an empirical growth, and by those who suppose it eternal and fundamental to Spirit. That virtue must be followed for its own sake— and otherwise our motive is not virtuous—is only another way of saying that we conceive virtue to be our highest good. Kant made the treatment of individuals as ends the primary law of morals. But the existence of morals depended on the Categorical Imperative. And the obligation of this on the moral agent—his recognition of it as binding—was equivalent to an assertion that *he* adopted it. The adoption must not be conceived as optional or morality would become capricious ; but it must be conceived as self-realization, or it would be unmeaning to speak of the agent, or his motive, as virtuous.

Now it is not recognition of this kind which the individuality of the object demands. The object as real claims to be considered as an end in itself, not because we shall in that way best fulfil our own ends, but in its own right. And this prevents perfect unity, for volition can acquiesce in nothing which claims in its own right, and which is entirely indifferent as to whether its claim is convenient to the subject or not. It can grant only recognition analogous to that which some moralists give to the duty of kindness to animals, when they deny that the lower animals have any rights to be violated, but recommend kindness to them as producing a desirable state of mind in the agent. And to such recognition as this, the This of the object will appear alien and inharmonious.

In the same way, the differentiation also must be imperfect.

That part of the object which is brought into unity with the subject is only a part, and the omission, though only of an abstraction, renders what is left abstract only. It is not in the objects themselves that we find satisfaction, but in the results of the objects as affecting ourselves. The objective world may be said to resemble for us the fragments of a child's dissected map. Only their external relations to ourselves and to one another have any significance for us. They are individuals, they live from within outwards. But as we find satisfaction in them, we are aware of them from without inwards, and their centre, instead of being a living unity is a dead abstraction. We fail, then, here as in knowledge, to do justice to the independence of the object.

And, as in knowledge, we find that the harmony is imperfect. We found there that the rationality of things depended in the long run on the immediate fact that they are what they are. So here we find that their righteousness—their response to the demands of our own nature—depends on the same fact. And, for volition as well as for knowledge, this immediate presents itself as a contingent. The immediate is as non-friendly as it is non-rational, and retains always the possibility of becoming actually hostile, as of becoming actually irrational. The immediacy of the object is for us a dead abstraction, and we are haunted by the possibility of its having had other qualities than those which it has as a matter of fact. Our method of looking at it has brought it and its qualities into an unreal independence of one another, in which their connection appears contingent. And such a possibility of disharmony is itself disharmony. To expect, however faintly, an evil, is an evil itself.

The possibility is indeed a meaningless one. To say that the righteousness of the universe is contingent on the universe as a whole being what it is, is equivalent to saying that it is not contingent at all. The condemnation must fall on volition itself, since it is unable to bring about complete harmony, owing to its regarding as a defect what is not really a defect. Like knowledge, it slanders the universe. The immediate is necessary for all satisfaction. The inherent

PHILOSOPHICAL STUDIES

contingency of the immediate can be shown to be a delusion. But it is a delusion that volition cannot get rid of. If it is balked in its attempt to treat everything as a means it declares its work imperfect, and, if it could ever succeed in its attempt, it would find its work destroyed.

To sum up. If this analysis has been correct, it will prove that neither knowledge nor volition can completely express the harmony of Spirit, since their existence implies that an immediate object does exist, while their perfection would imply that it did not. At the same time the dialectic assures us that the complete harmony must exist, since it is implied in the existence of any harmony at all, which again is implied in the undeniable existence of knowledge and volition. We must therefore look to find the complete expression of the harmony, which will be the ultimate form of Spirit, elsewhere.

Of the nature of this form we are now in a position to say two things. In the first place, it must synthesize the opposition which has been pointed out to exist between knowledge and volition, in so far as knowledge accepts the object, and volition the subject, as valid in the case of a disagreement. In the second place, it must be able to recognize the immediate without finding it to be necessarily alien or contingent.

This is all we can tell of the nature of the ultimate form of Spirit by general reasoning. And if that ultimate form is something of which, in our present lives, we can have no consciousness, it will be all that we can tell about it at all. But if we find that part of our present experience answers these tests, we may infer that the Absolute, though far more perfect, is in nature similar to this experience, and again, that this part of our lives, though doubtless greatly deficient in purity and intensity, is a fully concrete reality, requiring to be developed only, to reach perfection, and not like knowledge and volition, to be synthesized and transformed.

Can we find any such experience ? Knowledge and volition have been tried and found wanting. The only remaining independent element of consciousness is feeling, that is, pleasure and pain. This however will not serve our purpose. It does not enable us to regard an immediate object as not alien, for it has nothing to do with objects at all. It is a pure self-reference of the subject. And this, while it makes it in some ways the most intimate and personal part of our lives, prevents it from ever being self-subsistent, or filling consciousness by itself. For our self-consciousness only develops by bringing itself in contact with an external object. The definition of the Absolute Idea shows that the appreciation of an object is necessary to Spirit. Feeling therefore is only an element in states of consciousness, not a state by itself. We are conscious of relations to an object, and in this consciousness we see an element of pleasure or pain. But pleasure or pain by itself can never make the content of our minds.

The one thing left is emotion. For our present purpose, we may perhaps roughly define emotion as a state of consciousness tinged with feeling, or rather, since feeling is never quite absent, a state of consciousness, in so far as it is tinged with feeling. Here we have all three elements of consciousness. We are aware of the existence of an object; since we are brought in relation to it, we recognize it as more or less harmonizing with our desires, and we are conscious of pleasure or pain consequent on the greater or less extent to which knowledge and volition have succeeded in establishing a harmony. The state of mind may be a mere aggregate of three independent activities. In that case it will be useless for us. But it may turn out to be the concrete unity from which the three activities gained their apparent independence by illegitimate abstraction.[1] If so, it may not impossibly be the synthesis for which we are searching.

It is clear that no emotion can be the ultimate form of Spirit, unless it regards all objects as individual spirits. For the dialectic shows us that, till we regard them thus, we do not regard them rightly. And the dialectic tells us also, that we

[1] [In *The Nature of Existence*, II, ch. xli, McTaggart adopts the latter alternative, holding that ' the cogitation of that to which the emotion is directed, and the emotion towards it, are the same mental state, which has both the quality of being a cogitation of it, and the quality of being an emotion directed towards it.' This theory of Emotion is analogous to Dr. G. E. Moore's view of Volition, cf. *Principia Ethica* : Cambridge, 1922, p. 136.—*Ed.*]

do not regard them rightly till we know them to be in complete harmony with ourselves, and with one another. To regard all that we find round us as persons, to feel that their existence is completely rational, and that through it our own nature is realized, to experience unalloyed pleasure in our relations to them—this is a description to which only one emotion answers. We saw in the first part of this essay that the only value and interest of knowledge and volition, when pushed as far as they would go, lay in love. Here we go a step farther. If anything in our present lives can resolve the contradictions inherent in knowledge and volition, and exhibit the truth which lies concealed in them, it must be love.

Let us examine how far this hypothesis agrees with the tests mentioned above. In the first place, the absolute form of Spirit must transcend the opposition between knowledge and volition as to the side of the relation which is to be considered valid in case of discrepancy. Neither side in the Absolute must attain any pre-eminence over the other, since such pre-eminence has only meaning with regard to the possibility of imperfection.

Neither side has the pre-eminence in love. It is not essential to it that the subject shall be brought into harmony with the object, as in knowledge, nor that the object shall be brought into harmony with the subject, as in volition. It is sufficient that the two terms should *be* in harmony. The subject refuses here to be forced into the abstract position of either slave or master. To conceive the relation as dependent on the conformity of the subject to the object would ignore the fact that the subject has an ideal which possesses its rights, even if nothing corresponds to it in reality. To conceive the relation, on the other hand, as dependent on the conformity of the object to the subject, would be to forget that the emotion directs itself towards persons and not towards their relations with us. When, as in volition, the harmony results from the conformity of the object to the subject, any interest in the object as independent can only exist in so far as it realizes the end of the subject, and is so subordinate. But here our interest in the object is not dependent on our interest in the subject. It is identical with it. We may as well be said to value ourselves because of the relation to the object, as the object because of its relation to ourselves.

This complete equilibrium between subject and object is the reason why love cannot be conceived as a duty on either side. It is not our duty to love others. (I am taking the unusual, and almost indecent, course of using the word love, in an abstract essay, to mean what it meant for Dante and Tennyson.) It is not the duty of others to be lovable by us. In knowledge and volition, where one side was to blame for any want of harmony, there was a meaning in saying that the harmony ought to be brought about. But here, where the sides have equal rights, where neither is bound to give way, no judgment can be passed. You can only say that the absence of the harmony proves the universe to be not yet perfect.

And, as this harmony subordinates neither side to the other, it is so far qualified to completely express the Absolute. It needs for its definition no reference to actual or possible defects. It is self-balanced, and can be self-subsistent.

Let us pass to the second test. Can we find here anything that will undo the havoc which the existence of the This has worked with knowledge and volition? The immediacy of the object we cannot hope to transcend. With it would vanish all mediation and all reality. But can we find here some point of view which will save us from the necessity of regarding the immediate as the contingent and the alien? I believe that we can.

We must remember, in the first place, that there is already present in knowledge and volition, though not as their object, an immediate which does not appear to us contingent and alien. This is the immediate reality of the self as subject. (When the self becomes an object of knowledge, it has the characteristics of other objects, and presents the same difficulties as they do, cp. above, p. 242–3). We are as certain of the uniqueness, reality, and immediacy of our own selves, as we are of the same qualities in outside objects. Yet we feel no opposition, no alienation, between the abstract self and its abstract qualities. If we look at ourselves as if they were something outside ourselves, we lose this advantage. But the self in its characteristic position—as the centre of our consciousness—has no discord between its immediate reality and its mediated qualities.

Why is this ? It seems to be attributable to the fact that we see the subject in its concrete unity—the only way in which we can see anything as it really is. There is, of course, no need to bring the subject into unity with itself. And there is, therefore, no necessity to distort it, by analysing it into its two elements, each of which, if considered as an independent reality, would contradict the other and be self-contradictory. We see the two elements in the unity in which they really exist, in which they have no self-subsistence as against one another, and in which they show no opposition or contradiction.

But the object has to be brought into harmony with the subject. Knowledge and volition can only do this by producing or demonstrating the community of the What of the two sides. There is no community of the This, for the nature of the This is to be unique. Hence knowledge and volition, dealing with the What, and leaving the This as an untreatable residuum, have erected the two sides into two pseudo-independent realities. Hence the contradiction which haunts them. For the two sides, as abstracted from the concrete whole, imperiously postulate one another, and we can see that either by itself is unmeaning. Yet to bring them side by side is useless. A concrete unity cannot be restored by the mere juxtaposition of its elements, when by illegitimate abstraction they have acquired illegitimate independence. Such an attempt would be as useless as the stitching together of Cassim after the robbers had once cut him up. And so it follows that the two sides, while demanding one another, equally reject one another, and appear at once essentially connected and essentially alien. Our difficulty with the object lies in our simultaneously holding that the two sides are reciprocally implicated, which is true, and that they may be considered as independent, which is a delusion inseparable from the method used to approach the object. But in the case of the subject this delusion does not appear, and the contradiction does not arise.

If we could regard the object as we regard the subject it would appear from what has been said that our difficulties would vanish. Now the dialectic assures us that every object, which can come into relation with us, is in reality a self-conscious and individual spirit—that is a subject. We may now go a step farther, and say that, if we can regard the object as it regards itself, we shall have attained our end.

Now I submit that, since love is concerned with the object as a person, and not merely the results of the object on the subject, it does look at it as it would look at itself. The interest that I feel in my own life is not due to its having such and such qualities. I am interested in it because it is myself, whatever qualities it may have. I am not of course interested in myself apart from all qualities, which would be an unreal abstraction. But it is the self which gives the interest to the qualities, and not the reverse. With the object of knowledge or volition, on the other hand, our interest is in the qualities which it may possess, and we are only concerned with the This—under which form the self of the object appears in knowledge and volition—because without it the qualities could not exist. But in the harmony which we are now considering, we do not, when it has been once reached, feel that the person is dear to us on account of his qualities, but rather that our attitude towards his qualities is determined by the fact that they belong to him.[1]

In support of this we may notice, in the first place, that love is not necessarily proportioned to the dignity or adequacy of the determining motive. This is otherwise in knowledge and volition. In volition, for example, the depth of our

---

[1] [The distinction is important. Cf. *The Nature of Existence*, II, ch. xli ; especially section 465. We must distinguish ' between an emotion being because of a quality and in respect of a quality. And my contention is that while love may be because of qualities, it is never in respect of qualities.'—*Ed.*]

satisfaction ought to be proportioned to the completeness with which the environment harmonizes with our ideals and to the adequacy with which our present ideals express our fundamental nature. If it is greater than these would justify it is unwarranted and illegitimate. But a trivial cause may determine the direction of very deep emotion. To be born in the same family, or to be brought up in the same house may determine it. It may be determined by physical beauty or by purely sensual desire. Or we may be, as we often are, unable to assign any determining cause at all. And yet the emotion produced may be indefinitely intense and elevated. This would seem to suggest that the emotion is directed to the person, not to his qualities, and that the determining qualities are not the ground of the harmony, but merely the road by which we proceed to that ground. In that case it is natural that they should bear no more necessary proportion to the harmony than the intrinsic value of the key of a safe does to the value of the gold inside it.

Another characteristic worth attention is the manner in which reference to the object becomes almost equivalent to reference to self. We have seen above that all volition implies a self-reference, that however disinterested the motive it can only form part of our life in so far as the self finds its good in it. Now here we seem to come across a state of things in which the value of truth and virtue for us seem to depend on the existence of another person, in the same way as they unquestionably depend for us on our own existence. And this not because the other person is specially interested in truth and virtue, but because all our interest in the universe is conceived as deriving its force from his existence. This is, I suspect, the real meaning of Lovelace, ' I could not love thee, dear, so much, loved I not honour more.' The context indicates that his meaning was, not that honour was dearer to him than his lady, but that his love for her was the motive which gave strength to his sense of duty, independently of, or even opposed to, any desire or interest of hers.

And a third point which denotes that the interest is emphatically personal is found in our attitude when we discover that the relation has been based on some special congruity which has subsequently ceased to exist, or which was wrongly believed in, and never really existed at all. In knowledge and volition such a discovery would put an end to the relation altogether. To go on believing that a thing was rational or satisfactory, because it was so once, or because we once believed that it was so, would be recognized at once as an absurdity. If the cause of the harmony ceases, the harmony ceases too. But here the case is different. If once the relation has existed, any disharmony among the qualities need not, and, we feel, ought not, to injure the harmony between the persons. If a person proves irrational, or imperfect, this may make us miserable about him. It may make us blame him, or, more probably, make us blame God, or whatever substitute for him our religion may allow us. But it will not make us less interested in him, it will not make us less confident that our relation to him is the meaning of our existence, less compelled to view the universe *sub specie amati*. As well might any imperfection or sin in our nature render us less interested in our own condition, or convince us that it was unimportant to ourselves.

It often happens, of course, that such a strain is too hard for affection, and destroys it. But the distinction is that while such a result would be the only proper and natural one in knowledge and volition it is felt here as a condemnation. Knowledge and volition ought to yield. But love, we feel, if it had been strong enough, might have resisted, and ought to have resisted.

It may be urged with considerable force that all these phenomena are compatible with a theory which should attribute them, not to the adequacy with which the fundamental nature of Spirit is here displayed, but to errors and delusions of the human mind, which are well known to psychology. It may be said that the disproportion of the grounds and the intensity of affection merely shows the same want of judgment which, in volition, often makes us see our good in some trivial or unworthy aim. The tendency of affection to regard its entire interest in the universe as centred and mirrored in a single person may be (and has been) ascribed to insanity. And its tendency to persist when the cause which first originated it has departed may be treated as a case of that irrational conservatism which leads us to esteem a building, a rite, or an office, when all ground for esteem has departed.

To refute this, if it can be refuted, would take far more psychological knowledge than I possess. I am not bound to attempt it. For I have not asserted that the existence of these characteristics proves that love is the adequate expression of the Absolute. I have only maintained that these characteristics must be found in any such adequate expression, and that they are not found in any part of our present experience, except in this. Here or nowhere, therefore, can we at present find any representation of the Absolute. It may be added that all that psychological analysis could possibly do would be to prove, not that love had not these characteristics, but that it had them through a mistake, and not through superior penetration. The most that could follow from this would be a conclusion that the absolute state of spirit would differ from love in being better founded. It would be equally true, that the two states, though founded, one on delusion and one on reality, would present fundamentally similar features. At the worst, then, the case would be that we had here an unwarranted anticipation of the Absolute, which would gain its warrant as the universe developed further. And the difference between such an anticipation and an incomplete manifestation (which because of its incompleteness must always be more or less unwarranted) is scarcely perceptible.

It would seem then, that we have here reached a standpoint from which we are able to regard the object as it regards itself. We are able to regard the history and content of the object as a manifestation of its individuality, instead of being obliged to regard the individuality as a dead residuum in which the content inheres. We are able to see the object from within outwards, instead from without inwards. And so its claims to independence and substantiality become no more alien or inharmonious to us than our own.

This recognition of the independence of the object is

absolute. In knowledge and volition that independence was recognized to some extent. In volition, in particular, and more especially in those higher stages in which volition becomes moral, we saw that our own satisfaction depends on realizing the independence and the rights of others, and treating them, not as means, but as ends. But the reasons why this was necessary were always relative to our own self-development. Even with virtue, the ultimate ground of each man's choice of it must always be that he prefers it to vice. And hence this recognition as ends was itself a subordination as means, and the absolute assertion of itself as end, which the object itself made, continued to be something alien and inharmonious.

The position here is different. The subject is no longer in the same position of one-sided supremacy. In knowledge and volition it exists as a centre of which the world of objects is the circumference. This relation continues, for without it our self-consciousness and our existence would disappear. But conjoined with it we have now the recognition of the fact that we ourselves form part of the circumference of other systems of which other individuals are the centre. We know, of course, all through life, that this must be so. But here for the first time we come consciously and essentially into this relation. We are not only part of some one else's world in his eyes, but in our own. And we feel that this dependence on another is as directly and truly self-realization as is the dependence of others on us. All through life self-surrender is the condition of self-attainment. Here, for the first time, they become identical. The result doubtless seems paradoxical. But any change which made it simpler would render it, I think, less correspondent to facts. And if, as I have endeavoured to show, knowledge and volition carry in them defects which prevent our regarding them as ultimate, we need not be alarmed for our formula of the Absolute, should it appear paradoxical to them. It would be in greater danger if they could fully acquiesce in it.

With such a formula our difficulties cease. Here we have perfect unity between subject and object, since it is in the whole object, and not merely in one element of it, that we find satisfaction. And, for the same reason, the object attains its rights in the way of complete differentiation, since we are able, now that we are in unity with the whole of it, to recognize it as a true individual. Again, even unmeaning doubts of the completeness and security of the harmony between subject and object must now vanish, since not even an abstraction is left over as alien, on which scepticism could fix as a possible centre of discord.

It may seem unreasonable to represent the ultimate perfection of Spirit as existing in love, and in love only. For such a uniformity would be impossible in the present stage of our development. Emotion has now only justification and meaning in so far as it springs from, is surrounded by, and results in, acts of knowledge and volition, which remain such and never pass into a higher stage. This, however, is due to the imperfection, and not to the nature of the case. At present there is much of reality in which we are unable to perceive its spiritual nature. Whenever we do recognize a self-conscious individual we can only come into relation with him in so far as that other reality, still conceived as matter, which we call our bodies, can be made organic to our purposes. And finally, even when we have recognized reality as Spirit, the imperfection of our present knowledge leaves a large number of its qualities apparently contingent and irrational. Thus every case in which we have established a personal relation must be surrounded by large numbers of others in which we have not done so. And as all reality is interconnected, the establishment and maintenance of this relation must be connected with, and dependent on the imperfect relations into which we come with the surrounding reality. And, again, the same interconnection brings it about that the harmony with any one object can never be perfect, till the harmony with all other objects is so. Thus our relations with any one object could never be completely absorbed in love—leaving no knowledge and volition untranscended—until the same result was universally attained.

But there is no reason that it should not be attained completely, if attained universally. It is entitled to stand by itself, for it is, as we have seen, self-contained. It does not require a reference to some correlative and opposed activity to make its own nature intelligible, and it does not require any recognition of the possibility of discord. It is the simple and absolute expression of harmony, and, when once the harmony of the whole universe has become explicit, it is capable of expressing the meaning of the whole universe.

Before this ideal could be attained, it is clear that sense-presentation, as a method of obtaining our knowledge of the object, would have to cease. For the only data which are given to us through sense-presentation are purely immediate. To construct a faithful picture of the object, which contains the elements both of immediacy and mediation, it is necessary to combine these data by means of categories found in our own minds. And we have seen (cp. p. 254–5) that the attempt to reconstruct the object from the elements of which it is composed cannot restore its concrete unity, but, to some extent, leaves the elements merely side by side, and therefore contradictory. In a complete harmony the object would have to be seen at once in its full reality, as in the so-called 'intellectual intuition' by which, according to some of the older metaphysicians, God perceives the world.

Such an intuition would be incompatible with knowledge and volition. For the action of these forms consists in the mediation of the immediate. It is only by their method of performing this process that they are distinguished from one another. If the object were presented to us as it really is, no process would be necessary to bring about harmony.

Whether such a relation with external objects would be compatible with emotion we cannot decide. Clearly we can never experience it, so long as our souls only act through our bodies, and to inquire what will happen when they do not, would exceed even the licence I have allowed myself in this essay. I will only say that I do not see any imperative reason why they should not be compatible. The impossibility to receive any direct information except about the immediate element of the object rests, so far as we can see, on nothing but the impossibility of receiving any other information through our physical senses. Now physical senses may be necessary means of information while much of the reality, of which we desire to be informed, still takes the shape of matter, and the rest is only known to us in so far as it acts through material bodies. But it seems quite possible that the necessity, which spirits are at present under, of communicating with one another through matter, only exists because the matter happens to be in the way. In that case, when the whole universe is viewed as spirit, so that nothing relatively alien could come between one individual and another, the connection between spirits might very possibly be direct. And, with no imperfect medium to hinder or distort it, it does not seem incredible that the whole nature of the object, and not merely immediate data, should be presented at once.[1]

It may, again, be remarked of the adequate realization of the Absolute, that it must be timeless. For if it were conceived as realized during a finite period of time, the existence of any cause sufficient to determine it to cease at the end of

[1] [McTaggart proposes lengthy and positive arguments in the second volume of *The Nature of Existence* which he claims yield high probability for the suggestions made in this paragraph. He tries to establish, firstly, that there is no impossibility in one self directly and veridically perceiving another self and its parts ; secondly, that in the final (non-temporal) stage of a self's existence it will know clearly and completely selves not so known in its present experience. ' And, as of every substance that we know we shall know clearly and distinctly all its parts to infinity, we shall know clearly and distinctly an infinitely greater number of substances than at present. Our knowledge, also, of all these substances will have the intensity and directness of apparent perception, while at present much of it is in the less vivid form of apparent judgment. There will be emotion towards every substance which we perceive, and the sum of that emotion will be much greater than any in our present experience. . . . Thus the amount of our consciousness which is clear and distinct will be infinitely greater than at present, and its intensity will be greater than at present, so that the good arising from it will be a very great good as compared with our present experience. . . . Again, all good would depend on a single characteristic of the self— its perception of selves and their parts. And the perception of selves and their parts constitute the entire content of each self. Thus we get an absence of conflict, and a positive unity in the internal nature of the self. . . .' (*op. cit.*, pp. 430–1).—*Ed.*]

the period would be incompatible with complete harmony. On the other hand, to imagine it as realized through unending time would be to take the indefinite extensibility, which is all that we can truly predicate of time, as if it were equivalent with actual endless extent. And Hegel has taught us that the infinite of endless repetition cannot be taken as an ultimate term in any valid explanation.

That knowledge and volition should ever become timeless would appear impossible. For their work is to deal with reality which is first presented to them in the form of an unconnected manifold. To grasp a mere plurality like this apparently requires a succession of acts of apprehension ; and succession, of course, involves time. I am very far from venturing to assert that emotion could become timeless. Indeed, we can scarcely at present attach the faintest definite meaning to the words. But I think that the reasons, which make us definitely assert the impossibility of such a change in the previous case, do not apply here. For if, in emotion, we are able to come into contact with the object as it really is, we shall find no disconnected manifold. The object is not, of course, a mere blank unity. It is a unity which manifests itself in multiplicity. But, the multiplicity only exists in so far as it is contained in the unity. And, since the object has thus a real unity of its own, it might perhaps be possible to apprehend the whole of it at once, and not to require that successive apprehension which the synthesis of a manifold, originally given as unconnected, would always require.

It is true, of course, that we cannot conceive the Absolute as connection with a single other person, but rather, directly or indirectly, with all others. But we must remember, again, that the very fact that all reality must be conceived as in perfect unity, forces us to consider individuals not as a mere numerical or mechanical aggregate, but as forming a single whole, only differing from an organism because its parts are far more intimately connected than those of any organism can be. The various individuals therefore must be conceived as forming a differentiated and multiplex whole, but by no means as an unconnected manifold. It might therefore be practicable to dispense with successive acts of apprehension in contemplating the complete whole of the universe, as much as in contemplating the relative whole of a single individual. And in that case, we can see no positive reason why the highest form of emotion should not be free from succession, and from time.

I should be inclined to say, personally, that even at present, the idea of timeless emotion is one degree less unintelligible than that of timeless knowledge and volition—that the most intense emotion has some power of making time seem, if not unreal, at any rate excessively unimportant, which does not belong to any other form of mental activity. But this is a matter of introspection which every person must decide for himself.

How such great and fundamental changes can be made—how knowledge and volition are to pass into love, and a life in time into timelessness—may well seem doubtful. Even if we grant that it must be so, the manner in which the transition can possibly be effected would present many difficulties. But all such transitions, we may reflect, must necessarily appear strained and artificial, till they have taken place. The transition is from two relatively abstract ideas to a more comprehensive one, which synthesizes them. Till the synthesis has taken place, the abstractions have not yet lost the false appearance of substantiality and independence which they acquired by their abstraction from the whole. Till the synthesis has taken place, therefore, the process by which the two sides lose their independence and distinction must appear something, which, although inevitable, is also inexplicable. It is not till the change has been made that we are able to fully realize that all the meaning of the lower lay in the higher, and that what has been lost was nothing but delusion. So, in this case, we must remember that we are not building up love *de novo* out of knowledge and volition, but merely clearing away the mistakes which presented the former to us in the form of the latter. We are not constructing, but discovering. The only reality, if our theory is correct, is in the timeless and absolute harmony. We have not to construct it from the imperfect harmonies now around us, but only to show that these are misrepresentations of it.

I have only left myself room for a few brief words on the more practical aspects of the question. And, in the first place, it will be necessary to meet an objection which will naturally occur to a theory which places the perfection of Spirit in love only. It may be said that the extent and intensity in which this element enters into man's life is not a test of his perfection. Some people who have comparatively little of it we consider as far higher than others who have much. And, which is perhaps a more crucial instance, we find cases in which we regard as a distinct advance a change in a man's life which diminishes his devotion to individuals in comparison with his ardour for abstract truth or abstract good.

The existence of such cases cannot be denied, but need not, I think, be considered incompatible with what has been said. Any harmony which we can attain at present must be very imperfect, and postulates its own completion, at once because of its partial success and of its partial failure. Now the principle of a dialectic is that Spirit cannot advance in a straight line, but is compelled so to speak, to tack from side to side, emphasizing first one aspect of the truth, and then its complementary and contradictory aspect, and then finding the harmony between them. In so far, then, as the harmony is at any time imperfect, because it has not fully grasped the opposites to be reconciled, it can only advance by first grasping them, and then reconciling them. The difference must be first recognized, and then conquered, and between the first stage and the second the harmony will be impaired. The concrete whole may be cut up into the abstract generality of religion and the abstract particularity of passion ; it may be cut up into the abstract submission of the search for truth and the abstract assertion of the search for good ; it may be cut up into abstract intensity deficient in breadth and abstract extension deficient in depth. When any of these divisions happen the harmony will disappear, and yet the change will be an advance, since we shall have entered on the only path by which the harmony can be perfected. In that harmony alone we live. But here, as everywhere in this imperfect world, the old paradox holds good. He who seeks to save his life shall lose it. He who loses his life, for his life's sake, shall find it. (I have ventured to recast the historical form of this maxim.)

The result of the whole investigation would seem to come to this—that it is by love only that we can fully enter into that harmony with others which alone constitutes our own reality and the reality of the universe. We conceive the universe as a spiritual whole, made up of individuals, who have no existence except as manifestations of the whole, as the whole, on the other hand, has no existence except as manifested in them. The individuals, again, find their meaning and reality only in their connection with one another. And this connection is not to be conceived as a mechanical or arbitrary collection of particulars, but as exhibiting some plan or principle, in which the self-differentiation of the universal into the particular, has become so perfect, that from the idea of the whole we could determine any part, and from any part we could determine all the others. The relation in which each individual, as subject, finds himself to the others as objects, is one in which subject and object are in perfect equilibrium and perfect harmony. And in so far as love fulfils its own ideal, it has fulfilled this ideal also. Knowledge and volition, on the other hand, only represented the true connection adequately in so far as they are approximations to and abstractions from love ; in so far as they differ from it and claim independence, they fail either to realize the true connection of reality or to fulfil their own ideal. Our conclusion then is extravagant enough. Love is not only the highest thing in the universe, but the only thing. Nothing else has true reality, everything which has partial reality has it only as an imperfect form of the one perfection.[1]

---

[1] [In *The Nature of Existence*, ii, ch. lxv, McTaggart modified his position on this point. Cf. § 850 : '. . . those thinkers are right who attribute an unique and supreme goodness to love. . . It cannot, I think, be taken as the only good. It seems to me as in-

This love cannot be what is generally called love of God.[1] To discuss this question fully would take us into all the reasons which could be urged—I believe successfully—in favour of the proposition that Idealism finds the ultimate reality of the universe in a unity of persons and not a personal unity. Nor can I stop to inquire whether the word love can be applied to the relations of the finite with the infinite, with any real

dubitable that certain other emotions are good, and that virtue, knowledge, pleasure, and fullness of life are good, as that love is good. Nor can we say that all other goods are dependent on love.' Nor is it true that love is incommensurably better than any other good, for the smallest conceivable increase in love would not be better than the greatest possible increase in knowledge, virtue, pleasure, or fullness of life. Love would, however, hold this supreme and unique position if it were ' capable of being so good, that no possible goodness arising from knowledge, virtue, pleasure, or fullness of life could equal it.' This view, ' which has been held by many people, mystics and non-mystics,' McTaggart believes to be true, and ' to follow from contemplating the nature of love, on the one hand, and of the other qualities on the other hand ' (p. 437). Contemplating the supreme goodness of love in the final stage of the self's existence, and its relation to the goods and evils it encounters in the pre-final stages, McTaggart concludes *The Nature of Existence* with this reflection : ' Nor can we limit the evils which may meet us in this future any more than we can limit its duration. . . . All we can say is that this evil, however great it may be, is only passing ; that our lives are, with however much oscillation, gradually approximating to a final stage which they will some day reach ; and that the final stage is one in which the good infinitely exceeds, not only any evil co-existent with it, but all the evil in the series by which it is attained. And thus the very greatness of the evil which we endure gives us some slight anticipation of the greatness of the good which outweighs it infinitely. Of the nature of that good we know something. We know that it is a timeless and endless state of love—love so direct, so intimate, and so powerful that even the deepest mystic rapture gives us but the slightest foretaste of its perfection. We know that we shall know nothing but our beloved, and those they love, and ourselves as loving them, and that only in this shall we seek and find satisfaction. Between the present and that fruition there stretches a future which may well need courage. For, while there will be in it much good, and increasing good, there may await us evils which we can now measure only by their infinite insignificance as compared with the final reward.'—*Ed.*]

[1] [The problems which confront the theist who would accept McTaggart's evaluation of love are clearly and skilfully indicated by Dr. R. Leet Patterson in his article, ' McTaggart's Contribution to the Philosophy of Religion,' *Philosophy*, VI, 23 ; July, 1931.—*Ed.*]

meaning—whether such an emotion could have any closer resemblance to what is ordinarily known as love, than the dog-star, to use Spinoza's illustration, has to a dog.

But we may briefly notice that whether God is conceived as immanent in the universe, or as external to it, an emotion directed towards Him could not be the universal activity for which we have been looking. In the second of these two cases, it would follow that a God, on whom a universe was dependent, would be necessarily also dependent on the universe (cp. Hegel's *Encyclopædia*, Section 95). Such a limited being could scarcely be regarded as adequate to be the sole object of the only real activity of spirit. Moreover on this hypothesis the universe has an existence separate from, though dependent on, the existence of God. And consequently the other parts of the universe must be held to be in connection with ourselves somehow—a condition which could not be realized in an emotion connecting each of us individually with God.

If, on the other hand, we regard God as immanent in the universe, and as manifesting himself by its means, the difficulty takes another form. God is then the principle of unity in the universe. But the unity, we have seen, is as unreal without the differentiation, as the differentiation is without the unity. A mere God therefore, not incarnate in man, is as unmeaning an abstraction and contradiction as a mere man who should not be an incarnation of God. And an emotion directed to what is unreal and contradictory cannot be an adequate expression of the reality of all things. Nor can we say that it is God that we love in man. It is not more the merely divine than the merely material. The incarnation is not here a divine condescension, as in various religious systems. The abstractly divine is as much below the concrete individual as is the abstractly material, and it is the concrete individual which alone can give us what we seek for.

Again, though differentiation has no right as against the concrete whole, it is independent as against a mere unity. And therefore, if we could come into relation with the unity as such, it would not connect us with the differentiated parts of the universe, and could not therefore be a relation adequately expressing all reality.

We can, if we choose, say that our love is *in* God, meaning thereby that it cannot, at its highest, be conceived as merely subjective and capricious, but that it expresses the order of the universe, and is conscious that it does so. It is more than religion, but it must include religion. The invocation which conquered the spirits of the Beryl was two-sided : ' Love, for thy sake. In thy name, O God.' But this is not love of God. The relation is between persons, and God is conceived only as, so to speak, their common quality.

If we cannot, properly speaking, love God, it is still more impossible to love mankind. For mankind is an abstraction too, and a far more superficial abstraction. If God was only an abstraction of the element of unity, at least he was an abstraction of the highest and most perfect unity, able to fuse into a whole the highest and most perfect differentiation. But mankind represents a far less vital unity. It is a common quality of individuals, but not, conceived merely as mankind, a living unity between them. The whole nature of the individual lies in his being a manifestation of God. But the unity of mankind is not a principle from which the differences of its individuals can be deduced. The human race, viewed as such, is only an aggregate, not even an organism. You might as well try to love an indefinitely extended Post Office Directory. And the same will hold true of all subordinate aggregates—nations, churches, and families.

We must come back to the meaning of the word before it got into the hands of the thinkers for whom the highest is synonymous with the most abstract. It must mean for us, as it means for the world, the love that one person feels for one other person. At the same time we must guard against confounding it with the special forms which it assumes at present. At present it makes instruments of sexual desire, of the connection of marriage, or of the connection of blood. But in so far as these depend on any determining cause outside love itself, they cannot be the ultimate forms under which it manifests itself. Love for which any cause can be assigned carries the marks of its own incompleteness upon it. For all relations, all reality, must, I have tried to show, have been changed and transformed into love. Thus there will be nothing left outside to determine it. Love is itself the relation which binds individuals together. Each relation it establishes is part of the ultimate nature of the unity of the whole. It does not require or admit of justification or determination by anything else. It is itself the justification and determination of all things. The nearest approach to it we can know now is the love for which no cause can be given, and which is not determined by any outer relationship, of which we can only say that two people belong to one another—the love of the *Vita Nuova* and of *In Memoriam*.

No doubt an emotion which should be sufficient, both in extent and intensity, to grasp the entire universe, must be different in degree from anything of which we can now have experience. Yet this need not make us feel any essential difference between the two, if the distinction is only one of growth, and not of generic change. The attempt to imagine any communion so far reaching—extending, as we must hold it to do, to all reality in the universe—is no doubt depressing, almost painful. But this arises, I think, from the inability, under which we at present lie, to picture the ideal except under the disguise of a ' false infinite ' of endless succession. However much we may *know* that the kingdom of heaven is spiritual and timeless, we cannot help *imagining* it as in time, and can scarcely avoid imagining it as in space. In this aspect the magnitude of the field to be included naturally appears as something alien and inimical to our power of including it. We are forced too, since our imagination is limited by the stage of development in which we at present are, to give undue importance to the aspect of number, as applied to the individuals in the Absolute. If we look at it from this standpoint the briefest contemplation is bewildering and crushing. But number is a very inadequate category. Even in everyday life we may see how number falls into the shade as our knowledge of the subject matter increases. Of two points on an unlimited field we can say nothing but that they are two in number.   But if we were considering the relation of Hegel's philosophy to Kant's or of Dante to Beatrice, the advance which we should make by counting them would be imperceptible.   When everything is seen under the highest category, the Absolute Idea, this process would have been complete.   All lower categories would have been transcended, and all separate significance of number would have vanished.   And the dead weight, produced by the conception of an infinite number of things to be brought into unity, would vanish with it.

We must remember too, once more, that the Absolute is not an aggregate but a system.   The multiplicity of the individuals is not, therefore, a hindrance in the way of establishing a harmony with any one of them, as might be the case if each of them was an independent rival of all the rest.   It is rather to be considered as an assistance, since our relations with each will, through their mutual connections, be strengthened by our relations with all the others.   ' The complex reverberation of sympathy,' to use a characteristic phrase of Dr. Sidgwick's in a somewhat different context, is always a fact of vital importance.   And when the friction, which is necessarily incident to a world of matter and of undeveloped spirit, was no longer a hindrance to its action, the indefinite extension of individual sympathy, although no doubt incomprehensible, need scarcely be considered incredible.

It would be useless to attempt to deny that the conclusions I have endeavoured to support are hopelessly mystical.   In admitting this I shall be thought by many people to have pronounced their condemnation.   But mysticism is not so easily to be got rid of.   The attempt to join in a vital unity things which the consciousness of everyday life regards as separate—and this is mysticism—is inherent in philosophy, which can neither disregard the difference, nor be contented without the unity.   And when we consider that all things which we are accustomed to think of as different, are joined in a unity by the very fact that we think of them, and that a difference without unity, or a unity without a difference, are unmeaning terms, we may perhaps suspect that, if mysticism is a reproach, it is not so much philosophy which deserves the blame, as the reality which philosophy endeavours to represent.

A mysticism which ignored the claims of the understanding would indeed be doomed. ' None ever went about to break logic, but in the end logic broke him.' But this cannot be said of a mysticism which starts from the standpoint of ordinary life, and only departs from it in so far as that standpoint shows itself not to be ultimate, but to postulate something beyond itself. To transcend the lower is not to defy it. It is only such a result which will complete the work of Idealism, if it is to be completed. And it is only in this sense that I have ventured to indicate the possibility of finding, above all knowledge and volition, one all-embracing unity, which is only not true, only not good, because all truth and all goodness are but distorted shadows of its absolute perfection—' das Unbegreifliche, weil es der Begriff Selbst ist.'

XI

AN ONTOLOGICAL IDEALISM

Ontologically I am an Idealist, since I believe that all that exists is spiritual. I am also, in one sense of the term, a Personal Idealist. For I believe that every part of the content of spirit falls within some self, and that no part of it falls within more than one self; and that the only substances are selves, parts of selves, and groups of selves or parts of selves.

On the other hand, I should say that epistemologically I was a Realist. I should say that knowledge was a true belief, and I should say that a belief was true when, and only when, it stands in a relation of correspondence to a fact. I do not think that this particular relation of correspondence can be defined further, but it may be remarked that it is not a relation of copying or of similarity. Of facts I should say that whenever anything is anything, using both ' anything ' and ' is ' in the widest possible sense, it is a fact that it is so.

I should define philosophy as the systematic study of the ultimate nature of reality. The phrase ' *ultimate* nature ' distinguishes philosophy from science, which systematically studies the nature of reality, but not its ultimate nature.

Reality appears to me to be an indefinable quality, for which Being is another name. Nothing is unreal. When we say that the present Duke of London is unreal, what we mean is that the description ' the present Duke of London ' is a description which applies to nothing.

Existence appears to me to be another indefinable quality, which is such that all which is existent is necessarily real, but all which is real is not necessarily existent. It has been said that propositions, possibilities, qualities, and relations are real without being existent. I do not think that the independent reality of propositions or possibilities can be justified. But qualities and relations (which may be grouped together under the general name of characteristics) are in themselves real without being existent. The qualities and relations of existent substances, however, may be called, as such, existent.

I have confined myself to a study of the nature of existence. It is the existent alone which has any practical interest for us. And the nature of the existent involves the nature of all other reality, since, taking any quality x, it is clear that each existent thing must have either that quality or the quality not-x, whose nature depends on the nature of x.

I have divided my system into two parts. The first admits only two empirical premises—' something exists,' and ' what exists is differentiated.' The rest of it professes to be entirely *a priori*. In the second part the results obtained in the first part will be applied to those general characteristics which empirical observation tells us are, or appear to be, true of various parts of the existent.[1]

We know empirically that something exists. This is given us in perception. (I use the words ' perception ' and ' awareness ' in the senses in which they are defined by Mr. Russell in his *Mysticism and Logic*.) And if it should be denied or doubted that anything existed, then the very assertion of or denial or doubt would show that, at least, the assertion in question existed.

Existence is a quality. And it is evident that whatever exists must have some quality besides existence. The conception of quality is indefinable. For every positive quality, x, there is a negative quality, not-x, and one member of this pair can be predicated of everything that exists. Some qualities are Simple, and do not admit of analysis. Others are Compound, consisting of an aggregate of simple qualities.

---

[1] The first part is contained in vol. I of *The Nature of Existence*, published in 1921. The second part will occupy vol. II of the same work, which I hope to publish in 1926 or 1927. [Posthumously published by Dr. C. D. Broad in 1927.—*Ed.*]

Others are Complex, which do not consist of simple qualities, but can be analysed and defined by means of simple qualities and simple relations. (Negative qualities are complex.) The compound quality which is an aggregate of all the non-compound qualities possessed by anything may be called the Nature of that thing.

I hold that the existence of qualities involves the existence of Substances. I should define a substance as that which has qualities and is related, without being itself either a quality or a relation, or having qualities or relations among its parts. (The first part of this is the traditional definition of substance. The last part is added [1] to exclude facts.) By this definition many things would be called substances which are not usually called so, such as a sneeze or the group consisting of all red-headed archdeacons.

Is there only one substance, or are there more? Here, for a second time, and the last in the first part of my system, I appeal to perception, which shows us that more substances than one exist. But, at the same time, all the substances which exist may be taken together as a single substance.

Since there are more substances than one, they must exist in relations to one another—though, of course, relations also exist between qualities and relations, just as both qualities and relations have qualities. The conception of relation is indefinable, like the conception of quality. It is as fundamental as the conception of quality, and it is impossible to dispense with either of them in favour of the other.

Every relationship generates a derivative quality in each of its terms—the quality of being a term in that relationship. In the same way a derivative relation is generated between any quality and the substance which has it, and between every relation and each of its terms. Thus infinite series of characteristics are generated, but these infinite series are not vicious.

[1] [The latter part was added to meet Professor G. E. Moore's objection that the definition of Substance in *The Nature of Existence*, vol. I, does not preclude facts from being substances. Thus, by his emendation here, McTaggart presumably wishes to insist that facts do have, though substances do not have, qualities or relations among their parts.—*Ed.*]

S*

It seems clear to me that two substances cannot have exactly the same nature. (The difference, however, may not be a difference in original qualities, but may consist entirely in a difference in original relations, together with the difference in the derivative characteristics generated by those relations.) This result may be called the Dissimilarity of the Diverse.

Substances, being particular, cannot be defined, but they may be described. A description which applies only to one substance is an Exclusive Description of it. An exclusive description which is entirely in terms of qualities and relations, without introducing undescribed substances, I call a Sufficient description. Since no two substances have exactly the same nature, every substance has an exclusive description, and it can be shown to follow from this that, to avoid a vicious infinite series, every substance must have a sufficient description.

Some characteristics clearly imply others, since it is sometimes true that, if one substance has the characteristic X, that substance, or another which stands to it in some definite relation, will have the characteristic Y. This may be called Intrinsic Determination. But besides this there is a relation between all the characteristics of the same substance, such that, if any one of them were not a characteristic of that substance, we could not assert that any others of them were characteristics of that substance. This relation I have called Extrinsic Determination.

The nature of a substance may be regarded as a unity compounded of the particular characteristics which constitute it. But it may be regarded with equal truth as a unity which is manifested in those characteristics.

We now pass from the consideration of single substances to the consideration of Groups. By a Group I mean any collection formed of substances, or of collections of substances, or of both. The substances or collections which form the collection are Members of the group. A group is distinguished from a Class, which is determined by a class-concept, while a group is determined by denotation. Any combination of substances or groups is a group, however trivial or unimportant the similarities and connections between its members.

We must distinguish between the members and parts of a group. If we take the group of all the counties in Great Britain, Surrey is both a member and a part of it. England and Whitechapel are parts, but not members. The relation of Whole and Part appears to me to be indefinable.

At this point we must introduce two further conceptions. A Set of Parts of any whole is any collection of its parts which together make up the whole, and do not do more than make it up, so that the whole would not be made up if any of those parts, or of their parts, should be subtracted. A group may have many sets of parts, and I use the term Content of the Group to designate that plurality which is identical in the various sets of parts of a Group.

It follows from the definitions of a substance and a group that every group is a compound substance, but that several groups may be the same compound substance, e.g., the group of the counties of England and the group of the parishes of England are the same compound substance.

There is no group which contains all other groups, but there is one substance which contains all other substances. This substance is the Universe.

By means of the conception of the universe we can show that extrinsic determination is more extensive than was previously asserted, and that every fact about any substance extrinsically determines every fact about every other substance.

I pass to a position which is very vital to my system—the position that no substance is simple. It is possible that a substance is simple in some of its dimensions, but it could not be simple in all of them. This proposition appears to me to be self-evident and ultimate. I do not, therefore, attempt to defend it by direct arguments, though I believe that it is possible, by various explanations, to remove certain objections which might naturally be made to it.

Every substance, therefore, will have an infinite number of sets of parts. When two sets are such that no part in the second falls within more than one part of the first, while at least one part of the first set contains two or more parts of the second, I call the first set Precedent to the second, and the second Sequent to the first.

But now a difficulty arises. When the occurrence of the quality X determines intrinsically the occurrence of either the quality Y or the quality Z, but does not intrinsically determine whether it shall be Y or Z which does occur, let us say that X Presupposes the one of the two, Y or Z, which does actually occur. X may have more than one presupposition, and two of them may be such that when one of them is fixed to one of the alternatives, it implies the fixing of the other to one of the alternatives. Let us define the Total Ultimate Presupposition of X as being the aggregate of all the presuppositions of X after all those have been removed, the fixing of which is implied in the fixing of any of those which remain.

It is clear that whatever has a presupposition must have a total ultimate presupposition. But I maintain that it can be demonstrated that the sufficient descriptions of the members of any set of parts of a substance, would, except on one condition, have a presupposition without a total ultimate presupposition, which is absurd. The one condition on which this could be avoided must therefore be true. And that condition is that there must be some description of any substance, A, which implies sufficient descriptions of the members of all its sets of parts which are sequent to some given set of parts.

I think that there is only one way in which this result can be attained. Let A have a set of parts, B and C. Let it be true, in the first place, that each of these parts has a set of parts corresponding to each set of parts of A. In the second place, let it be true that the correspondence is of the same sort throughout, and that it is such that a certain sufficient description of C, which includes the fact that it is in this relation to *some* part of B, will determine a sufficient description of the part of B in question. And in the third place, let it be true that the correspondence is such that, when one determinant is part of another determinant, then any part determined by the first will be part of a part determined by the second.

I write B ! C for that part of B which corresponds to C, and B ! C ! D for that part of B which corresponds to that part of C which corresponds to D, and so on. I call such correspondence a Determining Correspondence, since by it, with the help of sufficient descriptions of B and C, we can determine a sufficient description of B ! C. I speak of C as the Determinant of B ! C, and of B ! C as the Determinate of C, or as determined by C. I say that B ! C ! D is Directly Determined by C ! D, and Indirectly Determined by D. I call A a Primary Whole, and B a Primary Part. I call B ! C a Secondary Part of the First Grade, B ! C ! D a Secondary Part of the Second Grade, and so on.

If the conditions mentioned above are fulfilled, it follows that sufficient descriptions of the primary parts will determine sufficient descriptions of parts of parts of A through an infinite series. We shall then have fulfilled the only condition, by fulfilling which it is possible to escape from the contradiction which would otherwise be involved in the infinite divisibility of substance. And as there seems no other theory which would fulfil this condition, I hold that we are entitled to regard the theory of determining correspondence as true, and to assert that the universe consists of one or more primary wholes, which, again, consist of primary parts, whose further parts are determined by determining correspondence.

It is not necessary, in order to establish determining correspondence, that each primary part should have parts corresponding to *all* the primary parts in its primary whole. It might have parts corresponding only to a certain number of them—e.g. to B and C, when the primary whole contained B, C, D, and E. Nor is it necessary that every primary part should be a determinant at all—though, of course, every primary part must be a determinate.

If, as I believe, causation is to be defined as a relation of intrinsic determination between the occurrence of existing qualities, it follows that determining correspondence is a causal relation, and, consequently, that a network of causal relations spreads through every primary part of the universe, though it does not follow that the occurrence of *every* existing quality is causally determined.

Determining correspondence also involves a classification of the content of the universe—into primary wholes, primary parts, secondary parts of the first grade, of the second grade, and so on. It can be shown that this classification is based on qualities which are of fundamental importance, and it may therefore be called the Fundamental System of the Universe.

In order that the secondary parts may be differentiated by determining correspondence, it is necessary that the primary parts should be differentiated independently of determining correspondence. This could happen in several ways. It might happen by a difference in original qualities, or by a difference in the sort of relations in which they stand to other things. Or, again, it might happen by a difference in the terms to which they stood in certain relations—though this last method of differentiation could not be the only method applicable to all primary parts, since that would involve a vicious infinite.

I now pass to the second part of my philosophy—as yet unpublished [1]—in which the results obtained in the first part will be applied to those general characteristics which empirical observation tells us are, or appear to be, true of various parts of the existent. In this part of the system it is impossible to hope for the absolute demonstration of positive results. The most that we can do is to show that certain empirically-known characteristics will meet the *a priori* requirements of the first part, and that no other characteristic which we know or can imagine will do so. But this will not assure us that the universe does possess these characteristics. For there may be others, which we have never experienced or imagined, which could also satisfy the *a priori* requirements. And it may be these latter which are found in part or all of the existent. But although we cannot attain absolute demonstra-

[1] [This 'second part' occupies Vol. II of *The Nature of Existence*.—*Ed.*]

tion here, we may, I think, attain reasonable certainty. (With negative results we may be able to reach absolute demonstration. If we are certain *a priori* that nothing with the quality *x* can be real, we can be certain that any empirically-known characteristic, which involves the quality *x*, cannot be true of reality.)

It seems to me that one-empirically-known characteristic which cannot really belong to anything that exists is the characteristic of Time. I can only briefly summarize the argument which leads me to this conclusion. It is : that nothing can be really in time unless it really forms a series of Past, Present, and Future (which may be called an A series), as well as a series of Earlier and Later (which may be called a B series). But the A series involves a contradiction. For every term of it is both past, present, and future. And, on the other hand, the three predicates are incompatible. But, again, we cannot regard the time series as totally erroneous. The terms which appear to us as a temporal series connected by the relation ' earlier than,' really do form a non-temporal series connected by another relation. (This I call the C series. It follows from what I have said that things are really in a C series, but not really in any A or B series.) [1]

We must also, I think, hold that nothing which exists can have the quality of being matter. My positive reason for holding this conclusion is that it appears impossible for anything which has the quality of materiality to have that determining correspondence between its parts which we have seen that all substances must have. This conclusion, however, can be supported by showing (as I have endeavoured to show in the third chapter of *Some Dogmas of Religion*) that the positive arguments put forward for the existence of matter are untenable.

It also seems inevitable that we should reject the reality of sense-data—I do not mean that we must deny that we have objects which we perceive, but that we must hold that those

---

[1] A fuller exposition of this argument may be found in my article ' The Unreality of Time,' *Mind*. 1908. [Cf. V, pp. 110-131, of the present volume.—*Ed.*]

objects have not the nature which is usually connoted by the name, sense-data. The ground for this assertion is, again, that nothing which has the quality of being a sense-datum can have determining correspondence between its parts. This position, like that of the unreality of time, involves that perception is sometimes erroneous. (I use Perception to mean the direct awareness of any substance.) The unreality of matter does not involve erroneous perception, since we never perceive anything as being material, though we judge it to be material.

What, then, shall we say about spirit? What, in the first place, do we mean by spirit? I should say that spirituality is the quality of having content—in the sense previously defined—all of which is content of one or more selves. I should say that the quality of being a self is a simple quality which is known to me because I perceive—in the strict sense of the word—one substance as possessing it. This substance is myself.[1]

With regard to selves, I hold, further, that a self can be conscious without being self-conscious, and that it is possible for a self not to be self-conscious. I also hold that it is impossible for one self to be part of another self, or for two selves to have any common part.

The activities which spirits have, or appear *prima facie* to have, are perceptions, awareness of characteristics, judgments, assumptions (the Annahmen of Meinong), images, volitions, and emotions. By perceptions, as I have said, I mean the awareness of any substance. But, since we can base judgments as to the characteristics of substances on our perceptions of those substances, we must conclude that, although we cannot perceive *that* the substance A has the characteristic X, we can perceive the substance A *as having* the characteristic X.

There are three propositions about perception for which, I think, good reasons can be given. The first is that there is no intrinsic impossibility in a self perceiving another self, or a part of another self. The second is that a perception is

[1] Cp. my article on 'Personality,' in the *Encyclopædia of Religion and Ethics*. [See III, pp. 69–96, in the present volume.—*Ed.*]

282

part of a percipient self. The third is that a perception of the part of a whole *can* be part of a perception of that whole. Then it follows that perception could be a relation of determining correspondence. We might have a primary whole, all of whose primary parts were selves, each of whom perceived all or some of the selves in the primary whole, and also perceived all the parts of each self it perceived. And it might be the case that each self had only one perception of each perception, and that he had no other contents but these perceptions. And in this case sufficient descriptions would be determined, within each self, of parts within parts to infinity. For each part would be sufficiently described by the description that it was the perception which a given self had of a given self, or of a given perception within a given self. In order that this should be the case, it would be necessary that each self should have a sufficient description which did not depend on determining correspondence. Such a description might be based either on qualitative or quantitative differences between the selves (or both), combined possibly with differences in relations.

It can be shown, further, that, while perception can thus give us determining correspondence, neither judgments, assumptions, images, nor awareness of characteristics can do so. There must be some substances whose parts admit of determination to infinity by determining correspondence. For there can be no substance which does not meet this requirement, and we know that there are some substances. Only three sorts of substance appear to be given us in experience—matter, sense-data, and spirit. We do not know, and we cannot imagine, any others. We have seen that no substance can really be matter or sense-data. This does not absolutely prove that all substances, or any substances, are spirits. For perhaps some, or all, substances are of some other nature which we do not know and cannot imagine. But although we have not here any absolute demonstration, we have, I think, good reason to believe that all reality is spiritual—in other words, that nothing exists except selves, groups of selves, and parts of selves.

What, then, about volition and emotion? I hold, in

accordance with a view suggested by Dr. Moore,[1] that a desire or an emotion is primarily a cogitation of the object of desire or emotion, which has the further quality—ultimate, and irreducible to any other sort of quality—which makes it a desire or an emotion. I hold that perceptions, which are cogitations, can be volitions and emotions.

Each of us has a perception of at least one other self. And I think that good reason can be shown for concluding that the relation in which a self stands to a self which it perceives is a relation of love—the percipient self loving the perceived self. By love I mean what is generally meant by the word—an emotion felt by one person towards another person.

This is the fact which decides all other emotions. If I love A, I shall regard myself with reverence, because I love him. If I indirectly perceive B, by perceiving A's perception of him, then, since I love A, and A loves B, I shall regard B with a feeling which may be distinguished from love by calling it affection. And I shall regard with complacency the parts of selves whom I regard with love, self-reverence, or affection.

There remains volition. Our perceptions cannot be ungratified volitions, since their objects exist. But are they gratified volitions, or not volitions at all? This question is answered by our last result. We cannot but acquiesce in the existence of what we regard with love, self-reverence, affection, or complacency; and the essence of volition is acquiescence.

If our conclusions are correct, the universe consists of selves, arranged in one or more primary wholes, whose whole content consists in their perceptions of themselves and of each other—perceptions which have emotional and volitional qualities such as those in our present experience, but, there is reason to believe, much more intense in quantity than they are in our present experience. Are such selves immortal? If we take immortality to mean endless existence in time—and I think it should be taken in this way—it is clear that

---

[1] [Cf. G. E. Moore, *Principia Ethica*, ch. iv, D., and more particularly, Moore's review of A. Messer's *Empfindung und Denken*, in *Mind*, 1910, p. 400.—*Ed.*]

selves cannot be really immortal, since they are not really in time. But the question still remains whether, when they appear *sub specie temporis*, their lives will appear as having or not having an end in time.

If the universe—the whole of that which exists—is of this nature can it include a self who is God ? I use ' God ' to designate a being who is a self, who is good, and whose power is such that, whether he does or does not create all other selves, his volition can profoundly affect them.

It is clear to begin with that there can be no one who is really the creator of the universe, since the created must be in time, even if the creator could be timeless, and since nothing is in time. Nor could there even be a being who, *sub specie temporis*, appeared as a creator. For this there are three reasons. In the first place, both God and the other selves would be primary parts, and they could not be dependent on God in any way in which God was not dependent on them. In the second place, God's volitions respecting them, like all volitions of all primary selves, would be cogitatively perceptions, and therefore they would depend on their objects, and not their objects on them. In the third place, I think that it can be proved that, *sub specie temporis*, all selves begin simultaneously, so that God could not appear to be prior to the other selves in time.

The first and third of these objections do not apply to the view that God, while not creating the rest of the universe, controls it, but the second objection would apply to this hypothesis alone.

But, it might be said, it is certainly the case that the volitions of selves do appear to affect the state of the rest of the universe. And could there not be some self whose volitions had the appearance—which, though only an appearance, would be a *phenomenon bene fundatum*—of influencing the rest of the universe so profoundly that he would properly be called a god ? There might be such a being, but there seems no evidence which should make his existence probable. And it must be noticed that, if our theory is true, the force of the argument from design would be greatly weakened, if not entirely destroyed, since it can be shown that a certain amount of order, and, as we shall see later, a certain direction towards the good, follows from the intrinsic nature of existence, and so does not suggest a conscious designer as its only possible cause.

It is clear that, if this is the real nature of what exists, it appears to be something very different from what it is. (1) It appears to include matter and sense-data, while really it includes nothing but spirit. (2) I appear to perceive myself, parts of myself, sense-data, and nothing else. But in reality I do not perceive sense-data, and I do perceive other selves and their parts. (3) I appear to have judgments, assumptions, and images, when in reality the whole content of myself consists in presentations. (4) Many of my volitions and emotions appear to be judgments, assumptions, or images, while in reality they are all perceptions. (5) All that I perceive appears to be in time, while in reality nothing is in time. Can we explain how reality should appear to be so different from what it really is ?

This will involve our accepting the possibility of erroneous perception. Even if part of our cognition consisted of judgments, some of the errors in appearance mentioned above must be put down to perception. And, if our theory is true, all our cognition is really perception, and so all error must fall in perception. But is it not an essential and self-evident characteristic of perception that there is no possibility that it should be erroneous ? And, if we remove this characteristic from anything, do not we thereby declare that it is not perception ?

But when we look more closely we see that our certainty as to the correctness of perception is only that what I perceive exists, and exists as I perceive it, *at the time at which I perceive it*, and there is no certainty about any other time. Now we have seen that time is unreal. The condition ' at the time at which I perceive it ' must be translated into something else before it gives us the truth. And if that translation should allow for erroneous perception, we shall have achieved our end. It is clear, therefore, that the explanation of all error must be closely associated with the appearance of time.

It is only possible for me here to state what my theory is, omitting both the arguments which seem to me to render it impossible to accept various alternative theories, and also the exposition of the way in which I think that this theory does explain satisfactorily in detail the difference of the appearance from the reality.

The content of all selves, as we have seen, forms a system of perceptions which is determined by determining correspondence, and is in two dimensions—one dimension being the series of primary parts, secondary parts of the first grade, secondary parts of the second grade, and so on infinitely, while the other dimension is the series of parts in each grade. I believe that each of these parts is divided in another dimension into a series of other parts. The parts in this dimension are not determined by determining correspondence, and so must be simple parts, though, so far as I can see, there is nothing to determine whether their number is finite or infinite. (The series, as we shall see, is bounded at both ends, but might contain an infinite number of parts if there were no next terms.)

I hold that in any perception, G ! H, all these parts are states of misperception by G of H, while G ! H, of which they are parts, is a correct perception by G of H. (By a correct perception I mean one which, while not necessarily perceiving H as having all the qualities which it does have, perceives it as having some of the qualities which it does have, and does not perceive it as having any qualities which it does not have.)

Each of these states in the misperception series of G ! H will be a misperception of H as a whole. H, like G, will have such a series within him and will be perceived by G as having it. But part of the erroneous element of G's perception of H will be to regard this C series as a B series, and consequently H will be misperceived by G as existing in time. (G, of course, can also perceive himself, in his perception G ! G, and so misperceive himself as existing in time.)

287

Any perception in G will perceive at present whatever in H is at the same stage in the series as itself. It will perceive as future or as past whatever is at a different stage in the series. The only perceptions which are apparent perceptions— that is, which appear to be, as they are, perceptions—are *some* of those which are at the same stage in the series as their percepta. All others appear, not as perceptions, but as judgments, assumptions, or images. But even perceptions which are at the same stage of the series as their percepta, appear in some cases, not as perceptions, but as judgments, assumptions, or images.

What is the relation which connects the terms of the series— the relation which, when misperceived as temporal, appears as the relation of earlier and later? In view of the fact that the terms of the series are all states of misperception, while the whole of which they are parts is a state of correct perception, I believe that it can be shown that the terms of the series, though each a part of the whole, do not form a set of parts of the whole, and that no two of them can be mutually outside each other. The only alternative is that, of any two terms in the series, one must include the other.

We have thus an Inclusion Series, whose terms are related by the relation ' included in,' and the last term of which will be G ! H itself, which includes all the others. All the terms of this series, with the exception of G ! H itself, which is correct, form a Misperception Series. And when the series is itself misperceived as being in time, the whole Inclusion Series acts as a C series—i.e. the series which is misperceived as a B series. The last member, however, G ! H, can never appear as present. For it could only appear as present to a term which was at the same stage in a series as itself, i.e. was a final term in a series. And as the final terms are not misperceptions, they could not perceive anything as being in time.

It follows from the fact that the inclusion series appears as the time series, that the time series is limited at both ends, and that a finite number of durations which are next terms to each other will exhaust it, in the sense that from any point of it we shall reach either end of the series in a finite time.

When we consider what is meant by the time series in different selves having a common C series, it follows that (in either direction) the final terms of the time series of all selves will appear, *sub specie temporis*, to be simultaneous.

We have seen that the relations ' inclusion of ' and ' included in ' appear, *sub specie temporis*, as ' earlier than ' and ' later than.' But which of them appears as which ? It appears clear that, in the time series, the relation ' earlier than ' is more fundamental than the relation ' later than,' since it arranges the terms in the order of actual change. And when we look into the exact nature of the inclusion series, there is good reason, I think, to regard the relation ' included in ' as more fundamental to it than the relation ' inclusive of.' And from these two results, I think that it is reasonable to conclude that it is the relation ' included in ' which appears as the relation ' earlier than.'

Then, in the inclusion series of H, it is H itself (which includes all the other terms, and is included in none of them), which, when the series appears as a temporal series, will appear as the latest term. (As this term contains all the content which is to be found in any part of the series, it may be called the whole of the series.) From the standpoint of any other term it will appear as future—never as past or present. From its own standpoint, however, it will not appear as present, but as timelessly eternal. For this case is not in the misperception series, and so cannot misperceive itself as in time.

It follows that the whole is, not really future, since nothing is really temporal, but as really future as my breakfast to-morrow is future.

We return to the question of immortality. After a finite time (speaking *sub specie temporis*), each self reaches the term of the whole, beyond which there is no other. But that term is the end of the time series. When this term is looked at from the standpoint of any earlier term, *sub specie temporis*, it will be perceived as unending (which it is, since there is nothing beyond it in that direction), and as being in time. And since we shall reach a state which *sub specie temporis* is

289

an unending time, it will follow that, *sub specie temporis*, we are immortal. We are not really immortal, in the sense in which I have taken the word, but this is not because our lives really end (which they do not), but because their unendingness is not an unending duration in time. Thus the view, which has been maintained by some Christians, that heaven is both timeless and future, is not necessarily contradictory.

On the other hand, while, *sub specie temporis*, our lives never end, they do begin. For in this direction the birth of the series is a zero of content, which is not a term of the series of inclusive contents. And therefore the whole series will, in this direction, be limited by something outside itself, and so will appear as beginning in time.

How long, for each of us, the part of the series before, or after, the present life, is in comparison with that life, we cannot tell. But there seem empirical reasons for supposing that it is very great—that is that, *sub specie temporis*, a great length of time has passed from the beginning of time to the birth of my present body, and a great length will pass from the death of my present body till the attainment of the final term. There seem reasons to suppose that both these periods are divided up into a plurality of lives, separated from one another, as the present life of each of us is separated from all that goes before and all that goes after.[1]

What can we say of the value in the universe, if our theory of the nature of the universe is true ? People do not agree as to what qualities of the existent give it value. But I think that there would be general agreement that they would not include anything not included in the following list : knowledge, virtue, the possession of certain emotions, happiness, extent and intensity of consciousness, and harmony.

We decided of the final states of the inclusion series—those states which were the wholes of the determining correspondence parts, as distinguished from their parts in the discussion of inclusion—that in them the whole content of each self would consist in perceiving selves and their parts, and perceiving them correctly, that all their perceptions would be states of

---

[1] Cp. *Some Dogmas of Religion*, ch. iv.

acquiescence in what was perceived, that each self would love all the other selves he perceived, and that this would determine his emotions toward himself, towards the selves perceived by the selves whom he perceived, and to the parts of all selves. Now if this state of things is judged by any or all of the criteria of goodness enumerated in the last paragraph, it will be very good. It will not possess complete good, which is impossible, since there is always a degree of good greater than any given degree of good, but it will possess very much greater good than we ever now experience, and the good will be unmixed with evil.

In all the other stages of the inclusion series, which are states of misperception, and whose nature will therefore be different, there is no guarantee that the states will be very good, or unmixed with evil. And since our present life is within those stages, we know empirically that they are partly good and partly bad.

Can we estimate all the values in the universe, including both the final and the pre-final stages ? The pre-final stages appear, *sub specie temporis*, as finite in time, the final stage as infinite in time. The value of any stage varies, *cæteris paribus*, according to its duration in time. But, as the final stage does not appear to itself as in time at all, we cannot infer directly that the value of the final stage is infinitely greater than that of all the rest. I think, however, that good reasons can be given for holding that the limitation or non-limitation of value depends on boundedness or unboundedness, and not on whether this appears *sub specie temporis* or not. In that case the final stage will have infinitely more value than the aggregate of all the others. And as the final stage is unmixed good, and the others are mixed good and evil, the universe as a whole and every self in the universe, is infinitely more good than bad, although the evil—what there is of it—is just as real as the good.

There is, then, a state of very good and unmixed good, which, *sub specie temporis*, must be regarded as lying in the future, and as being reached in a finite time, while it is itself endless. But the time required to reach it may have any finite length, however great, and we do not know how much evil may await us during that period. What we do know, if our conclusions are correct, is that all the evil of the future and the past are surpassed infinitely in value by the good which lies at the end of time.